THE SUPREME COURT AND
THE USES OF HISTORY

CHARLES A. MILLER

THE SUPREME COURT AND THE USES OF HISTORY

THE BELKNAP PRESS OF
HARVARD UNIVERSITY PRESS
CAMBRIDGE, MASSACHUSETTS, 1969

TO MY PARENTS

CONTENTS

THE SUPREME COURT AND
THE USES OF HISTORY

CHAPTER I

INTRODUCTION

In the spring of 1964 the United States Supreme Court decided the case of Bell v. Maryland.[1] Robert Mack Bell and his companions had been arrested on trespass charges for "sitting in" at a restaurant in Baltimore in order to protest its policy of racial segregation. In the Supreme Court the protesters argued that their arrest was unconstitutional. They claimed, in part, that the framers of the fourteenth amendment had intended that the amendment outlaw racial discrimination in places of public accommodation. The state of Maryland argued that the framers of the amendment had no such purpose in mind. The six justices of the Supreme Court who were willing to take a position on this issue divided evenly: three of them, citing numerous historical sources from the 1860's, agreed that the sit-ins were constitutional; the other three, citing the same historical sources almost page for page, denied it.[2]

Why did the parties to the case and the justices of the Court consider, indeed assume, that history was relevant to a proper constitutional decision? Why did they disagree so completely on the meaning of the constitutional history when they relied on the same historical sources? Were the justices consciously distorting or only taking justifiable liberty with their materials? Does it make any difference? These are the kinds of questions which this study seeks to answer.

The problem of the Supreme Court's use of history as a principle of adjudication in constitutional law is, in formal terms, a problem of legal theory. But because the principle involved here is history, the field constitutional law, and the tribunal the Supreme Court, the problem is as much the concern of historians and political scientists as of constitutional theorists. Yet for the most part, the

1. 378 U.S. 226 (1964).
2. The use of history in the sit-in cases is the subject of Chapter VI.

Supreme Court's use of history has been treated, if at all, by lawyers. It has not been given much attention by either historians or political scientists.

In political science, where the entire field of public law is relatively less significant than it was several decades ago, the most representative approaches to the Constitution emphasize either the political context of the work of the Supreme Court or the political values espoused by the justices. The present situation, as one political scientist put it, reflects "the profession's diminished interest in law and its indifference toward history." [3] In history the outlook is much the same. A recent discipline-conscious article deplored the quality of history used by the Supreme Court in its opinions and suggested that historians had unfortunately abandoned the fertile field of constitutional history to men with the wrong training — political scientists and lawyers. The article concluded, in the words of its title, that for historians it was "time to reclaim" the field of the Constitution.[4] A leading intellectual historian suggested that the problem is much larger. He wrote, without regard to professional discipline: "Of all the basic institutions of our society, our laws are probably still least studied as if they were part of the main stream of our history." [5] In short, we are learning as little about law from historians as about history from political scientists. The role of history in constitutional law is often lost in the middle.

The decline of the historical approach to constitutional law is in part paralleled by the decline of the other traditional route to constitutional understanding, that of legal or doctrinal studies, formerly common to political science journals and law reviews but now largely restricted to the latter. As the Supreme Court has entered new areas and made relatively clean breaks with the past, older cases appear to have little relevance to current issues. The search for an exclusively law-oriented jurisprudence applicable to the Constitution now seems futile. The formal studies which do appear today are likely to be incorporated into wider political and social contexts or to be prescriptive in their orientation, showing judges a legal road to a social Elysium. The legal mind, like the

3. William M. Beaney (book review), *American Political Science Review,* 60 (1961), 634.
4. Paul L. Murphy, "Time to Reclaim: The Current Challenge of American Constitutional History," *American Historical Review,* 69 (1963), 64–79.
5. Daniel J. Boorstin, *The Mysterious Science of the Law* (Boston: Beacon Press, 1958), p. v.

historical mind, is giving way in constitutional law to the political mind.[6]

Whichever way the trends in constitutional law are moving, the subject of this study requires that fair consideration be given to all three attitudes of thought, political, historical, and legal, to see how they fit into contemporary American constitutional law. American history, especially political history, has long played a role in the opinions of the Supreme Court, but there has been little writing more recent than nineteenth-century commentaries on the Constitution in which the Court's use of history has been discussed. The one major, indeed exhaustive, twentieth-century treatment of the subject is written from a strictly legal point of view. In a series of five law review articles in 1938 and 1939 the late Jacobus ten Broek undertook to analyze the "admissibility and use by the United States Supreme Court of extrinsic aids in constitutional construction." [7] He wrote: "Whenever the United States Supreme Court has felt itself called upon to announce a theory for its conduct in the matter of constitutional interpretation it has insisted, with almost uninterrupted regularity, that the end of constitutional construction is the discovery of the intention of those persons who formulated the instrument or of the people who adopted it." [8]

Organized around the topics of admissibility of "extrinsic evidence" in constitutional construction and the roles of the debates of the constitutional convention, of the history of the times, and of contemporaneous exposition of the Constitution, ten Broek's analysis has a formalistic cast. But at virtually every point the author demonstrates that the Court as a whole, and sometimes individual justices, have resorted to suspect, if not invalid, and to inconsistent, if not incompatible, methods and explanations in applying the theory of "intent of the framers" to the interpretation of the Constitution. The

6. A leading statement of the contemporary approach is Martin Shapiro's study of "political jurisprudence," *Law and Politics in the Supreme Court* (Glencoe, Ill.: The Free Press, 1964).

7. This was the title of the first article, appearing in *California Law Review*, 26 (1938), 287–308. The others, all entitled "Use by the United States Supreme Court of Extrinsic Aids in Constitutional Construction," appear in *California Law Review*, 26 (1938), 437–54, 664–81; and 27 (1939), 157–81, 399–421. They total over one hundred pages and are substantially the same as ten Broek's unpublished doctoral dissertation, "The Intent Theory of Constitutional Construction and Nondocumental Sources," University of California, Berkeley, 1940.

8. *California Law Review*, 27 (1939), 399.

intent theory of constitutional construction, ten Broek concludes, is one of the Supreme Court's "fundamental doctrinal fallacies." [9]

Ten Broek's study is significant not merely because it is thorough, or because it implies that the intent theory of constitutional interpretation is a miserable legal fiction without even the virtue of logic in application, or because it demonstrates how history can provide a magnificent smoke screen for the "real" reasons behind the Court's decisions. It is equally significant because it has failed to make a dent in the way the Supreme Court announces its decisions. The reason for the failure is probably associated with the difficulties encountered by the realist and sociological jurisprudence current when ten Broek wrote his articles. One of the important achievements of this jurisprudence was to abolish, in theory, the notion that judges discover law rather than make it.[10] But realist jurisprudence did not prompt judges to sprinkle their opinions with remarks pridefully owning that they had made the law they declared. Instead, they have persisted in claiming that the values their opinions may espouse are not their own but those of "the law" to which they have looked for guidance. In particular, they have continued to search for and ground their decisions on "the intent of the framers" of the Constitution. The Supreme Court's use of history as a principle of adjudication is evidently based on deeper needs of the American polity than legal criticism will be able to overcome.

Historical, in contrast to legal, criticism takes another approach to the Court's reliance on history as a method of constitutional interpretation. Historians are essentially concerned with determining partial and often tentative truths about the past and with interpreting their findings to the present. When historians study opinions of the Supreme Court, they are not concerned with principles of adjudication but with interpretations of the American past. There are innumerable historical studies of this sort. They typically focus on a particular clause of the Constitution and are often designed to refute the Supreme Court's version of history. They seldom, how-

9. *Ibid.*, 421.

10. John Marshall had stated it classically: "Courts are the mere instruments of the law, and can will nothing." Osborn v. Bank, 9 Wheat. 738, 866 (1824). For the practical differences that may result from holding one side or the other of this question, see Zechariah Chafee, Jr., "Do Judges Make or Discover Law?" *Proceedings of the American Philosophical Society*, 91 (1947), 405–20. There is one remarkable official exchange, between Justices Black and Clark, on making and discovering law. Linkletter v. Walker, 381 U.S. 618, 622–29, 643 (1965).

ever, analyze in any depth how or why the Supreme Court utilizes history, either in particular cases or in constitutional law in general.[11] There have been a very few broader discussions of the role of history in constitutional law. One of them is a short section in the only modern book-length consideration of the principles of constitutional adjudication.[12] The others are separate articles devoted to the practical and theoretical difficulties of relying on the materials of 1787–89 as a guide to twentieth-century constitutional interpretation.[13] In recent years the wide-ranging "activist" Supreme Court has often used history in its reformulation of constitutional law, and criticism of the Court in general has at times been directed towards its use of history in particular. In "Clio and the Court: An Illicit Love Affair" the constitutional historian Alfred Kelly discusses the varieties of uses to which the Court has put history in recent years, examining critically several areas of contemporary

11. Three outstanding exceptions to this may be mentioned: Alexander M. Bickel, "The Original Understanding and the Segregation Decision," *Harvard Law Review*, 69 (1955), 1–65; Mark DeWolfe Howe, *The Garden and the Wilderness: Religion and Government in American Constitutional History* (Chicago: University of Chicago Press, 1965); John P. Roche, "The Expatriation Cases: 'Breathes there the Man, with Soul so Dead . . . ?' " *Supreme Court Review* (1963), 325–56. There has been one systematic attempt, under the direction of Sister Marie Carolyn of Catholic University, to note, according to eras in Supreme Court history, all the significant uses of history in constitutional law. On the whole, the results are good surveys of limited perception. The published essays of the series are Marie Carolyn Klinkhamer, "The Use of History in the Supreme Court, 1789–1835," *University of Detroit Law Journal*, 36 (1959), 553–78; and John J. Daly, *The Use of History in the Decisions of the Supreme Court, 1900–1930* (Washington, D.C.: The Catholic University of America Press, 1954). The unpublished essays, all master's theses at Catholic University, are James E. Welch, "Roger B. Taney: Historical Allusion in his Supreme Court Decisions" (1950); Joseph A. O'Brien, "The Use of History in the Supreme Court, 1864–1873" (1950); John J. Daly, "The Use of History in the Supreme Court, 1873–1887" (1950); and Sister Ellen Mary Harnett, "The Use of History in the Supreme Court under Charles Evans Hughes" (1956). A logical source of research on the Supreme Court's use of history, the *American Journal of Legal History*, is of quite limited value. Legal historians are apparently not inclined to look for public or political significance in their own profession.

12. Willard Hurst, "The Role of History," in Edmond Cahn (ed.), *Supreme Court and Supreme Law* (Bloomington: Indiana University Press, 1954), pp. 55–58.

13. William Anderson, "The Intention of the Framers: A Note on Constitutional Interpretation," *American Political Science Review*, 49 (1955), 340–52; John G. Wofford, "The Blinding Light: The Uses of History in Constitutional Interpretation," *University of Chicago Law Review*, 31 (1964), 502–33.

constitutional law.[14] Kelly concludes that inept and perverted history has aided the Warren Court in announcing pathbreaking decisions, and that "law office history" has been concocted to give the opinions the trappings of scholarship and seeming roots in the past while serving the ends of modern "libertarian idealism."

The quality of the Court's opinions and its use of history are not, however, of interest only to constitutional scholars and lawyers. The public authority of the Supreme Court is one of the distinguishing features of American political life. This authority is maintained through the general acceptance of the Court's decisions and the reasons offered for these decisions. When the Court's work is scrutinized in public, that is, when the Court's authority is being confirmed or criticized, the use of history is also a matter of concern. The Constitution itself is a product of the nation's past, and the Supreme Court, as the accepted interpreter of the Constitution, has become a public interpreter of American political history.

The public recognizes this role of the Court. The Court's use of history has been questioned in the press.[15] Publications of the Virginia Commission on Constitutional Government, an official state agency, are permeated with historical analysis to refute the reasoning of the Supreme Court on various issues. The civil rights revolution has forced a large-scale confrontation with the American past in which the Supreme Court has been intimately involved, from the 1954 school segregation cases to the present.[16] The Supreme Court's use of history in constitutional law, then, which seems at first a topic in jurisprudence or history or political science, is also, and perhaps more importantly, a topic in political sociology.

This study takes into account both the jurisprudential and the political-sociological roles of history in constitutional law. Following this Introduction, Chapter II proposes a theoretical framework in which to view history as a principle of constitutional adjudication. In this context history is seen as one of several vehicles which

14. *Supreme Court Review* (1965), 119–58.
15. See, for example, Philip B. Kurland, "The Court Should Decide Less and Explain More," *New York Times Magazine*, June 9, 1968, p. 34, and esp. p. 124; "In the 13th Year of the 'Warren Revolution,'" *U.S. News & World Report*, June 20, 1966, pp. 48–53; Arthur Krock, "History Rewritten on the Bench," *New York Times*, Nov. 28, 1965, p. E–9; Anthony Lewis, "A Tough Lawyer Goes to the Court," *New York Times Magazine*, Aug. 8, 1965, p. 11, and esp. p. 67.
16. Brown v. Board of Education, 347 U.S. 483 (1954); Jones v. Alfred H. Mayer Co., 392 U.S. 409 (1968). In general, see Chapter VI.

judges use to explain the outcome of a decision, and, at the same time, as one of several political values which judges may carry internally or rely on explicitly in voting as they do.

Chapters III through VII are case studies in the Supreme Court's use of history. History is used in these chapters as the main focus for viewing five twentieth-century issues of constitutional law.[17] Each issue centers on a single case or closely related series of cases in which, to judge by the opinions, history has played an important role in reaching or explaining the conclusion of the Court. The cases involved are significant ones — they do not need their extended historical discussions to save them from obscurity — and they are unrelated to each other, thus permitting a wide discussion of history, historical interpretation, and the methods and purposes of using history in constitutional law. The studies appear in order of complexity of the historical problems they present.

In the light of the material provided by the case studies, Chapter VIII examines more theoretically the two sides of the basic problem posed by a written constitution, constitutional intent and constitutional change. In order adequately to understand the social function of the Supreme Court's use of history, Chapter IX provides a survey of the attitude of the American public towards history, towards the Constitution, and towards the Supreme Court. The concluding chapter presents both a summary and an evaluation of the uses of history in constitutional law.

17. American courts also make considerable use of legislative history, and legislative and constitutional history may overlap in constitutional cases. (See, for example, Chapters III and VI.) But the distinction between the two types of history, one referring to the Constitution, with all its political symbolism, and the other to ordinary law, is essential. The political significance of the Supreme Court's use of history is almost always derived from the Court's authority to interpret the Constitution, not statutes. This study is concerned with history as a principle of adjudication in constitutional, not in statutory, law.

CHAPTER II

PRINCIPLES OF ADJUDICATION
IN CONSTITUTIONAL LAW:
HISTORY AND OTHERS

The Judicial Mind and Judicial Principles

"I get letters, not always anonymous, intimating that we are corrupt. Well, gentlemen, I admit that it makes my heart ache. It is very painful, when one spends all the energies of one's soul in trying to do good work, with no thought but that of solving a problem according to the rules by which one is bound, to know that many see sinister motives and would be glad of evidence that one was consciously bad." [1] These words are from a talk by Justice Holmes in 1913. "No thought but that of solving a problem according to the rules by which one is bound" — is this to be believed? One may believe Holmes's sincerity and still question his proposition as applied to constitutional law.

In the first place, most of constitutional law does not admit of having the justices give "no thought" to anything but a legal problem and legal rules. Lower court judges who hear cases involving constitutional questions are bound by rules — the rules of the Supreme Court. And Supreme Court justices are relatively bound by law in nonconstitutional issues. But while judges in traffic courts or in bankruptcy proceedings may be able to concentrate on the relation between the facts of the case and "the law," justices hearing arguments on constitutional issues can seldom do so.

In the second place, what are "the rules" to which one is bound? Compared to other fields of law, constitutional law knows relatively few rules. In the area of procedure the Supreme Court, like other

1. Oliver Wendell Holmes, *Collected Legal Papers* (New York: Harcourt, Brace and Howe, 1920), p. 292.

courts, is fairly inflexible. But substantively its freedom is large. In a constitutional system which recognizes a wide scope for judicial review, these limits are set by the political and judicial values of the justices and the nature of the cases which come before them. In one case Justice Jackson candidly declared that neither the Constitution nor any other legal source offered a guide to the judges; it was a matter, he said, "on which we can find no law but our own prepossessions." [2]

In assessing the question whether Supreme Court justices determine the outcome of cases according to the rules by which they are bound or according to their own prepossessions, one is concerned in part with the problem of "judicial sincerity" — the degree to which justices really believe what they write in their opinions and how well they are able to convince others that opinions are decided for the reasons stated. It is the problem of judicial principles and the judicial mind.

Those who wrote Justice Holmes of the sinister motives behind Supreme Court decisions were certainly not wrong if they suggested that the reason for a decision might not be the same as the reasoning in the opinion. The "real" reason behind casting a vote one way rather than another may very well be obscured from the public — and even from the judge himself. "The decision," as Justice Holmes himself once pointed out, "will depend on a judgment or intuition more subtle than any articulate major premise." [3] But when a judge is denied a clear view of the "real" reasons for what he does, this is typically a matter of more psychological than judicial significance. What counts in the public life of the judicial system is the opinions of the judges as a form of public communication. For this communication to take place, it must be at a level where it is, at least in the long run, both functional and credible. The Supreme Court's opinions and the authority behind them exist and operate in a public world. What is said in the opinions must ultimately be accepted by and make sense to the people to whom they are addressed, regardless of how the decisions come about or the opinions happen to be written.

If it is still asked whether justices, although not "consciously bad," do not sometimes hide their values and therefore their "real" reasons behind a ceremonial screen of opinion-writing, the answer is yes.

2. Concurring in McCollum v. Board of Education, 333 U.S. 203, 238 (1948).
3. Dissenting in Lochner v. New York, 198 U.S. 45, 76 (1905).

Supreme Court opinions are in part a cover-up for something else. Several decades ago the Court supported a philosophy of laissez-faire capitalism, a philosophy not always made explicit in Court opinions. Today the Court is a source of democratic equalitarianism, a creed often implied rather than stated. But discerning these broad values demonstrates that constitutional law and currents of political and social theory are interrelated; it does not show that the courts are consciously dissembling.

Yet the *process* by which a judge reaches his decision and formulates his reasoning into an opinion is a psychological phenomenon, the understanding of which may aid in explaining the notion of judicial principles. It is this process, the "cause" of decision and of the determination how to explain it in an opinion, which often lies at the root of judicial criticism. Benjamin Cardozo quotes the British political scientist and sociologist Graham Wallas on this process of judicial reasoning: "When . . . I asked an American judge, who is widely admired both for his skill and for his impartiality, how he and his fellows formed their conclusions, he . . . laughed, and said that he should be stoned in the street if it were known that, after listening with full consciousness to all the evidence, and following as carefully as he could all the arguments, he waited until he 'felt' one way or another." [4]

Yet judges are not embarrassed to construct and reconstruct reasoning for their conclusions after having reached them. Judges might be stoned in the street for practicing the courtroom illogic of the Queen of Hearts, who demanded "Sentence first — verdict afterwards," but not for being born with the mental processes of normal mortals. Over a century ago, in a book on the rules of legal interpretation, Theodore Sedgwick pronounced judgment that holds today: "How is it to be expected that we can, with success, lay down rules which are generally to govern the operations of the mind? The attempt is ingenious, metaphysically curious, but of little practical utility in the study of the science of the law. What is required [is] . . . that complete education of the mind, which lead[s] it to a correct result, wholly independent of rules, and, indeed, almost unconscious of the process by which the end is attained." [5]

4. Quoted in *The Paradoxes of Legal Science* (New York: Columbia University Press, 1928), pp. 60–61.
5. *Treatise on the Rules Which Govern the Interpretation and Application of Statutory and Constitutional Law* (1857), quoted in Paul H. Sanders and

The "complete education of the mind" does not stop at a complete legal education. It refers to an entire system of social and political principles and values.[6] It is these values, plus the rules of the judicial process to which Justice Holmes referred, plus the facts of a case before the judge, which form the materials or sources of decision.[7] The three sources of decision — values, rules, and facts — combine to focus on the mysterious "act of deciding." While the sources of decision are rationally comprehensible, the act of deciding is not. But after that act, adjudication becomes understandable once more when the opinion of the court, the explanation of decision, is handed down.[8]

Judicial opinions are the most permanent and public manifestation of the work of the courts, and they are the chief demonstration that reasoning is the essential element of the judicial process. Opinions cannot be dismissed as sham.[9] The function of opinions is to

John W. Wade, "Legal Writings in Statutory Construction," *Vanderbilt Law Review*, 3 (1950), 573.

6. For finely wrought expressions of the role of a liberal education in the making of constitutional law, see Learned Hand, *The Spirit of Liberty* (New York: Knopf, 1952), e.g., p. 81.

7. This threefold analysis of the judicial process is reflected in the work of the philosopher Morris Cohen and of the historian Daniel Boorstin. Cohen qualified the proposition that judges make law on the basis of their own value systems by saying that judges could not make law as they pleased: "Every one who is engaged in making or creating something is limited by the rules of the process and the nature of the material." Quoted from an article of 1915 in Cardozo, *The Paradoxes of Legal Science,* p. 56. A parallel to this division is provided by the outline of Boorstin's study of William Blackstone and eighteenth-century British jurisprudence. The three parts of his book are entitled "Nature," "Reason," and "Values." *The Mysterious Science of the Law* (Boston: Beacon Press, 1958).

8. See in general Julius Stone, *Legal System and Lawyers' Reasoning* (Stanford: Stanford University Press, 1964), pp. 301–37.

9. There are two principal arguments for treating judicial opinions as sham:
a. "The whole point of the opinion-writing ritual is to provide acceptable rationales which will protect the justices from personal criticism — and even from personal responsibility — for their decisions." Glendon Schubert, *The Judicial Mind: Attitudes and Ideologies of Supreme Court Justices 1946–1963* (Evanston: Northwestern University Press, 1965), p. 14.

b. "The alleged logic of Constitutional Law is equally amorphous, equally unconvincing, equally silly whether the decisions the Court is handing down are 'good' or 'bad,' 'progressive' or 'reactionary,' 'liberal' or 'illiberal' . . . No matter in which direction the legal wand is waved, the hocus-pocus remains the same." Fred Rodell, *Woe Unto You Lawyers!* (New York: Reynal & Hitchcock, 1939), pp. 98–99.

As to the first: If the "whole point" of opinion-writing is the protection of the judges, it has been a miserable failure, as everything from law journals convince the judge, the parties, and the public that cases are rightly decided.[10] They serve to uphold the moral power of the courts, without which the judiciary would be ineffectual.[11] Moral power also depends, of course, on the weight of tradition, the authority of the government as a whole, and on the mystery of the law, particularly the reverence generally accorded the Constitution. But the prestige of the judiciary in America does not, as it does in other legal systems, depend on the moral authority of the individual judge, or the sanctions of tribal elders, or the unquestioned authority of religious scriptures and their interpreters. It is related to the quality of the opinions of the courts as statements of reasoning. When the reasoning of an opinion fails adequately to support the decision in a case, it is the entire judicial process that suffers. People do take judicial reasoning seriously, and they are not fools nor being fooled in doing so, at least no more than in other forms of communication or with respect to other strands that form the web of a political culture.

One of the most intense, and often baffling, controversies in recent American jurisprudence has centered precisely on the point of adequate judicial reasoning in reaching decisions.[12] Justices of the Supreme Court have also stressed the importance of reasoning in

---

to "Impeach Earl Warren" billboards can attest. The alternative to writing opinions, writing no opinions at all, is impracticable in American jurisprudence. And if the Supreme Court really desires protection, the European practice of handing down only unanimous opinions would be a much more efficacious method than the American custom of concurring and dissenting opinions.

As to the second: Not only is it unlikely that nine justices would exhaust themselves to produce hocus-pocus; it is impossible that the parties to the case, the legal profession, and the public at large would accept judicial opinions and reasoning as a conjurer's trick.

10. For evidence that judges may change their votes *after* deciding because an opinion "won't write," or because of the persuasiveness of a dissenting opinion, see Paul A. Freund, "An Analysis of Judicial Reasoning," in Sidney Hook (ed.), *Law and Philosophy: A Symposium* (New York: New York University Press, 1964), p. 288; and Robert H. Jackson, *The Supreme Court in the American System of Government* (Cambridge, Mass.: Harvard University Press, 1955), p. 15. Justices Black, Douglas, and Murphy changed their minds publicly in the flag-salute cases. Jones v. Opelika, 316 U.S. 584, 623–24 (1942).

11. See, e.g., Edward H. Levi, "The Nature of Judicial Reasoning," in Hook, *Law and Philosophy*, pp. 280–81; and Charles Evans Hughes, *The Supreme Court of the United States* (New York: Columbia University Press, 1928), pp. 64–65.

12. Much of this is the prelude and aftermath of Herbert Wechsler, "Toward Neutral Principles of Constitutional Laws," *Harvard Law Review*,

their work.[13] "This is one of those cases," Justice Jackson once wrote, "in which the reasons we give for our decision are more important to the development of the law than the decision itself." [14] The reasons of decision become constitutional principles, and as principles they acquire a force of their own. As Jackson said on another occasion, they stand around "like a loaded weapon" waiting to be fired when the constitutional occasion arises.[15]

The absence of reasoning in the form of a coherent argument is as detrimental to the Court's legal function and political role as the formulation of poor doctrine. Both reflect an inability to appreciate the power of opinions not as judicial commands but as judicial reasoning.

In the 1930's Justice Harlan Stone complained to Professor Felix Frankfurter about one of the opinions of the conservatives of the "old Court": "It just seems the writer and those who united with him didn't care what was said, so long as the opinion seemed plausible on its face . . . I can hardly see the use of writing judicial opinions unless they are to embody methods of analysis and of exposition which will serve the profession as a guide to the decision of future cases. If they are not better than an excursion ticket, good for this day and trip only, they do not serve even as protective coloration for the writer of the opinion and would much better be left unsaid." [16]

Five hundred years ago the English jurist John Fortescue could

73 (1959), 1–35. The problem has also received serious attention in the press. See, e.g., Alexander M. Bickel, "Is the Warren Court Too 'Political?'" *New York Times Magazine,* Sept. 25, 1966, p. 30; and Philip B. Kurland, "The Court Should Decide Less and Explain More," *New York Times Magazine,* June 9, 1968, p. 34.

13. For an instance of this from a jurist untouched by modern legal thinking, see Chief Justice White lamenting the fact that the Court offered no reasons for its conclusions in the National Prohibition Cases, 253 U.S. 350, 388 (1920). The "pertinacious pursuit of the processes of Reason in the disposition of the controversies that come before the Court" is the main lesson of Justice Frankfurter's valedictory to his colleagues. 371 U.S. iv (1962).

14. Dissenting in Craig v. Harney, 331 U.S. 367, 394 (1947).

15. Dissenting in Korematsu v. United States, 323 U.S. 214, 246 (1945).

16. Quoted in Alpheus T. Mason, *The Supreme Court: Vehicle of Revealed Truth or Power Group, 1930–1937* (Boston: Boston University Press, 1953), p. 41. The case referred to is Colgate v. Harvey, 296 U.S. 404 (1935). It was overruled in Madden v. Kentucky, 309 U.S. 83 (1940). For a complaint against the "new Court," expressed in similar language, see Justice Roberts dissenting in Smith v. Allwright, 321 U.S. 649, 666–70 (1944).

proclaim: "Sir, the law is as I say it is, and so it has been laid down ever since the law began; and we have several set forms which are held as law, and so held and used for good reason, though we cannot at present remember that reason." [17] But today the reason of the law is either remembered or constructed; at all events, it is given. The law is not majestic enough in the American system to endure for good but unexplained or unexplainable reason. Law, indeed, may be considered the application of reason in general to the governance of human affairs. And judges recognize this. In judicial decisions this appears as reasoning, as the careful explanation, within the rules of the process, of why a case has been decided as it has.

Principles as Vehicles of Judicial Reasoning

"If you have the decision," a judge is quoted as saying, "reasons will be found to be as plentiful as blackberries." [18] The judge is as correct as his analogy: blackberries, even when plentiful, may be unripe or overripe, and they are always surrounded by thorns. In constructing a judicial opinion, in other words, one must be careful to pluck only the appropriate reasons and to go about it in the least painful manner. As Justice Holmes one warned: "Every question of construction is unique, and an argument that would prevail in one case may be inadequate in another." [19]

Although the judicial opinion is written with a foregone conclusion in mind, it is written in a carefully arranged order so that its arguments, separately and together, support the conclusion in a way that is natural to our ways of thinking about law. This "naturalness" is primarily a matter of social and legal conditioning. But it also contains elements of an informal logic, a logic of presentation. The logic of presentation resembles only faintly a sequence of "if-then" statements; it is perhaps nearer the classical study of rhetoric. [20] This logic is a pattern of argument, usually including several separate lines of reasoning, that leads to a single conclusion. Each

17. Quoted in David Mellinkoff, *The Language of the Law* (Boston: Little, Brown, 1963), p. v.

18. The judge is quoted in J. Walter Jones, *Historical Introduction to the Theory of Law* (Oxford: Clarendon Press, 1965), p. 195.

19. United States v. Jin Fuey Moy, 241 U.S. 394, 402 (1916).

20. For a discussion of the relation of classical rhetoric to law, see Huntington Cairns, *Legal Philosophy from Plato to Hegel* (Baltimore: The Johns Hopkins Press, 1949), pp. 151–60.

of the paths may be considered as a principle of adjudication in the sense of being a vehicle for deciding cases. Principles of adjudication as vehicles in constitutional law include the constitutional text, constitutional and other legal doctrines, precedent, social facts, and history. In view of the purpose of this study the first four of these will be given relatively brief treatment.

Constitutional text. The first step in the construction of written documents, whether literary or legal, is to consult the document itself. If a legal document is supposed to control the outcome of a case and its unadorned text is perfectly plain, then legal interpretation stops right there. It is difficult to disagree with Justice Noah Swayne's remark a century ago: "If the language be clear it is conclusive. There can be no construction where there is nothing to construe." [21] But as Justice Holmes stated, this is "rather an axiom of experience than a rule of law," and very few cases have come to a conclusion in as short order as the axiom suggests.[22] Although some causes of the Constitution are perfectly clear today, most have required considerable interpretation. The constitutional text continues as the touchstone of interpretation, but it is not by itself sufficient as a principle of adjudication.[23]

Doctrine. Constitutional doctrines are formulas extracted from a combination of the constitutional text and a series of related cases. Typically stated in shorthand fashion, they may be used almost as an emendation on the constitutional text. A good example of a constitutional doctrine developed in the nineteenth century is the "Cooley doctrine," which set at rest the pendulum swings of Supreme Court opinion on the extent to which states could exercise control over interstate commerce in the absence of congressional legislation. The Cooley doctrine forbids states to legislate on sub-

21. United States v. Hartwell, 6 Wall. 385, 396 (1868).
22. Boston Sand and Gravel Co. v. United States, 278 U.S. 41, 48 (1928).
23. Nineteenth-century commentaries contain extensive discussion of how to interpret the constitutional text. The problem was then considered to be very similar to that of statutory interpretation, and, indeed, much contemporary writing on statutory construction is applicable, with modification, to the text of the Constitution. See Charles P. Curtis, "The Role of the Constitutional Text," in Edmond Cahn (ed.), *Supreme Court and Supreme Law* (Bloomington: Indiana University Press, 1954), pp. 64–70. A comprehensive symposium on statutory construction appears in *Vanderbilt Law Review*, 3 (1950), 365–584. Law review articles and notes on the subject appear continuously, among them Felix Frankfurter, "Some Reflections on the Reading of Statutes," *Columbia Law Review*, 47 (1947), 527–46.

jects that are "in their nature national, or admit only of one uniform system, or plan of regulation." [24] An example of a twentieth-century doctrine is that of "one person, one vote," the simplest expression of the meaning of the fourteenth amendment with respect to legislative apportionment.[25]

Neither the Cooley doctrine nor the apportionment rule is self-interpreting. But as doctrines they are intermediaries between the Constitution and a case that may come before the Court. Once established they may be resorted to as principles of adjudication with high authority. Because their purpose is to relate the abstractions, generalizations, or obscurities of the Constitution to the concreteness of a case, constitutional doctrines are subject to some flexibility and adaptability without becoming either verbal ornament (as the text of the Constitution may appear to be) or dead-end conclusions (as the outcome of a single case often is).[26]

Precedent. One of the distinctive features of the common law system is the use of precedent, or previously decided cases, in the determination of later cases. Precedents may be used as examples or as sources of insight into particular legal problems. But they may also become binding legal authority for later cases which a court considers similar. When this happens, the court is following the doctrine of stare decisis.[27] In constitutional law stare decisis has

24. Cooley v. Board of Port Wardens of Philadelphia, 12 How. 299, 319 (1851).

25. The reapportionment cases are the subject of Chapter VII.

26. Doctrines, like the cases from which they are derived, are particularly appropriate to Benjamin Cardozo's "method of philosophy" or "rule of analogy," according to which the principles derived from cases expand and contract by posing as analogies for new situations that come before the courts. *The Nature of the Judicial Process* (New Haven: Yale University Press, 1921), pp. 9–50. They also fit what Edward Levi terms a process of "moving classification" in judicial reasoning and what Julius Stone has called "categories of illusory reference" necessary to the judicial process. Levi, "The Nature of Judicial Reasoning," in Hook, *Law and Philosophy*, pp. 266–73; Stone, *Legal System*, pp. 235–300.

Constitutional law also uses doctrines originally formulated in other fields of law. The "clear and present danger" formula is a notable example. There are in addition a number of Court-designed standards for accepting cases to adjudicate or for disposing of them. See, e.g., Justice Brandeis concurring in Ashwander v. Tennessee Valley Authority, 297 U.S. 288, 346–48 (1936); Alexander M. Bickel, "The Passive Virtues," *Harvard Law Review*, 75 (1961), 40–79; John P. Roche, "Judicial Self-Restraint," *American Political Science Review*, 49 (1955), 762–72.

27. Historically, it was only after the practice of citing previously decided cases had been established that stare decisis as a rule of law developed. See

been applied with much less rigor than in other fields of law, on the theoretical ground that it is the Constitution which is the basic standard and not the previous decisions of the Court. The practical justification for the ease with which precedent, as stare decisis, is ignored in constitutional law is that constitutional cases deal with momentous social and political issues that only temporarily take the form of litigation, and these issues cannot be dealt with on the same terms as other legal problems. Constitutional law has great need for the continuity and certainty that the doctrine of stare decisis can provide, and precedents have been dispensed with only over strong dissent. But since constitutional law depends even more on its soundness than its firmness, in a conflict between precedent and progress, precedent will, more quickly than in other fields of law, yield to progress.[28]

Social evidence. Since its earliest days the Supreme Court has taken notice of social facts in its opinions and has used them as a principle of constitutional adjudication. But only in the twentieth century has the principle become generally recognized and, at the same time, the subject of controversy.[29]

Social and economic legislation of both state and federal governments, beginning in the late nineteenth century, has provided the chief test of the Supreme Court's willingness to recognize the signifi-

---

Frederick G. Kempin, Jr., "Precedent and Stare Decisis: The Critical Years, 1800–1850," *American Journal of Legal History*, 3 (1959), 28–77.

28. The literature on the use of precedent in constitutional law is enormous. Among the most instructive essays are Charles Aiken, "*Stare Decisis*, Precedent, and the Constitution," *Western Political Quarterly*, 9 (1956), 87–92; Ralph F. Bischoff, "The Role of Official Precedents," in Cahn, *Supreme Court and Supreme Law*, pp. 76–83; Louis B. Boudin, "The Problem of *Stare Decisis* in our Constitutional Theory," *New York University Law Quarterly Review*, 8 (1931), 589–639; William O. Douglas, "Stare Decisis," *Columbia Law Review*, 49 (1949), 735–58 (Justice Douglas states on p. 737 that stare decisis "must give way before the dynamic component of history"). The writings of Benjamin Cardozo, particularly *The Nature of the Judicial Process* and *The Paradoxes of Legal Science,* contain wise treatment of the role of precedent and stare decisis in law generally.

29. In the nineteenth century, for instance, it seemed natural for the Court to hold, contrary to both precedent and constitutional intent, that federal maritime jurisdiction extended to all navigable waters, not just to those affected by ocean tides. Chief Justice Taney wrote that a decision he was overruling had been handed down "in 1825, when the commerce on the rivers of the west and on the lakes was in its infancy, and of little importance, and but little regarded compared with that of the present day." The Genesee Chief v. Fitzhugh, 12 How. 443, 456 (1851), overruling The Thomas Jefferson, 10 Wheat. 428 (1825).

cance of factual situations in constitutional adjudication. In the *Lochner* case the Court declared invalid a New York law limiting the working hours of bakers, with the assertion that the legislation involved "neither the safety, the morals, nor the welfare of the public." [30] To overcome such an outlook on welfare legislation, Louis Brandeis presented a brief (in a case decided three years later) which contained more than a hundred pages of statistics and other documentary material in support of the reasonableness of a state labor law affecting women. The Brandeis brief succeeded. The Court agreed that the mass of evidence was persuasive in determining "the extent to which a special constitutional limitation" would go, even though "technically speaking" the evidence was not constitutional authority.[31]

The Brandeis brief did not assume that all constitutional limitations could be overcome by evidence from the social world. This, indeed, offers theoretical justification for the failure of the technique in many cases where it has been applied. It did succeed, however, in the watershed decision between the "old" and "new" Courts in 1937, and this victory was its undoing.[32] In the new era, when the Court assumed that social legislation was constitutional rather than unconstitutional, the Brandeis brief was no longer necessary. When the burden of argument fell to those who had to prove a negative (that a statute was invalid on the grounds of factual evidence), the task became almost impossible.[33]

The momentous exception to this state of affairs is the school desegregation decision of 1954, and it proves the rule.[34] One of the major points of controversy about this decision has been that it contains statements, and one footnote in particular, pointing to sociological and psychological rather than traditional legal principles as

30. Lochner v. New York, 198 U.S. 45, 57 (1905).

31. Muller v. Oregon, 208 U.S. 412, 420–21 (1908).

32. For five members of the Court, Chief Justice Hughes wrote: "We may take judicial notice of the unparalleled demands for relief which arose during the recent period of depression and still continue to an alarming extent despite the degree of economic recovery which has been achieved." West Coast Hotel Co. v. Parrish, 300 U.S. 379, 399 (1937). The conservative minority succinctly but unavailingly replied: "The meaning of the Constitution does not change with the ebb and flow of economic events." 300 U.S. at 402.

33. See, e.g., Robert G. McCloskey, "Economic Due Process and the Supreme Court: An Exhumation and Reburial," *Supreme Court Review* (1962), 34–62. On general limitations of the Brandeis brief see Paul A. Freund, *The Supreme Court of the United States* (Cleveland: World, 1961), pp. 150–54.

34. Brown v. Board of Education, 347 U.S. 483 (1954).

the basis of adjudication. Despite the use of social science evidence in the Supreme Court for a century and a half, opponents of the decision expressed shock at the technique, and defenders of the decision were surprisingly weak. There were several reasons for this. First, psychology and sociology seemed qualitatively different fields from economics and public health, two of the important disciplines that had been relied on before. The findings seemed, and were, less scientific, and they were therefore more suspect. Second, the debatable evidence was used to support a negative proposition, as if certain facts which showed unwisdom could at the same time demonstrate unconstitutionality. Finally, the use of the evidence suited the basic argument of the Court's opinion, that a change in social climate over the decades is sufficient to change constitutional interpretation. This argument seemed to many, including integrationists, an unnecessary acceptance of constitutional relativism. The same principle could be employed at a later date to undo the decision; the justices would only have to be convinced that the latest findings in the social sciences showed that racial separation was beneficial.[35]

In expanding the school desegregation decision to other fields the Court has implicitly recognized the force of this criticism. Instead of presenting more evidence and conclusions from the social sciences, it has followed the prudent course of relying on the precedent of the original desegregation decision.[36] Contemporary social experience,

35. Among the pertinent analyses of the question are Edmond Cahn, "A Dangerous Myth in the School Segregation Cases," in Lenore L. Cahn (ed.), *Confronting Injustice: The Edmond Cahn Reader* (Boston: Little, Brown, 1966), pp. 329–45 (originally published 1955); Kenneth B. Clark, "The Desegregation Cases: Criticism of the Social Scientist's Role," *Villanova Law Review*, 5 (1959–60), 224–54; Jack Greenberg, "Social Scientists Take the Stand," *Michigan Law Review*, 54 (1956), 953–70; Joseph Tanenhaus, "Social Science in Civil Rights Litigation," in Milton Konvitz and Clinton Rossiter (eds.), *Aspects of Liberty* (Ithaca: Cornell University Press, 1958), pp. 91–114. A concise history of the Brandeis brief from its origin in the *Muller* case through the *Brown* decision is Alpheus Thomas Mason, "The Case of the Overworked Laundress," in John A. Garraty (ed.), *Quarrels That Have Shaped the Constitution* (New York: Harper and Row, 1964), pp. 176–90.

36. A list of these cases may be found in *The Constitution of the United States of America: Analysis and Interpretation* (Washington: Government Printing Office, 1964), p. 1306. The practice has not been followed when the Court has dealt with the right of Negroes to nondiscriminatory service in places of public accommodation. See Chapter VI. And it has not been followed when lower courts have held unconstitutional de facto segregation in the public schools. See, e.g., the 180-page opinion of Judge J. Skelly Wright in Hobson v. Hansen, 269 F. Supp. 401 (U.S. Dist. Ct. for D.C. 1967).

whether offered as fact or impression or left unmentioned entirely, continues to influence constitutional adjudication. But it must be recognized as a vehicle of interpretation that is not suitable for all cases.

History. The final vehicle used to decide cases in constitutional law is history. For purposes of this study history may be defined as that which, in the opinions of the Supreme Court, is believed to be true about the past — about past facts and past thoughts.[37] From the Supreme Court's first terms to the present, history has played a large role in constitutional adjudication. It is perhaps too much to claim, as Justice Horace Gray did in 1895, that the "question [in this case], like all questions of constitutional construction, is largely a historical question," but concerning no other principle could such a claim even be proposed.[38] Indeed, each of the previously discussed principles of adjudication may be seen under the aspect of history: the constitutional text because it is an eighteenth-century document; constitutional doctrine because it is a distillation of the Court's past decisions and practices; precedent because it is judicial history; and social facts because they are, in effect, the materials of contemporary history. More generally, the nature of law, particularly constitutional law, and the function of the Supreme Court in American society both contain a large element of viewing the present in terms of the past. They both have the historical question built into them.

The most restricted form of history used in constitutional law is that which is internal to a particular case, its factual background. All other history used by the Court is external to the case. By the time a case reaches the Supreme Court the facts are seldom in dispute, yet the opposing briefs and majority and minority opinions almost always present this internal history in different ways.[39] The Court has

37. History is also, of course, what is actually true about the past, what happened at the time regardless of what anyone later believes about it. Among historians this is a common distinction, and it is one sometimes necessary to observe in analyzing the Court's uses of history. But the Court itself does not make the distinction, and, as Chapters IV–VII demonstrate, the Court's uses of the past are primarily a function of its own beliefs.

The reason for distinguishing facts (physical events) from thoughts (mental events) is that, while the historical sources giving evidence of either are largely the same, the first is almost always agreed upon by the Court, but the second, especially in the form of the contemporaneous significance of facts, is often not.

38. Sparf v. United States, 156 U.S. 51, 169 (1895).

39. One of the most vivid examples of this is United States v. Shipp, 214 U.S. 386 (1909), in which the Court divided 5–3 solely on a question of fact. In

said that its duty "is not limited to the elaboration of constitutional principles; we must also in proper cases review the evidence to make certain that those principles have been constitutionally applied." [40] This means that the Court may sometimes review issues of fact, by which it means "basic, primary, or historical facts." [41]

Once outside the background of an individual case, history is immensely varied. For purposes of analysis it may again be divided into two categories: history internal to the law and history external to the law. This distinction, like many distinctions, is blurred at the boundaries but clear at the center. History internal to the law consists of precedents, which have already been discussed, and legal history. Legal history pertains to the history of legal terms and doctrine, legal systems, and judicial practices.

In American history the most important broad topic in legal history dealt with by the courts has been the extent to which the English common law was "received" as the law of the colonies and, later, of the states. Like many issues in legal history, the nineteenth-century argument over the reception of the common law was not a legal issue alone but was embroiled in politics. Like other legal receptions it was conditioned by cultural attitudes towards the home country of the system — in the American case the attitude towards England — but the issue was argued in terms of law. At one point, indeed, the opposition to British law was so great that several states enacted legislation forbidding the courts from even citing prerevolutionary British cases. Ultimately the country succumbed to the Anglo-Saxon heritage, but with the qualification that the law adopted

---

its 17-page opinion the majority held: "Only one conclusion can be drawn from these facts, all of which are clearly established by the evidence, — Shipp not only made the work of the [lynch] mob easy, but in effect aided and abetted it." 214 U.S. at 423. In an eight-page dissent three justices concluded: "A careful consideration of the case leaves [us] with the conviction that there is not one particle of evidence that any conspiracy had ever been entered into or existed on the part of the sheriff, as charged against him." 214 U.S. at 426.

"In my experience in the conference room of the Supreme Court of the United States, which consists of nine judges," declared Justice Samuel Miller in the late nineteenth century, "I have been surprised to find how readily those judges come to an agreement upon questions of law, and how often they disagree in regard to questions of fact." Quoted in Barbara Frank Kristein (ed.), *A Man's Reach: The Philosophy of Judge Jerome Frank* (New York: Macmillan, 1965), p. 208. See also Paul A. Freund, "Review of Facts in Constitutional Cases," in Cahn, *Supreme Court and Supreme Law*, pp. 47–51.

40. New York Times Co. v. Sullivan, 376 U.S. 254, 285 (1964). See also the cases there cited.

41. Townsend v. Sain, 372 U.S. 293, 309 n. 6 (1963).

would have to measure up to the "civil and political condition" of America.[42]

Recent cases in which the Supreme Court has used legal history to decide constitutional issues have been no less enmeshed in politics, and the result, quite naturally, has been to make legal history the subject of political manipulation in briefs and in court opinions.[43] One example will indicate the close relationship between politics and legal history in constitutional law. In 1964 the Supreme Court decided a case in which the Governor of Mississippi, when cited for criminal contempt by a federal court for disobeying injunctions relating to the desegregation of the state university, had insisted that he was guaranteed a jury trial by the Constitution.[44] His expectation was that a jury of fellow Mississippians would not convict him but independent federal judges probably would. This is the political context of the case. But half of the Supreme Court's opinion, plus a twenty-three page appendix of "statutes and cases relevant to the punishment for contempt imposed by colonial courts," is devoted to

42. The phrase comes from Murray's Lessee v. Hoboken, 18 How. 272, 277 (1855), in which a unanimous Court interpreted authoritatively for the first time the due process clause of the fifth amendment. The opinion examined in detail "settled usages and modes of proceeding existing in the common and statute law of England, before the emigration of our ancestors . . ." *Ibid.* Among the literature on the reception see Ford W. Hall, "The Common Law: An Account of its Reception in the United States," *Vanderbilt Law Review,* 4 (1951), 791–825; Roscoe Pound, *The Formative Era of American Law* (Boston: Little, Brown, 1938); Charles M. Haar (ed.), *The Golden Age of American Law* (New York: Braziller, 1965), pp. 423–52.

Justice Joseph Story in the nineteenth century and Justice Felix Frankfurter in the twentieth made the most scholarly and sustained use of legal history in their legal opinions. For a study of a more obscure justice in the same tradition see Robert M. Spector, "Legal Historian on the United States Supreme Court: Justice Horace Gray, Jr., and the Historical Method," *American Journal of Legal History,* 12 (1968), 181–210.

43. This matter has been approached in several ways. L. J. Downer, in "Legal History — Is it Human?" *Melbourne Law Review,* 4 (1963), 1–16, pleads for the freedom of legal history from relevance to contemporary law in order to upgrade its status as history. William F. Swindler, "Legal History — Unhappy Hybrid," *Law Library Journal,* 55 (1962), 98–110, speaks of the strained relations among lawyers, historians, and political scientists in the presentation and uses of legal history. Frederick B. Wiener covers the subject widely and pungently in an address to the British society for legal history, the Selden Society. *Uses and Abuses of Legal History: A Practitioner's View* (London: Bernard Quaritch, 1962). James R. Wiggins provides a specific example to support his general comments in "Lawyers as Judges of History," *Proceedings of the Massachusetts Historical Society,* 75 (1964), 84–104.

44. United States v. Barnett, 376 U.S. 681 (1964).

legal history. In the end, the Court denied the official's claim. The major dissenting opinion in the case relied largely on the same authorities cited in the majority's appendix but concluded that legal history supported the claim of a constitutional right to a jury trial in these circumstances.[45]

Somewhere on the borderline between legal history, which is internal to the law, and general political history, which is external to the law, lies the history used in two important classes of cases heard by the Supreme Court: disputes between states and litigation involving Indian tribes. In no other fields of public law does history play so decisive a role, a role and a decisiveness accepted by all parties to the litigation as well as the Court. The history most referred to in these cases is that of surveys and treaties, claims and possessions, political and economic activities and control.

The principle for the use of history in boundary cases was stated by Justice Stone. Decisions of the Court have established, he said, "either expressly or by example that in the interpretation of a treaty or grant between two states for the settlement of a boundary dispute the nature and the history of the controversy must be considered." [46] In most boundary cases the history has not only been considered, it has been the controlling factor. In an early case between Rhode Island and Massachusetts, Chief Justice Taney requested reargument in order principally to have more historical material presented to the Court.[47] In one of the cases involving the most important boundary dispute in the twentieth century, that between the United States and several states over ownership of the tidelands oil in the Gulf of Mexico, Justice Harlan wrote for the Court: "Both sides have presented in support of their respective positions a massive array of

45. A separate dissent of Justice Black held that the framers of the Constitution intended to provide jury trial in all criminal cases and that legal history was not relevant to a determination of the issue. The case is critically discussed in Sheldon Tefft, "United States v. Barnett: ' 'Twas a Famous Victory,' " *Supreme Court Review* (1964), 123–36. Two other recent cases worth comparing with *Barnett* from the standpoint of the uses of legal history in constitutional adjudication are Fay v. Noia, 372 U.S. 391 (1963), and United States v. Johnson, 383 U.S. 169 (1966). The first of these is sharply criticized in Lewis Mayers, "The Habeas Corpus Act of 1876 — The Supreme Court as Legal Historian," *University of Chicago Law Review*, 33 (1965), 31–59; and Dallin H. Oaks, "Legal History in the High Court — Habeas Corpus," *Michigan Law Review*, 64 (1966), 451–72.

46. Vermont v. New Hampshire, 289 U.S. 593, 605 (1933).

47. Rhode Island v. Massachusetts, 13 Pet. 23 (1839); Rhode Island v. Massachusetts, 14 Pet. 210 (1840).

historical documents, of which we take judicial notice, and substantially agree that all the issues tendered can properly be disposed of on the basis of the pleadings and such documents." [48]

In disputes concerning American Indian tribes the courts have also considered and often decided cases principally on the basis of historical materials. The judicial attitude and its reasoning were stated in a typical Indian treaty case in the Supreme Court: "We may look beyond the written words to the history of the treaty, the negotiations and practical construction adopted by the parties . . . Especially is this true in interpreting treaties and agreements with the Indians; they are to be construed, so far as possible, in the sense in which the Indians understood them and 'in a spirit which generously recognizes the full obligation of this nation to protect the interests of a dependent people.' " [49] This generous recognition of the full obligation to protect the interests of a dependent nation may sound strange, condescending, or even hypocritical in the face of the military force, political expediency, and social neglect which have bulked large in the history of the white man's relations with the Indians. But it has been white man's law that has provided the chief source of security for the Indians, and beyond an appeal to conscience and legal documents the best evidence in most Indian cases is the testimony of history, especially the use, possession, practice, and expectation concerning the lands. Because a human community and its fortunes are usually involved, rights to large areas of land, whether contested by states or by Indian tribes, are adjudicated cautiously and with particular respect to the materials of the past.[50]

The final form of history to be considered as a principle of con-

48. United States v. Louisiana, 363 U.S. 1, 12–13 (1960). Justice Black, dissenting in part, agreed that this was the proper method of deciding the controversy: "We must look to the claims, understandings, expectations and uses of the States throughout their history." 363 U.S. at 90. The same considerations prevailed in the companion case, United States v. Florida, 363 U.S. 121 (1960). The standard authority on boundary questions is Charles Warren, *The Supreme Court and the Sovereign States* (Princeton: Princeton University Press, 1924).

49. Choctaw Nation v. United States, 318 U.S. 423, 432 (1943). The internal quotation is from Tulee v. Washington, 315 U.S. 681, 684–85 (1942).

50. The most famous Indian cases in American history, on the dispute among Georgia, the Cherokee Indians, and the United States, relied extensively on history, though the decisions were ultimately based on lesser legal points. Cherokee Nation v. Georgia, 5 Pet. 1 (1831); Worcester v. Georgia, 6 Pet. 515 (1832). The standard work on Indian law, Felix S. Cohen, *Handbook of Federal Indian Law* (Washington: Government Printing Office, 1942), bears out the large role of history in this field of law.

stitutional adjudication is general history. General history, which is external to the law, includes political, social, economic, and cultural history. It has been an accepted guide to constitutional interpretation since the establishment of the nation. The distinguishing feature of general history is the scope it gives the Supreme Court for policy choices.[51] General history not only takes the justices into fields where their training and knowledge may be limited, but it also invites the avoidance of the more strictly legal principles of decision. The use of general history may seem to confess the inadequacy of the traditional tools of law for deciding cases. More than this, the political authority of the Court often endows it with a certain intellectual authority. By writing history into its opinions the Court contributes to the public's view of the American past as much as, and sometimes even more than, professional historians and other historical writers do. When the Supreme Court has the chance to tell us what American history is, history becomes more than a tool of decision. It affirms or denies the significance of past events for the activities of the present. While this may be of little consequence in the field of legal history, it is not so in general history. With the increased scope and power granted the Court by the use of history goes the increased responsibility in the handling of historical materials.[52]

In terms of its use by the Supreme Court, general history may be seen as both the history which serves to explicate the meaning of the original Constitution (and the amendments) as drafted and ratified and the history which serves to reveal conditions in the nation since the ratification, conditions that the justices believe have a bearing on later interpretation of the Constitution. Typically, the history concerned with the formation and ratification of the Constitution serves to restrain the Court in its decisions. It shares this feature with two other principles of adjudication: the constitutional text and precedent. In contrast, the use of continuing or "ongoing" history allows the Constitution to move with the prevailing temper of the country and may therefore be considered forward-looking. The evidence of ongoing history merges into contemporary observation at no clearly

51. This is the point of Willard Hurst, "The Role of History," in Cahn, *Supreme Court and Supreme Law*, p. 58.
52. This is one of the lessons of Mark DeWolfe Howe's study of church-state relations in constitutional law. *The Garden and the Wilderness: Religion and Government in American Constitutional History* (Chicago: University of Chicago Press, 1965). See also Howe's "Split Decisions," *New York Review of Books*, July 1, 1965, p. 14.

definable date. It eventually yields to the use of social evidence as a principle of adjudication.

The difference between the two types of general history can be expressed in another way. The history that searches for the "original understanding" of a constitutional clause is a history that recognizes and places a high value on the "intent theory" of documentary interpretation. The intent theory holds that a document, such as the Constitution, should be construed in agreement with the intentions of the person or persons who wrote it. To discover these intentions for the Constitution one must turn to the history of the late eighteenth century. Since it is the Constitution that commands the Supreme Court to decide one way or another, since the Constitution should mean what it was intended to mean, and since intent is ascertainable only by resort to historical material, history as intent is essentially history as command. The other history, ongoing history, is not to be viewed as determining the command of the Constitution but as demonstrating the currents and lessons of experience. Ongoing history does not say "this is what was expected," but "this is what the nation has become." [53]

The Supreme Court has availed itself liberally of both "intent history" and ongoing history since its first sessions, changing the techniques only as new perspectives, documents, and professional standards have influenced opinion-writing. For two reasons an essential identity between intent history and ongoing political history existed during the early years of the Court. First, there was a relative absence of source material concerning the Constitutional Convention. Second, the events surrounding the adoption of the Constitution were merged in the minds and experience of the justices with the early history of the national period.[54] But when memory could no

---

53. Chapter VIII examines the problems of constitutional intent and constitutional change at greater length.

54. John Marshall is the best example of this. His devotion to George Washington and the cause of American nationalism was the result of his experience during the Revolution. He argued for the adoption of the Constitution at the Virginia ratification convention. He was envoy to Paris, member of Congress, and Secretary of State before becoming Chief Justice. And in a five-volume *Life of Washington* he wrote a general political history of the country since the time of settlement. In short, the text of the Constitution was the distillation of a history that Marshall knew well; and his opinions on the Court, which contain abundant evidence of his historical interests, firmly established the validity of history as a principle of adjudication in constitutional law. See Marie Carolyn Klinkhamer, "The Use of History in the Supreme Court, 1789–

longer serve to explicate the original understanding of the Constitution and when ongoing history — the political, economic, and social changes since 1789 — pressed increasingly for recognition in constitutional law, the two types of history diverged permanently.

The *Dred Scott* case, the most inflammatory decision of the Court in the nineteenth century, provides perhaps the best single illustration of intent and ongoing histories in conflict. Chief Justice Taney for the Court and Justice Curtis in dissent turned the adoration of Clio into a ravishment. Although Taney's theory of constitutional construction was unequivocally historical, ongoing history played no role in his conception of how to use the past. He relied only on history as intent: "No one, we presume, supposes that any change in public opinion or feeling . . . should induce the court to give to the words of the Constitution a more liberal construction in their favor than they were intended to bear when the instrument was framed and adopted . . . Any other rule of construction would abrogate the judicial character of this court, and make it the mere reflex of the popular opinion or passion of the day." [55] On this basis the Chief Justice insisted that it was "necessary . . . to determine who were citizens of the several States when the Constitution was adopted." [56] After a long essay on American and European attitudes and practices with respect to Negroes, Taney decided that members of "this unfortunate race" were not intended to be citizens of the United States.[57]

Justice Curtis, on the other hand, argued not only that this was not the original meaning of the Constitution but that, with regard to the power of Congress to prohibit slavery in the territories, "a long series of acts of the gravest importance" had determined the constitutional issue in the years since 1789 in favor of the Negroes.[58] Chief Justice Taney may have had the better history, but Justice Curtis was the better historian, for he agreed to follow intent not only as contemporaneous meaning but also as potential for growth.

1835," *University of Detroit Law Journal,* 36 (1959), 553–78; Klinkhamer, "John Marshall's Use of History," *Catholic University Law Review,* 6 (1956), 78–96; Albert J. Beveridge, *The Life of John Marshall* (4 vols.; Boston: Houghton Mifflin, 1916–19), esp. III, 223–73; William A. Foran, "John Marshall as a Historian," *American Historical Review,* 43 (1937), 51–64.

55. Scott v. Sandford, 19 How. 393, 426 (1857).
56. 19 How. at 407.
57. Quotation, *ibid.*
58. 19 How. at 619.

He saw history as process, not only as event. He studied the stream and the flow, not merely the source.

The example of *Dred Scott* apparently confirms that history as intent is a restraining force in constitutional law and that ongoing history is the champion of progress. This is perhaps the natural implication of the difference between viewing history as event and viewing it as process. But because the Court writes opinions in order to explain its decisions and not with respect to developing a consistent philosophy of the uses of history, this natural implication has sometimes proved misleading and the roles of the two histories have been reversed. Intent history has been invoked in the name of change and ongoing history in the name of the existing order.[59]

Yet the considerable latitude of judicial choice that history offers as a vehicle of adjudication does not give it immunity from constructive criticism. On the contrary, this latitude invites careful study, within specific constitutional contexts, of the uses to which history is put. It is the reasoning of the Supreme Court, not the bare decisions, which imparts meaning to constitutional law. It is the validity of that reasoning which in large part determines the authority of the Constitution and the Court in the public mind.

Principles as Political Values

Why does the Supreme Court make the constitutional law that it does? Why do the justices of the Court vote as they do? The answers lie in the interaction between the values of the individual judges and the currents of the society in which they live, including the prevailing attitudes towards law, the judiciary, and the Supreme Court. The political values of the judges are also principles of adjudication. But these values are categories of belief, not of argument. While principles as vehicles explain how a decision was reached and refer to legal reasoning, principles as political values explain why a particular decision was made and refer to human reasons. Holmes declared seventy years ago that in doubtful cases which present "a conflict between two social desires" and for which precedent offers no solution "judges are called on to exercise the sovereign prerogative of choice." [60] Cases that reach the Supreme

---

59. This is one of the lessons that may be drawn from the case studies in Chapters V–VII.

60. *Collected Legal Papers*, p. 239.

Court are almost always such doubtful cases, and no judges exercise the sovereign prerogative of choice more than the justices of the Supreme Court.

In exercising the prerogative, Benjamin Cardozo said, a judge should give effect "not to his own scale of values, but to the scale of values revealed to him in his readings of the social mind." [61] Yet this test may fail, and then the judge must "look within himself." [62] When they look within, judges, like other men, find a view on the good society in America. In addition, judges, unlike most other men, hold views on the nature of the judicial function. To discover the views of judges one must go both behind the decision to the man and to the Court and forward from the opinion to the political and social impact of the case. Just as few judicial opinions present only one vehicle of adjudication, few decisions represent only one value. And because principles as values in adjudication conjoin to form a single political weltanschauung for each individual justice, classifying the components of the entire Court's political values is a distinctly synthetic operation, involving more than the classification of principles as vehicles of adjudication. Yet the results can clarify distinctions and aid in understanding the opinions of the Court. The following survey treats the value principles of adjudication under the following headings, with more attention, as before, reserved for the final one, which includes history: social philosophy, the role of government in society, the role of the judiciary in government, law and order, stability and change.

Social philosophy. There are two broad areas of social philosophy about which most informed citizens, not only judges, hold views. These are the organization and functioning of the economy, and the rights and roles of individuals and minority groups in society. The decisions of the Marshall and Taney Courts reflect, in part, the needs of a capitalist economy in a developing nation.[63] Leading cases of the time required states strictly to honor their land grants (as contracts); to respect the national banking system; to refrain from interfering with corporate rights — except in the interest of public improvements; to maintain debt laws unaltered with respect to previously

61. *The Paradoxes of Legal Science,* p. 55.
62. *Ibid.,* p. 56.
63. On constitutional history and the American economy in general, see Max Lerner, "The Supreme Court and American Capitalism," *Yale Law Journal,* 42 (1933), 668–701.

contracted agreements; and to permit corporations chartered elsewhere to do business within the states.[64]

From the 1880's to the 1930's the theory of laissez faire dominated the Court's thinking on economics. Justice Field, the most creative jurist to mold the constitutional basis for this outlook, quoted Adam Smith in his support and, at the end of his career, fulminated against "the present assault upon capital." [65] Judicial instruments, such as the labor injunction, and doctrines, such as "business affected with a public interest," "direct" versus "indirect" effect on interstate commerce, and the "rule of reason" in antitrust prosecutions, contributed to the prevailing economic philosophy of the Court and aided in overturning much social welfare legislation until the justices yielded to the New Deal in 1937. Since that time the Court has refrained from passing constitutional judgment on the substance of most economic legislation. But the impact of the Court through interpretation of the antitrust laws and the review of independent regulatory commissions has been substantial, regardless of the technically nonconstitutional nature of the decisions.[66]

The second area of social philosophy in which a judge's values may be relevant to constitutional adjudication concerns individual and minority rights. Race relations is the only one of these issues which reaches far back into the Court's history. Antebellum opinions on slavery were usually carefully restricted to legal and constitu-

64. The cases referred to are Fletcher v. Peck, 6 Cr. 87 (1810); McCulloch v. Maryland, 4 Wheat. 316 (1819); Dartmouth College v. Woodward, 4 Wheat. 518 (1819); Charles River Bridge v. Warren Bridge, 11 Pet. 420 (1837); Sturges v. Crowninshield, 4 Wheat. 122 (1819); Bank of Augusta v. Earle, 13 Pet. 519 (1837).

65. Adam Smith is quoted in Field's dissent in The Slaughter-House Cases, 16 Wall. 36, 110 (1873); the quotation in the text is from Field's concurring opinion in the income tax case, Pollock v. Farmers' Loan & Trust Co., 157 U.S. 429, 607 (1895). Even more outspoken for the rights of property, though less influential on the Court, was Field's nephew, Justice David Brewer. See, e.g., Brewer's opinions for the Court in Monongahela Navigation Co. v. United States, 148 U.S. 312 (1893); South Carolina v. United States, 199 U.S. 437 (1905). In the latter case Justice Brewer suggested that laissez faire was the intention of the framers of the Constitution. See also his dissent in Budd v New York, 143 U.S. 517 (1892).

66. For a good specialized study see Martin Shapiro, *Law and Politics in the Supreme Court* (Glencoe, Ill.: The Free Press, 1964), chap. 6, "Antitrust — The Supreme Court as Political Economist." One of the few economic areas in which the Court does pass judgment under the Constitution regards state acts that patently discriminate against interstate commerce. See in general Robert L. Stern, "The Problems of Yesteryear — Commerce and Due Process," *Vanderbilt Law Review*, 4 (1951), 446–68.

tional arguments in order to avoid public controversy, but in spite of that it was assumed that the justices were voting their political convictions on the matter. When the judiciary spoke out strongly in the mid-twentieth century, after decades of national somnolence on rights for Negro Americans, it was assumed once more that the Court was deciding the issue on the basis of political values. As if to demonstrate this, the Court's unanimity broke down when other political values, such as property rights and the need for public order, clashed too strongly with the justices' basic sympathy for the goals of the civil rights movement.[67] The political values of the justices have also been reflected in decisions affecting individual and minority rights, including free expression, church-state relations, rights of the accused, the "right of privacy," citizenship, and legislative apportionment. As in the case of race relations, the tendency has been to expand the rights of the individual or group until value principles collide with one another.[68]

The role of government. The justices' views on the role of government in society, though less directly affecting the litigants in a case than economic and social convictions, may also be essential in determining the decision of the Court. To understand the opinions of John Marshall and Joseph Story, for instance, it is necessary to recognize their political goal of binding the states into a permanent union through the interpretation of a legal document. Conversely, in the modern era when national unity was secure, it was one of Justice Brandeis' cherished principles that political and economic power be dispersed to the states.[69] Federalism is an even brighter thread in the opinions of Justice Frankfurter, where it is a value of adjudication in complete disregard of any interest-oriented jurisprudence of economic and social principles.

67. Property rights were at issue when the Court split in the sit-in cases. (See Chapter V.) The threat of violence led to a 5–4 decision in Adderly v. Florida, 385 U.S. 39 (1966).

68. An excellent example of this is the Court's handling of the Sunday blue laws, in which the power of the state to regulate business for the public welfare (to insure a day of rest) clashed with the right of individuals to be free of regulations that discriminate in favor of religion or among different religions. McGowan v. Maryland, 366 U.S. 420 (1961); Gallagher v. Crown Kosher Market, 366 U.S. 617 (1961); but cf. Sherbert v. Verner, 374 U.S. 398 (1963).

69. See Freund, *The Supreme Court of the United States,* p. 126. Holding that federal courts must follow state court decisions as to state law, Brandeis overturned a century-old decision of Justice Story, whose motivation was devotion to the national principle. Erie R. Co. v. Tompkins, 304 U.S. 64 (1938), overturning Swift v. Tyson, 16 Pet. 1 (1842).

Aside from their views on the allocation of power between states and nation, the justices also hold convictions on the exercise of power by government in general. The pronounced views against governmental authority which dominated the Court from Reconstruction to the New Deal are now reversed, and the Court permits almost any regulation by state or federal government, regardless of the particular legislative views of members of the Court. A crucial test of the Court's attitude toward the exercise of governmental power comes in times of economic and military emergency. On the national level the Court has usually upheld congressionally approved action, but, following a political principle descended from the revolutionary era, it has been less willing to permit the executive branch to exercise special powers on its own.[70]

The role of the judiciary. Half a century ago, when the godlike nature of Supeme Court justices was first coming under respectable intellectual attack, the most caustic intelligence among the scholars, Thomas Reed Powell, wrote: "Judges have preferences for social policies, as you and I. They form their judgments after the varying fashions in which you and I form ours. They have hands, organs, dimensions, senses, affections, passions. They are warmed and cooled by the same winter and summer and by the same ideas as a layman is."[71] Yet a most important attitude that a man brings to (or develops on) the bench concerns the judiciary itself: that judges ought not to be warmed and cooled by the same ideas as a layman is. In a dissent delivered shortly before the Supreme Court passed into a new era in the 1930's, Justice Stone wrote: "The power of courts to declare a statute unconstitutional is subject to two guiding principles . . . One is that courts are concerned only with the power to enact statutes, not with their wisdom. The other is that while unconstitutional exercise of power by the executive and legislative branches of the government is subject to judicial restraint, the only check upon our own exercise of power is our own sense of self-restraint."[72]

This is an influential modern statement of the role of the judge in

70. Relevant cases in this regard include Ex parte Milligan, 4 Wall. 2 (1866); Korematsu v. United States, 323 U.S. 214 (1945); Yakus v. United States, 321 U.S. 414 (1944); Youngstown v. Sawyer, 343 U.S. 579 (1952).

71. "The Logic and Rhetoric of Constitutional Law" (1918), in Robert G. McCloskey (ed.), *Essays in Constitutional Law* (New York: Knopf, 1957), p. 89.

72. United States v. Butler, 297 U.S. 1, 78–79 (1936).

the political system. But it is subject to qualification. First, it is not always easy to discern Stone's two principles in action. An opinion may protest that it is concerned only with legislative power and is deeply conscious of the need for self-restraint, and then proceed to declare a law unconstitutional. This is possible not only because it is the Court's duty to declare unconstitutional some legislation but also because, as the Constitution itself is revered as a fount of wisdom, even judges may not be able totally to disentangle what is wise from what is constitutionally permissible. The only tests of the proposition that the principles are taken seriously are their repeated declaration and evidence that a judge voted either to sustain a law he disapproved of or to overturn one he agreed with.[73] The second qualification of Justice Stone's statement is of a substantive nature and it was made by Stone himself. The limit of judicial self-restraint is reached, said Stone, when the democratic processes are thwarted. Under these circumstances "there may be narrower scope for the operation of the presumption of constitutionality," and the judiciary may step in long enough to correct the situation.[74]

Law and order. Law and order is a fourth major area of political values which affect the outcome of constitutional litigation. A judge's views in this area are especially important in cases concerned with legal procedure and cases involving the public peace. Although all members of the Court insist that legal procedure be fair, there is ultimately a point, already reached according to some, at which legal procedure stymies the apprehension and prosecution of criminals. If there is a real relationship between the incidence of crime and the rights of the accused, then judges are confronted with a situation in

73. Justice Holmes passes both of these tests better than any other member of the Court. Repeatedly expressing the view that his "agreement or disagreement has nothing to do with the right of a majority to embody their opinions into law," he would have upheld reform legislation which ran counter to his economic beliefs; and he struck down convictions in free speech cases in which the defendants held views he found personally revolting. The quotation is from Holmes's dissent in Lochner v. New York, 198 U.S. 45, 75 (1905). More recently Justice Frankfurter has been the Court's principal exponent of judicial self-restraint. Compare also the views of Justice Black dissenting in the leading birth-control case. Griswold v. Connecticut, 381 U.S. 479, 507 (1965).

74. The quotation is from Justice Stone's famous "footnote 4," United States v. Carolene Products Corp., 304 U.S. 144, 152 n. 4 (1938). The apportionment cases are an outstanding example of a conflict between the doctrine of judicial self-restraint and the "footnote 4" qualification of that doctrine. See Chapter VII.

which law may be magnified to such a degree that disorder is countenanced as a result. Judges must then make the difficult choice between two values that are normally linked together.

A conflict of political principles also occurs when law and order are invoked against the exercise of first-amendment rights of free expression. The fundamental issue in such cases is whether the democratic process is best maintained by upholding constitutional rights under conditions not likely to promote the intelligent consideration of public affairs, or by protecting civil peace, without which these rights become meaningless. Political agitation cases of the 1940's and 1950's, in which the justices almost uniformly abhorred the causes espoused, and cases stemming from the civil rights movement of the early 1960's, in which the Court manifestly approved of the political goals, have presented the conflict of principles between free expression and public peace most clearly.[75] The factors to which the Court looks in order to determine these civil liberties cases include the character of the speech (particularly its context and intent), the character of the official reaction to it, the public regulations for such speech, and whether the police acted against the speaker or against the crowd. But no matter how refined the treatment of the circumstances, the justices' values must ultimately play a role in the outcome.[76]

Stability and change. The justices' views on stability and change comprise a final philosophical attitude that affects constitutional law. Because of their position in society and their training in the law, judges tend to favor stability and the status quo.[77] For several

75. The earlier and later cases are also distinguishable in other ways. The political agitation group occurred in an era when the Court, like the country, was sensitive to comparisons with totalitarian countries where neither free speech nor the slightest disorder was permitted. The civil rights cases typically arose from situations in which the demonstrators adhered to the philosophy of nonviolence. Yet Justice Black, who had written the strongest opinions favoring free speech in the earlier cases, dissented in the later ones partly on the ground that the nobler the end the greater should be the Court's service to it by insisting on public order. See, e.g., Cox v. Louisiana, 379 U.S. 559, 584 (1965).

76. See in general Freund, *The Supreme Court of the United States,* pp. 57–91; Thomas I. Emerson, "Toward a General Theory of the First Amendment," *Yale Law Journal,* 72 (1963), 877–955; and the concurring opinion of Justice Frankfurter in Niemotko v. Maryland, 340 U.S. 268, 275–83 (1951).

77. Age by itself appears not to be correlated with a tendency towards either stability or change. President Roosevelt's court-packing plan proposed additions to the Court when justices failed to retire at seventy, and "the nine old men" were indeed old. But, if one omits Justice Roberts (as a "swing man") in the calculations, the four conservatives on the Court at the time

reasons, however, judges may be disposed towards change. Some justices of the Supreme Court have been appointed with the expectation that they would help bring about change in constitutional law.[78] In addition, the justices' personal backgrounds in politics or public affairs keep them informed of and often sympathetic to the major currents of society. Finally, independence in office encourages speaking out for change that may not yet be accepted by the country at large.

Inseparable from the justices' attitude toward stability and change is their attitude toward the past, and therefore toward history. In this regard history — respect for the past — may become a principle of adjudication or a political value of its own. Roscoe Pound has suggested that attempts to reconcile stability and change in law have proceeded along three lines: authority, philosophy, and history.[79] By authority Pound understood a "single ultimate unchallengeable author behind the legal order," such as God, or "the people." [80] By philosophy he understood an organizing plan or ideal to which law should conform, in particular the precepts of natural law as models for human law. And by history Pound meant the principles of growth and development traced through the past.

Although history has been used in support of the other two concepts, helping to identify the sources of authority and aiding in the explanation of philosophical systems, Pound saw the dominion of the three principles of legal theory in a rough chronological sequence. It was in the nineteenth century, under the influence of the German historical school, that history became a self-sufficient basis for the legal order. This school, which developed in reaction to the ideas of legal rationalism and the law of nature, stressed a study of past legal institutions in order to determine the law most appropriate for the present. History became a positive value in law. It was not merely a vehicle for explaining decisions. To Dean Pound, however, history was not an especially beneficial value. It disappeared

---

averaged 76 years and the four liberals 75½, which is to say there was no difference.

78. It is thought, for instance, that the appointments of Justices Strong and Bradley to the Court in 1870 were designed to reverse the decision declaring the Legal Tender Act unconstitutional. The justices appointed by Franklin Roosevelt were staunch New Dealers who immediately ratified social welfare legislation.

79. "Law and History," chap. 1 of *Interpretations of Legal History* (New York: Macmillan, 1923).

80. *Ibid.,* p. 3.

as a leading current in jurisprudence at the end of the nineteenth century, and in America it was replaced with pragmatism, a "revival of faith in action." [81]

The categories of Pound, without regard to his judgment on them, are instructive in viewing the work of the Supreme Court. Perhaps because the Court has been more attuned to social practice than to social theory and has been in existence only a short time relative to Pound's sweep of history, the attempt to place his categories in distinct historical periods needs modification for the history of American constitutional law, which is unnecessary for the history of jurisprudence. But to the extent that the Court is influenced by broad doctrines of legal and political philosophy its trends have borne out Pound's analysis. The Court put more faith in authority, and philosophy (natural law) in its first years, in history during the bulk of the nineteenth century, and in pragmatism in recent decades. In another sense, however, the justices have referred to all three categories throughout the history of the Court. The Constitution has stood for authority, economic and social theory for philosophy, the course of American development for history, and social evidence for pragmatism.

In reconciling stability and change in constitutional law today, authority and philosophy offer very little practical aid. Both the Constitution and "social philosophy" are vessels into which a judge may pour almost any content he wishes. But history and pragmatism can be of real use in analysis, for they carry within themselves attitudes towards stability and change. Under the pragmatic view an open future is insured by a continual re-evaluation of the present. Where the historical perspective is valued, stability is more probable.

Either of the two outlooks is compatible with American constitutional theory. On the one hand there is the Constitution that looks to the future, that is "intended to endure for ages to come." [82] On the other hand there is the Constitution that establishes political community, a fundamental law whose authority depends upon common experience and roots in the past. The difference between the two outlooks may be represented by the political philosophies of Edmund

---

81. Pound himself advocated an "engineering interpretation" of the law, a variety of pragmatism according to which jurists would lead legislatures and the courts in securing through the application of the social sciences various contemporary social interests. *Ibid.,* chap. 8.

82. Chief Justice Marshall in McCulloch v. Maryland, 4 Wheat. 316, 415 (1819).

Burke and Thomas Jefferson. Burke saw a "sacred veil . . . over the beginnings of all governments," regarded social continuity as a cardinal value, and tested civil institutions not by reason but by experience.[83] "With regard to this admired Constitution," Burke wrote of the British system, "we ought to understand it according to our measure, and to venerate where we are not able presently to comprehend . . . Let us follow our ancestors, men not without a rational though without an exclusive, confidence in themselves . . ." [84]

Thomas Jefferson thought otherwise. "I set out on this ground which I suppose to be self-evident," he had written James Madison in the flush of the French Revolution, " 'that the earth belongs in usufruct to the living;' that the dead have neither powers nor rights over it." [85] To Jefferson there was no mystery in the origin of government — it was a written constitution. Far from regarding continuity as the highest value, the right of revolution was meant to be exercised. Jefferson affirmed the worth of experience, but largely to point out what the nation should avoid and never as a guide unaccompanied by the philosophy of reason. "Some men," he wrote, as if in reply to Burke, "look at constitutions with sanctimonious reverence, and deem them like the ark of the covenant, too sacred to be touched. They ascribe to the men of the preceding age a wisdom more than human, and suppose what they did to be beyond amendment. I knew that age well; I belonged to it, and labored with it. It deserved well of its country . . . Laws and institutions must go hand in hand with the progress of the human mind. As that becomes more developed, more enlightened, as new discoveries are made, new truths disclosed, and manners and opinions change with the change of circumstances, institutions must advance also, and keep pace with the times." [86]

83. The quotation is from "Speech on the Impeachment of Warren Hastings, Second Day," *The Writings and Speeches of Edmund Burke* (12 vols.; Boston: Little, Brown, 1909), IX, 401.
84. "Appeal from the New to the Old Whigs," *Writings*, IV, 213.
85. Letter of Sept. 6, 1789, *Writings*, ed. Paul L. Ford (10 vols.; New York: Putnam's Sons, 1892–1899), V, 116 (emphasis omitted).
86. Letter to Samuel Kercheval, July 12, 1816, *Writings*, X, 42–43. In the terms used to describe history as a vehicle rather than as a value of adjudication, it may be suggested that Burke's history is ongoing history, so long as it goes back far enough, while Jefferson's is intent, so long as this is ratified by the living generation. Recent studies of Burke and Jefferson have shown that some revision is necessary with regard to their respective conservative and ra-

In determining the role of history in constitutional law the Supreme Court is choosing, symbolically, between Burke and Jefferson, and it typically attempts to choose them both. The Court expects to keep pace with the times while showing reverence for the Constitution and respect for tradition. It is grappling with the insight of Justice Holmes: "It ought always to be remembered that historic continuity with the past is not a duty, it is only a necessity" — with which neither Burke, who felt historic continuity a duty, nor Jefferson, who felt it no necessity, would have agreed.[87] And at the same time the Court heeds the emendation of Justice Frankfurter that judges "are under a special duty not to over-emphasize the episodic aspects of life and not to undervalue its organic processes — its continuities and relationships. For judges at least it is important to remember that continuity with the past is not only a necessity but even a duty." [88]

---

tionalist outlooks. But the contrasting image of the two men remains. See Gerald Wester Chapman, *Edmund Burke: The Practical Imagination* (Cambridge, Mass.: Harvard University Press, 1967); Daniel J. Boorstin, *The Genius of American Politics* (Chicago: University of Chicago Press, 1953), pp. 84–94; and H. Trevor Colbourn, "Thomas Jefferson's Use of the Past," *William and Mary Quarterly*, 15 (1958), 56–70.

87. *Collected Legal Papers*, p. 139.

88. "Some Reflections on the Reading of Statutes," *Columbia Law Review*, 47 (1947), 534–35. For an elegant statement of the "part history plays as the source of value in the law," see Charles E. Wyzanski, Jr., "History and Law," *University of Chicago Law Review*, 26 (1959), 237–44. Judge Wyzanski finds Jefferson "profoundly in error" in stating that "the world belongs to the living" (p. 244).

CHAPTER III

MINNESOTA MORTGAGE

MORATORIUM: THE OLD COURT AND

AN IMMUTABLE CONSTITUTION

Whereas, the severe financial and economic depression existing for several years past has resulted in extremely low prices for the products of the farms and the factories, a great amount of unemployment, an almost complete lack of credit for farmers, business men and property owners and a general and extreme stagnation of business, agriculture and industry, and

Whereas, many owners of real property, by reason of said conditions, are . . . threatened with loss of such properties through mortgage foreclosure and judicial sales thereof, and

Whereas, such properties have been and are being bid in at mortgage foreclosure and execution sales for prices much below what is believed to be their real values . . .

The Legislature of Minnesota hereby declares its belief, that [these] conditions . . . have created an emergency of such a nature that justifies and validates changes in legislation providing for the temporary manner, method, terms and conditions upon which mortgage foreclosure sales may be had or postponed.[1]

These words come from the preamble to an act of the Minnesota legislature passed in April 1933. In January 1934 the Supreme Court, by a five-to-four vote, upheld the constitutionality of the act in the case of Home Building and Loan Association v. Blaisdell.[2] Mr. and Mrs. John Blaisdell, landlords and residents of a large house in Minneapolis, had availed themselves of an act intended primarily for

1. Home Building and Loan Ass'n. v. Blaisdell, 290 U.S. 398, 421 n. 3 (1934), quoting from Chap. 339 of the Laws of Minnesota (1933).
2. 290 U.S. 398 (1934).

the relief of farmers. They had defaulted on mortgage payments on their home, and Home Building and Loan Association, in May 1932, had purchased the house at a foreclosure sale for $3700, an amount equal to the indebtedness remaining in the mortgage but substantially lower than the market value of the property. Unable to redeem the mortgage within a year of foreclosure, the period granted by legislation in effect at the time, the Blaisdells obtained through judicial proceedings the maximum extension of the redemption period allowed by the new law, two years. During this extension period they were to pay Home Building and Loan Association a reasonable monthly rent on the house.

The question before the Supreme Court was whether the proceedings authorized by the Minnesota law violated the contract clause of the Constitution: "No state shall . . . pass any . . . law impairing the obligation of contracts." [3] Chief Justice Hughes wrote a thirty-three-page opinion for the Court holding that the contract clause had not been violated. He was joined by Justices Brandeis, Stone, Roberts, and Cardozo. After a lengthy recital of the facts the Chief Justice explained the decision to uphold the statute as follows:

(1) "The policy of protecting contracts against impairment presupposes the maintenance of a government by virtue of which contractual relations are worth while, — a government which retains adequate authority to secure the peace and good order of society." [4] Minnesota had witnessed a number of riots by farmers against foreclosure sales, and the state pointed to these as evidence that the moratorium legislation was justified to preserve the good order of society.

(2) In order to secure such order, states may, in times of emergency like Minnesota's, exercise their powers to promote the welfare of their citizens in a way not permissible in ordinary circumstances: "While emergency does not create power, emergency may furnish the occasion for the exercise of power." [5]

3. Art. 1, sec. 10.

4. 290 U.S. at 435.

5. 290 U.S. at 426. This statement is devastatingly scrutinized by the dissent at 472–73. The Chief Justice did not dream up the doctrine for the occasion, however. Before the Depression Hughes had written: "The Supreme Court has recognized that the legislature may meet public emergencies by action that ordinarily would go beyond its constitutional authority." *The Supreme Court of the United States* (New York: Columbia University Press, 1928), p. 222.

(3) It is not "the occasion and general purpose" of the contract clause that fixes its precise scope, but the subsequent judicial interpretation of the clause and the course of American development.[6] There are three reasons for this. First, a capacity for evolution is basic to the American Constitution. Second, the Constitution contains two distinct kinds of clauses, specific and general. The general clauses, of which the contract clause is one, afford the Court only "a broad outline [for which] the process of construction is essential to fill in the details." [7] And third, under these circumstances, judicial construction, because it is more recent, is a better guide to the contemporary meaning of the Constitution than are the constitutional text and the history of its adoption.

(4) Cases decided under the contract clause "put it beyond question that the prohibition is not an absolute one." [8] Under the present emergency, these cases sanction the constitutionality of the limited and carefully drafted Minnesota statute.

The dissent in the *Blaisdell* case, slightly longer than the opinion for the Court, was written by Justice Sutherland. He was joined by Justices McReynolds, Van Devanter, and Butler. Point by point the dissent challenged the argument of the majority. In outline it held: (1) The stability of society requires that the meaning of a constitutional provision remain unchanged. (2) The application of a constitutional clause, as distinct from its meaning, may vary according to circumstances, but it depends upon "the nature of the power and the intent of the Constitution with respect thereto" whether an emergency may furnish the occasion for certain otherwise unconstitutional exercises of the power.[9] (3) Neither in its nature nor by its intent is the contract clause susceptible to special interpretation in emergencies: "The testimony of history [puts] . . . beyond the domain of uncertainty . . . that the clause of the Constitution now under consideration was meant to foreclose state action impairing the obligation of contracts *primarily and especially* in respect of such action aimed at giving relief to debtors *in time of emergency*." [10] (4) With respect to debtor legislation enacted in times of crisis, the

6. 290 U.S. at 428.
7. 290 U.S. at 426. On "two-clause theories" of constitutional interpretation in general, see below, pp. 162–67.
8. 290 U.S. at 428.
9. 290 U.S. at 473.
10. 290 U.S. at 465 (emphasis in the original).

cases decided under the contract clause do not permit an interpretation alternative to its original constitutional intent.[11]

The *Blaisdell* decision, a victory for the state's powers during an emergency, appeared to be significant both politically and legally, but in fact its significance lies elsewhere. In the context of the times *Blaisdell* represented the first defeat for the conservative justices of the Court after the coming of the New Deal. But it proved a misleading indicator of how the Court would treat social legislation occasioned by economic crisis, for until 1937, with few exceptions, the values of the *Blaisdell* minority prevailed, and state and federal legislation was declared unconstitutional. In the context of contract clause litigation the case has proved even more misleading. Instead of inaugurating an era in which impairments of contracts in favor of

11. Two of these cases deserve mention. The one most relevant to the situation in *Blaisdell* was Bronson v. Kinzie, decided ninety years earlier. 1 How. 311 (1843). In *Bronson* the Court held unconstitutional Illinois legislation which, with respect to a pre-existing mortgage that permitted unrestricted power of sale in case of default, required (a) sale for at least two thirds of the appraised value and (b) the right of redemption by the mortgagee within one year of the sale. The Court in *Bronson* felt that while the remedy for enforcing a contract might constitutionally be altered, this went so far that the obligation of the contract itself was impaired. Chief Justice Hughes distinguished the Minnesota case from the *Bronson* circumstances on two grounds: first, provision (a) was absent in the Minnesota statute; second, the extension of the redemption period in the Illinois situation was both unconditional (instead of under judicial supervision) and without concurrent rental payments. As Justice Sutherland pointed out in dissent, the conditions in Illinois during the depression that began in 1837 were very similar to those in Minnesota almost a century later. Hughes's attempt to distinguish the two statutes did no more than show that their wording was not identical.

The other important precedent for *Blaisdell* was nearer in time but more remote in subject matter. In the Rent Cases of 1921 and 1922 the Court held 5–4 that during a wartime housing shortage New York, under the police power, had the right to prevent the ejectment of tenants by landlords at the expiration of the leases so long as a reasonable rent was paid. Marcus Brown Holding Co. v. Feldman, 256 U.S. 170 (1921); Levy Leasing Co. v. Siegel, 258 U.S. 242 (1922). Of these cases Chief Justice Hughes says in *Blaisdell:* "Whatever doubt there may have been that the protective power of the State, its police power, may be exercised — without violating the true intent of the provision of the Federal Constitution — in directly preventing the immediate and literal enforcement of contractual obligations, by a temporary and conditional restraint, where vital public interests would otherwise suffer, was removed by our decisions relating to the enforcement of provisions of leases during a period of scarcity of housing." 290 U.S. at 440. This is a heavy burden to impose on such close decisions in a somewhat different field. As Justice Sutherland concluded in dissent: "Reasonably considered [the Rent Cases] do not foreclose the question here involved." 290 U.S. at 479.

debtors would be declared constitutional and the contract clause take on new importance in constitutional law, the case established no important precedent and almost bowed the contract clause out of constitutional law.[12] The significance of *Blaisdell* is that it is a classic example of a leading theoretical problem in constitutional interpretation: how to use history — history as the intent of the framers — as a principle of constitutional adjudication.

The history surrounding the inclusion of the contract clause in the Constitution is clear, particularly with respect to debtor legislation of the type at issue in *Blaisdell*. That history is unequivocally opposed to the decision of the Court. In *Blaisdell*, however, the opinion for the Court is unusual in that it does not invoke any of the common responses that have been developed in constitutional law to deal with obstinate historical facts. The first of these responses is to devise a different interpretation of history that would permit a different outcome for the case. A second is to dispute the clarity of the historical facts and to hold, on that basis, that history is of no real aid in settling the issue. A third response is to ignore history altogether. But Chief Justice Hughes admits that history is not on his side and proceeds to decide the case on other principles.[13]

The chief purpose of the contract clause, according to Hughes's accurate historical statement, was to alleviate "the widespread distress following the revolutionary period [which] had called forth in the States an ignoble array of legislative schemes for the defeat of creditors and the invasion of contractual obligations." [14] In dis-

12. On the contract clause in general see Benjamin F. Wright, *The Contract Clause of the Constitution* (Cambridge, Mass.: Harvard University Press, 1938); Robert L. Hale, "The Supreme Court and the Contract Clause," *Harvard Law Review*, 57 (1944), 512–57, 621–74, 852–92; *The Constitution of the United States of America: Analysis and Interpretation* (Washington: Government Printing Office, 1964), pp. 378–410; and El Paso v. Simmons, 379 U.S. 497 (1965), especially the dissent of Justice Black.

13. If the weight accorded a principle of adjudication in deciding a case may be roughly measured by the amount of space devoted to it in an opinion, then a comparison of the majority and minority *Blaisdell* opinions in this respect is instructive. The opinions are of approximately equal length, and each side makes the most of its respective strength. Chief Justice Hughes devotes two, but Justice Sutherland over twelve, pages to the history of the contract clause. When it comes to the facts and the context of the Minnesota law, the balance is heavily in the other direction. Approximately equal space is given in each opinion to precedent and other constitutional doctrines.

14. 290 U.S. at 427. The Chief Justice cites as authorities Max Farrand (ed.), *The Records of the Federal Convention of 1787* (1911); Jonathan Elliot (ed.), *Debates in the Several State Conventions on the Adoption of the Federal Con-*

sent, Justice Sutherland corroborates this conclusion at length. Quoting from historians of the period, Sutherland emphasizes the economic distress in America just prior to the Constitutional Convention.[15] Much of Justice Sutherland's description would apply virtually unaltered to the conditions in Minnesota in the early 1930's: men out of work, property sold at a fraction of its value, courts and judges stormed by mobs, agricultural produce destroyed rather than brought to market for low prices, and stay laws and installment laws enacted to cope with the difficulties.[16]

The history recounted by Justice Sutherland and agreed to by the Court is perfectly correct. But it is not the only correct historical interpretation of the contract clause, and from the viewpoint of twentieth-century constitutional law it is not necessarily the most relevant. In the Constitutional Convention the contract clause occasioned almost no debate, and very little in the state ratifying conventions. Antifederalist pamphlets were not concerned with it, and the discussion in *The Federalist*, where it might have been extensively defended and explicated, was brief, perfunctory, and very general.[17]

---

stitution (1861); *The Federalist,* No. 44; provisions of the Northwest Ordinance; John Marshall's *Life of Washington;* and works of historians George Bancroft and John Fiske.

15. Justice Sutherland's authorities, in addition to those cited by the Court, include David Ramsay, George Ticknor Curtis, John Bach McMaster, Edward Channing, Charles A. Beard, Charles Warren, and Allan Nevins. The Supreme Court had told the same history in a case over half a century earlier. Edwards v. Kearzey, 96 U.S. 595, 604–07 (1878).

16. A stay law prevents a creditor from collecting any part of the monies owed him for a specified period; an installment law permits a debtor to pay his debt by installments after the original payments have fallen due.

17. The subject is referred to specifically in only two places. In *The Federalist,* No. 7, Hamilton outlines the weaknesses of the Confederation: "Laws in violation of private contracts, as they amount to aggressions on the rights of those States whose citizens are injured by them, may be considered as another probable source of hostility." Hamilton, Madison, and Jay, *The Federalist,* ed. Benjamin F. Wright (Cambridge, Mass.: Harvard University Press, 1961), p. 118. In No. 44, when Madison discusses the cures proposed by the Constitution, he lumps the prohibitions against bills of attainder, ex post facto laws, and laws impairing the obligation of contracts all together in one paragraph and says nothing about any of them individually. The meager antifederalist literature on the contract clause is summarized in Wright, *The Contract Clause,* pp. 5, 13; and Cecelia M. Kenyon (ed.), *The Antifederalists* (Indianapolis: Bobbs-Merrill, 1966), pp. lxxxviii–xc. It should be noted that the months of greatest economic hardship caused by the scarcity of sound money were over by the time of the ratification debates. Justice Sutherland states that the contract clause was "strongly defended" by Hamilton and Madison (290 U.S. at 463), but this refers to the general argument for eco-

If the economic conditions were as calamitous as historians described; if economic considerations were of great significance in debates over the Constitution; and if stay laws and installment laws were common instances of state legislation designed to be prohibited by the contract clause, why then did the debtor class, which benefited from the legislation and was well represented in public debate, agree with the creditors that the contract clause was scarcely worth mentioning in the debate over the ratification of the Constitution?

One reason for this curious lack of debate seems to be that all concerned, federalists and antifederalists, debtors and creditors, recognized that the debtor relief laws were only symptomatic of the broader problem of an unstable currency. Much more attention, therefore, was devoted to the monetary clauses of the Constitution (which gave Congress the power to coin and regulate the value of money and to raise revenue through taxation and by borrowing) than to the contract clause.[18] Persons in need of money could scarcely expect to find a lender if the terms of the loan might be freely altered by legislative decree. It was to the advantage of both sides that relief laws become unnecessary (and therefore their prohibition unimportant). It was the underlying economic conditions, particularly matters of currency, that needed to be improved.[19]

If this interpretation is correct, then Justice Sutherland's history (and that of the Court) is right as to the particular impairment the framers of the Constitution had in mind, but it is irrelevant to the basic problem recognized by the people of the time. Pursuing this reasoning it might be argued, first, that in construing the contract clause the large purpose, the smooth functioning of the economy, should be more important in later constitutional adjudication than the specific means designed to promote this end in the 1780's; and second, that the debtor legislation of the 1930's was designed to effectuate the broader aims of the clause. According to the leading historian of the contract clause, "relief legislation of the Confedera-

nomic stability presented in *The Federalist,* not to the contract clause specifically. For the background of the clause, see Wright, *The Contract Clause,* pp. 3–26.

18. In fact, according to Benjamin Wright (*ibid.,* p. 15), many of the men of 1787–88 confused the contract clause with the monetary provisions of Article I, Section 10.

19. For a most discriminating treatment of the debtor and paper money problem in the struggle over constitutional ratification, see Jackson Turner Main, *The Antifederalists: Critics of the Constitution, 1781–1788* (Chicago: Quadrangle, 1964), esp. pp. 5–7, 26–27, 162–67, 259–81.

tion period was almost entirely the result of the existing shortage of a stable currency." [20] One hundred and fifty years later, when the same kind of legislation was enacted in Minnesota, economic conditions were completely different. Although in form the same, the laws passed in the two eras are seen to be opposite in significance when viewed in the light of the different economic conditions. The earlier relief legislation exacerbated economic instability. The modern relief laws were designed to bring economic instability to a halt, that is, to achieve the underlying aim of the contract clause. Could the Minnesota law not be upheld on the ground of agreement with the basic intention of the framers of the Constitution?

In economic terms, or in historical perspective, this argument is a justifiable one. But from a legal point of view it is distinctly uncomfortable and in some ways even disingenuous. Since justices of the Supreme Court are more sensitive to legal than to historical and economic arguments, it is not surprising that this interpretation of contract clause history does not appear in the *Blaisdell* opinions. It is quite naturally left unmentioned in the dissent, since it could only have harmed Justice Sutherland's narrowly focused historical argument. And though potentially present in the opinion of the Court, it is completely veiled in a survey of judicial precedents.[21] Yet at one level the broader history behind the contract clause meets precisely the constitutional point at issue in the case: how to base twentieth-century law on an eighteenth-century Constitution. And it meets this point in a way that avoids the historicism of the dissent without being trapped by the generalities of the majority.

The dangers of these generalities can easily be overlooked in admiring the candor and progressive tone of the opinion of Chief Justice Hughes. Writing shortly after the *Blaisdell* decision was announced, constitutional scholar Edward Corwin stated:

> The emergency met by the Minnesota statute is *not* the same type of emergency which the Convention of 1787 had in mind, and for the simple but irresistible reason that the *social environment has essentially changed since then.* But Justice Sutherland

20. Wright, *The Contract Clause*, p. 13.
21. The Chief Justice quotes from an early contract clause case: "a great part of the difficulties of the cause arise from not giving sufficient weight to the general intent of this clause of the Constitution, and subjecting it to a severe literal construction." Ogden v. Saunders, 12 Wheat. 213, 286 (1827), quoted in 290 U.S. at 428. But nothing is made of this statement in historical terms.

urges in refutation, the Constitution must be construed according to 'the intention of its founders.' The answer is twofold: First, that the Constitution's founders could never have had an intention as to something — social conditions of 1933, to wit — which they could not have imagined or foreseen; secondly, that their broader intention was that the Constitution should, as Marshall phrased it, 'be adapted to the various crises in human affairs,' this being the condition of its survival.[22]

According to this statement, it makes no difference what the specific intent of the contract clause is, nor even, one may add, what a "middle level" intent is (such as that proposed above). In determining the validity of the mortgage moratorium it is important only to consider the broadest purpose of the Constitution, and that with twentieth-century circumstances in mind.

The weakness of this argument, which is essential to the opinion of Chief Justice Hughes, is that if only the broadest purposes of the Constitution are to be used in its construction, judges are left completely free of the constitutional text, constitutional history, and judicial precedent. Under these conditions constitutional interpretation would quickly break down as an exercise in reasoning; there would be no justification for a written constitution at all. Neither Hughes nor Corwin argues this, nor would either of them have followed it to the extreme. But it is the logic inherent in the antihistorical, broad-purpose method of constitutional construction. If the Court moves more gradually through time, however, provisions such as the contract clause may undergo changes that leave them far from original intent but still integrated into contemporary constitutional law. This is what Hughes attempts to do with his survey of legal precedents, although he is not entirely successful. It is what the historical interpretation outlined above is also designed to achieve.

Although relegating the particular origins of the contract clause to as inconspicuous a place as possible, the Court opinion in *Blaisdell* does not say flatly that origins do not matter. It says only that they do not fix the "precise scope" of the contract clause.[23] While "the course of judicial decisions" [24] will serve to fix that scope from

---

22. "Moratorium Over Minnesota," *University of Pennsylvania Law Review,* 82 (1934), 313–14 (emphasis in the original).

23. 290 U.S. at 428.

24. *Ibid.*

a legal point of view, origins apparently do matter from a political point of view, for the historical background creeps back into the opinion of the Court in two guises, as if there were no keeping it out. First the Court professes to interpret the Constitution according to "the vision of our time." [25] But it simultaneously seeks the support of the vision of the framers. "We find no warrant for the conclusion," writes the Chief Justice, "that the founders of our Government would have interpreted the [contract] clause differently had they had occasion to assume that responsibility in the conditions of the later day." [26] The meaning of this statement lies in its rhetoric, for taken literally it is probably wrong and in any event unprovable. If we cannot move ourselves back to the time of the founders, runs the argument, then let us move the founders up to the present. One way or another, their approval is essential.[27]

History's second subtle appearance in the opinion of the Court is an extension of the first. It is a detailed attempt to obtain the approval of the founders and the Court's contemporary audience at the same time. The technique is to explain, ostensibly in terms of the contract clause, precisely what the difference is between the framers' time and our own. Such an explanation is designed to support the majority's basic theory that the Constitution evolves over time and that a change in social conditions makes a difference in constitutional interpretation that would be approved by the framers of the Constitution as well as by twentieth-century interpreters. It is, in short, an example of the use of ongoing history as a principle of constitutional adjudication after intent history has failed.

Yet the Chief Justice apparently fails to notice that the point of his statement of social change is not really applicable to the issue of the contract clause. He writes:

> The settlement and consequent contraction of the public domain, the pressure of a constantly increasing density of population, the interrelation of the activities of our people and the complexity of our economic interests, have inevitably led to an increased use of the organization of society in order to protect the very bases of individual opportunity. Where, in earlier days, it was thought that

25. 290 U.S. at 442.
26. 290 U.S. at 443.
27. Justice Sutherland proposed going back in time: "As nearly as possible we should place ourselves in the condition of those who framed and adopted [the Constitution]." 290 U.S. at 453.

only the concerns of individuals or of classes were involved, and that those of the State itself were touched only remotely, it has later been found that the fundamental interests of the State are directly affected; and that the question is no longer merely that of one party to a contract as against another, but of the use of reasonable means to safeguard the economic structure upon which the good of all depends.[28]

For the Supreme Court this is an unusual expression of long-range social perspective, but it merits analysis. If the first sentence is read as a statement of increasing economic interdependence in the course of American history, it is unexceptionable. But the second sentence borders on obscurantism when it suggests that the "interests of the State" are — or were — different from the concerns of the individuals and classes which make it up. This theory, which might be accepted by proponents of laissez faire in the late nineteenth century or by adherents of political pluralism in the twentieth, did not exist among the framers of the Constitution. The framers did not believe that the welfare of the state was something essentially different from the welfare of the people. Neither the facts nor the thinking about social conditions in the 1780's justifies the assertion that in those times the interests of "the State" were "touched only remotely" by the issue behind the contract clause. Behind both the Constitution and the contract clause lay the conviction that economic prosperity and the form of government enjoyed by Americans were intertwined. By failing to substantiate any theoretical difference between the eighteenth and twentieth centuries on the role of government in the economy, Chief Justice Hughes's statement of the practical differences suffers, and along with it the justification of the *Blaisdell* decision on the basis of historical change.

There are several lessons to be drawn from the mortgage moratorium case in regard to history as a principle of adjudication. First, constitutional history clearly contrary to the desired outcome of a case may be largely overcome by slighting it and appealing instead to the principle of an evolving Constitution. Second, the innately greater coherence of judicial reasoning afforded those who can point to an agreed-upon history — agreed upon even by the majority in this case — is damaging to the quality of the opposing opinion which

28. 290 U.S. at 442.

attempts to be contemporary in outlook. Third, a "mediating" history, between a particularistic account of the intent of the framers and a general expression of the basic purpose for establishing a constitution, may founder on the rock of accepted canons of constitutional construction. Such a history is neither legal enough in its method nor open-ended enough in its conclusions to satisfy the Supreme Court.

The dilemma posed by the problem of history in the *Blaisdell* case cannot be solved by fiat. Constitutional law must be justified by the Constitution, and the Constitution is not a body of rules freely floating in the present. In considering John Marshall's "it is *a constitution* we are expounding," the last word also needs emphasis.[29] Constitutional law is constitutional interpretation, interpretation which takes place around a definite document that limits by both its text and its traditions. The power of the courts to interpret the Constitution, and the expectation that they will supply cogent reasoning in justification of their interpretation, presents a dilemma of modernity peculiar to the American judiciary. No other nation possesses a written constitution (still in use) as old as America's, and no other nation worships its constitution with such reverence. Yet we expect the judiciary to be both contemporary and rational when expounding constitutional law.

The dilemma — or the embarrassment — of constitutional intent may seldom be as pronounced as in *Blaisdell*. But *Blaisdell* demonstrates excellently that the real source of the problem is a style of constitutional and judicial thinking which attempts to justify the present in terms of the past, even while rationalizing a progressive result. Several years after the mortgage moratorium decision a judicial "realist" stated the problem in this way:

> An example of the great difficulties caused by the travails of change in judicial method may be found in Chief Justice Hughes's long and involved opinion in the *Minnesota Mortgage Moratorium case* . . . Hughes started with an account of the views of the Founding Fathers, quoting the *Federalist*. Later on in the opinion, however, he quoted with approval Holmes's remark that the 'case before us must be considered in the light of our whole experience and not merely in that of what was said a hundred

29. McCulloch v. Maryland, 4 Wheat. 316, 407 (1819) (emphasis in the original).

years ago.' But Hughes still feels he must pay heavy attention to what was said by the Founding Fathers and in the early precedents a hundred years ago. He feels he must go through the arduous rigmarole of judicial ceremony which court tradition has hallowed, even when he is making a decision in the face of a national 'emergency.' There must be reason for hope that the newly appointed members of the Court will lead us out of the conventional morasses of opinion-writing.[30]

But the newly appointed justices did not break with the conventional morasses of opinion-writing. Neither the clinical destruction of the Court's use of history through legal scholarship[31] nor outright advocacy of forward-looking decisions has been able to tear up traditions of constitutional and judicial thinking deeply rooted in the American political culture. The ties of the Constitution are to the past, and when history calls the justices strain to listen.

30. Beryl Harold Levy, *Our Constitution: Tool or Testament?* (New York: Knopf, 1941), p. 244. The internal quotation comes from Justice Holmes for the Court in Missouri v. Holland, 252 U.S. 416, 433 (1920).
31. See above, pp. 3–4.

CHAPTER IV

PRESIDENTIAL REMOVAL POWER:

THE FIRST CONGRESS

AS CONSTITUTIONAL INTERPRETER

The Constitution provides that the President, "by and with the advice and consent of the Senate," may appoint certain classes of public officials, particularly ambassadors, members of the cabinet, and justices of the Supreme Court; and that Congress may "vest the appointment of such inferior officers as they think proper, in the President alone, in the courts of law, or in the heads of departments." [1] Except for possible conviction in impeachment proceedings, however, the Constitution is silent concerning the removal of men from public office. This chapter is concerned with the several attempts in American history to break this constitutional silence. In particular, it focuses on the attempts of the First Congress in 1789 and of the Supreme Court in Myers v. United States, a case decided in 1926.[2]

A few weeks after the inauguration of George Washington in April 1789 Congress began consideration of a bill to establish a department of foreign affairs — the present Department of State. The only significant question debated by the legislators was whether the Constitution, which expressed nothing, implied anything concerning the removal of the head of an executive department from office; and, regardless of the answer to that question, what, if anything, should be said about the removal of the secretary of foreign affairs in the bill under discussion. The language finally adopted by Congress provided that the chief clerk of the department would have custody of the official records "whenever the said principal officer shall be removed

1. Art. II, sec. 2.
2. 272 U.S. 52.

from office by the President of the United States." [3] This made it clear that the President might remove the officer. But the conditional clause and the passive voice masked an important issue: whether the removal power was the President's by virtue of the Constitution or by grant of Congress. Although Congress had not said so explicitly, the standard interpretation of the congressional action, at least so far as cabinet officers were concerned, was that the President had the constitutional power of removal; Congress had merely recognized the existence of the power already inherent in the chief executive.[4]

One reason why the First Congress had exerted little effort on its own behalf was that George Washington was President, and no legislator dared question his wisdom by denying him the right to remove a member of his own cabinet. On the next important occasion for public discussion of the removal power, however, the situation was quite different. It involved a controversial president and lower-ranking federal officials. Andrew Jackson exercised the removal power by displacing several hundred government officials for purposes of party patronage. This pronounced introduction of the spoils system into national politics brought an outcry by opponents, particularly on the part of the Senate, whose advice and consent was required for the appointments. A number of persons asked for a reconsideration of the "decision of 1789," as the action of the First Congress had come to be called.[5]

The next dispute over the removal power was the most important one in the country's history and brought about a reversal of the decision of 1789. The bitter feud between Andrew Johnson and the radical Republican Congress elected in the fall of 1866 produced the Tenure of Office Act, passed over the President's veto in March

3. 1 Stat. 28, 29.

4. Joseph Story cautiously wrote: "The final vote seems to have expressed the sense of the legislature, that the power of removal by the executive could not be abridged by the legislature; at least, not in cases where the power to appoint was not subject to legislative delegation." *Commentaries on the Constitution of the United States* (2 vols.; Boston: Little, Brown, 1858), II, 400.

5. Justice Story, no friend of Jacksonian politics, wrote in 1833: "This extraordinary change of system has awakened general attention, and brought back the whole controversy, with regard to the executive power of removal, to a severe scrutiny." *Commentaries,* II, 405. He documented his case in a footnote. In general, see Erik M. Eriksson, "The Federal Civil Service Under President Jackson," *Mississippi Valley Historical Review,* 13 (1927), 517–40. The controversy was sharpened by the dismissal of Secretary of Treasury William Duane for his refusal to withdraw the government deposits from the Bank of the United States.

1867. This act prohibited the President from removing officials whose appointments had been confirmed by the Senate unless that body expressly agreed to their removal. The violation of the act by the President, through the dismissal of Secretary of War Stanton, was one of the crucial charges of impeachment brought by the House of Representatives against Johnson in 1868. The issue of the removal power was clearly drawn. But it remained unresolved, as Johnson was acquitted and the Tenure of Office Act stayed in force.

The removal problem lay dormant until President Cleveland secured the repeal of the Tenure of Office Act in 1887, with certain exceptions. One of these exceptions was the provision that applied to postmasters, and in the 1920's, after President Wilson had dismissed the postmaster of Portland, Oregon, this exception occasioned the massive entry of the Supreme Court into the dispute between Congress and the Executive over the power of removal.[6] In Myers v. United States, a suit for the dismissed postmaster's back pay, the Court held that the Constitution gave the President the unqualified right to remove officials who had been appointed with the advice and consent of the Senate, without first obtaining the permission of that body. The postmaster removal clause was declared unconstitutional — and by implication the defunct Tenure of Office Act. The decision of 1789 was revived and confirmed as constitutional doctrine.

Chief Justice Taft, who wrote the opinion for the Court in the *Myers* case, felt the Court had "not had a case in two generations of more importance." [7] At the time, and excepting perhaps the income tax cases, this judgment appeared correct. The *Myers* case spent three years in the Supreme Court. It was argued twice, the second time by Senator George Wharton Pepper as invited amicus curiae for the Senate. The opinions of the justices take up almost 250 pages in the official reports.[8] It was indeed a monumental decision. Yet within a decade a unanimous Court had so limited the reasoning and

6. The postal laws had been revised and consolidated in the 1870's. Due to the codifier's care, the removal clause was carried over intact from, and made independent of, the Tenure of Office Act. It entered the twentieth century in these words: "Postmasters of the first, second and third classes shall be appointed and may be removed by the President by and with the advice and consent of the Senate and shall hold their offices for four years unless sooner removed or suspended according to law." 19 Stat. 78, 80.

7. From a letter to Justice Stone, quoted in Alpheus Thomas Mason, *Harlan Fiske Stone: Pillar of the Law* (New York: Viking, 1956), p. 229.

8. The opinions were also published in a separate book by the Government Printing Office.

effect of the *Myers* decision that the entire episode has been almost forgotten.[9] As revived here in order to examine the use of history by the Supreme Court, the case will be discussed under the following headings: the *Myers* decision in outline; the First Congress: justification for relying on it; the First Congress: its debate over the presidential removal power; interpretation of the "decision of 1789" prior to *Myers*; and history, the First Congress, and the decision in *Myers*.

The Myers *decision in outline.* The Supreme Court declared the clause requiring Senate concurrence for the removal of postmasters unconstitutional by a vote of six to three. The single opinion for the Court was written by Chief Justice Taft and concurred in by Justices Van Devanter, Sutherland, Butler, Sanford, and Stone. There were three dissenting opinions, by Justices Holmes, McReynolds, and Brandeis. Together, the opinions present a motley spectacle. The seventy-page opinion of the Court is diffuse and loosely organized.[10] Justice Holmes's three-paragraph dissent is lost between this opinion, on one side, and the two other minority opinions, of sixty and fifty-five pages each, on the other. The dissent of Justice McReynolds, although containing eighteen numbered sections, is as weak in structure as is the opinion of the Court. The dissent of Justice Brandeis is a struggle to maintain a text amidst the footnotes and perhaps a thousand citations to statutes, court cases, legislative debates, and other material.

The protagonists in the case are Taft and Brandeis. Their political values, their approaches to constitutional law, their definition of the issues in the case, and their views on the relevance of the "decision of 1789" stand in direct opposition to each other. The Chief Justice — former President and the author of *Our Chief Magistrate and His Powers* (1916), written during his years as a professor of constitutional law — had firm views on the nature and scope of the Presidency. Despite the fact that the case at hand dealt with a postmaster, Taft thought in larger terms, essentially in terms of cabinet members,

9. Humphrey's Executor v. United States, 295 U.S. 602 (1935). See also Wiener v. United States, 357 U.S. 349 (1958). The decision in *Myers* is still law, but the expansive reasoning in support of it no longer has constitutional validity. The obscurity into which the case has fallen can be appreciated by examining contemporary casebooks on constitutional law, which scarcely mention it except for its doctrinal excesses and place in history.

10. For an account of the preparation of the Court opinion, including the aid given the Chief Justice by Justice Stone, see Mason, *Harlan Fiske Stone*, pp. 222–31.

whose confidence and cooperation a President quite obviously and directly required in order to perform his duties. In deciding a case about the removal of a postmaster the Chief Justice felt it important to pronounce on the removal of all executive officers. If a single clause of the notorious Tenure of Office Act could survive, the entire law could be re-enacted whenever Congress wished to curb the President. This violated Taft's constitutional conception of the separation of powers and his view of the constitutional grant to the President of "the executive power."

On the other side was Justice Brandeis, who extended his economic conviction of "the curse of bigness" to politics and viewed with suspicion any attempt to grant the President more power than was absolutely compelled by the Constitution. The doctrine of the separation of powers, Brandeis said, was adopted "not to promote efficiency but to preclude the exercise of arbitrary power. The purpose was, not to avoid friction, but, by means of the inevitable friction incident to the distribution of the governmental powers among three departments, to save the people from autocracy." [11] Further, it was "of special value," Brandeis felt, that persons appointed to office by the President with the consent of the Senate be protected in their position.[12]

The political values of the Chief Justice and Justice Brandeis were reinforced by their approaches to constitutional interpretation. Justice Brandeis habitually narrowed constitutional questions before answering them, regardless of the values involved; and he focused on facts, context, and specific issues. He was a legal ecologist who studied one element in relation to its environment. The constitutional landscape of Chief Justice Taft, on the other hand, generally consisted of large independent features that were best viewed from a

11. Myers v. United States, 272 U.S. 52, 293 (1926).

12. 272 U.S. at 276. A personal element of recent history no doubt also contributed to the disagreement between the two members of the Court and strengthened their opposing views of the presidential removal power. In 1909 President Taft had upheld the dismissal by his Secretary of Interior of a subordinate who had publicly charged the Secretary with misconduct in office. A lengthy congressional investigation, attended with all the publicity the muckrakers could muster, pitted Louis Brandeis as attorney for the dismissed official against high officers of the Taft administration. Though the Secretary of Interior was ultimately exonerated by the congressional committee, he was eventually forced to resign, and the entire episode reflected discredit on the President and his closest advisers. See Alpheus Thomas Mason, *Brandeis: A Free Man's Life* (New York: Viking, 1946), pp. 254–81.

distance. He had faith, for instance, in the actuality of "the executive power." [13]

These contrasting views on how to go about deciding a case in constitutional law led to completely different statements of the issue in Myers v. United States. In the first sentence of his opinion the Chief Justice wrote: "This case presents the question of whether under the Constitution the President has exclusive power of removing executive officers of the United States whom he has appointed by and with the advice and consent of the Senate." [14]

Justice Brandeis' definition of the issue presents a sharp contrast: "May the President, having acted under the [postal] statute in so far as it creates the office and authorizes the appointment, ignore, while the Senate is in session, the provision which prescribes the condition under which a removal may take place? It is this narrow question, and this only, which we are required to decide. We need not consider what power the President, being Commander in Chief, has over officers in the Army and the Navy. We need not determine whether the President, acting alone, may remove high political officers." [15]

Once the difference between Chief Justice Taft and Justice Brandeis is clear with respect to political values, constitutional approach, and definition of the issues in the case, their difference with regard to the significance of the First Congress' "decision of 1789" in determining the outcome of the postmaster removal case should be obvious. The Chief Justice asserted that "the exact question which the House voted upon was whether it should recognize and declare the power of the President under the Constitution to remove the Secretary of Foreign Affairs without the advice and consent of the Senate." [16] And from "an examination of the record" he drew the general conclusion that "the vote [in 1789] was, and was intended to be, a legislative declaration that the power to remove officers appointed by the President and the Senate vested in the President alone." [17] Conversely, Justice Brandeis said simply: "The question of

13. For a survey of Taft's constitutional creed see Alpheus Thomas Mason, *William Howard Taft: Chief Justice* (New York: Simon and Schuster, 1964), pp. 236–66. For Brandeis, see Paul A. Freund, *The Supreme Court of the United States* (Cleveland: World, 1961), pp. 116–44.

14. 272 U.S. at 106.

15. 272 U.S. at 241. Justice McReynolds' statement of the issue was not so concise or controlled, but it amounted to the same thing. 272 U.S. at 178–79.

16. 272 U.S. at 114.

17. *Ibid.*

the great debate of 1789 is not before us." [18] In consequence of these outlooks on the relevance of the debate of the First Congress, the opinion of the Court devotes fifteen pages to that debate directly and alludes to it indirectly throughout; Justice Brandeis disposes of the debate in three tightly written pages and scarcely refers to it again.[19]

The First Congress: justification for relying on it. Elaborating on the presidential removal power in *The Federalist,* Alexander Hamilton wrote: "The consent of [the Senate] would be necessary to displace as well as to appoint." [20] In the absence of a determination of the issue in the constitutional text or at the Convention, this would appear sound authority. But Hamilton was overruled on the question by the First Congress, an equally knowledgeable but more binding authority on the meaning of the Constitution, and the Court in the *Myers* case builds its opinion around what it believes to be the congressional interpretation.[21]

The Chief Justice presents a full rationale for relying on the interpretation of the First Congress: "We have devoted much space to this discussion and decision of the question of the Presidential power of removal in the First Congress, not because a Congressional conclusion on a constitutional issue is conclusive, but, first, because of our agreement with the reasons upon which it was avowedly based; second, because this was the decision of the First Congress on a question of primary importance in the organization of the Government, made within two years after the Constitutional Convention and within a much shorter time after its ratification; and, third, because that Congress numbered among its leaders those who had been members of the Convention." [22]

The points of this rationale deserve consideration, beginning with what the Court says is *not* a reason for using the debates, namely that a congressional interpretation of the Constitution is conclusive. The First Congress, meeting well before a judicial monopoly on con-

---

18. 272 U.S. at 242.

19. The debates of the First Congress are treated in the opinion of the Court in 272 U.S. at 111–36, by Justice Brandeis at 284–86, and by Justice Mc-Reynolds at 193–99.

20. No. 77 (Wright ed., p. 485).

21. In addition, the Court insists that Hamilton changed his mind. 272 U.S. 136–39. This is cogently disputed by Edward S. Corwin, "Tenure of Office and the Removal Power under the Constitution," *Columbia Law Review,* 27 (1927), 370–71. Justices Brandeis and McReynolds cite Hamilton in support of their position. 272 U.S. at 208 and 293.

22. 272 U.S. at 136.

stitutional interpretation had been established, was under the impression that its conclusion on the issue would be binding. James Madison, the floor leader in the First Congress for the foreign affairs department bill, said at one point in the debate over the removal power: "If it relates to a doubtful part of the Constitution, I suppose an exposition of the Constitution may come with as much propriety from the Legislature, as any other department of the Government." [23] At another point Madison expressed the conviction that "the decision that is at this time made, will become the permanent exposition of the Constitution." [24] Yet in order to support its own authority to decide the *Myers* case, the Supreme Court had to reject this theory, while at the same time accepting the conclusions made by the First Congress in reliance on it. By denying the validity of the premise of the congressional debate but endorsing the validity of that debate's outcome, the Court's explanation of the significance of the First Congress as constitutional interpreter is flawed from the start.

The Court's first reason for using the congressional debate is "agreement with the reasons on which [the conclusion of the First Congress] was avowedly based." Assuming that the debate is relevant to the issue in *Myers*, this is of course a valid point. But the fact that the Court agrees with its own interpretation of the congressional discussion of the removal power does not insure the adequacy of that interpretation, and, as will be shown below, what happened in the First Congress and what the Court believes happened are not the same thing. The other reasons offered by the Court for relying on the First Congress reduce to the claims that that Congress is an authoritative (though not binding) constitutional interpreter because the decision of 1789 was "of primary importance in the organization of the Government"; because the First Congress met very shortly after the Constitutional Convention and ratification and therefore knew what both of these were all about; and because there was

---

23. *Annals of the Congress of the United States* (Washington: Gales and Seaton, 1834), I, 461. Madison was challenged by Congressman Smith of South Carolina, who thought such an exposition "an infringement on the powers of the judiciary." *Ibid.*, 470.

24. *Ibid.*, 495. For an account of the theory and practice of congressional authority to interpret the Constitution, including an extended discussion of how this was exercised in "the decision of 1789," see Donald G. Morgan, *Congress and the Constitution: A Study of Responsibility* (Cambridge, Mass.: Harvard University Press, 1966).

overlapping membership between the Constitutional Convention and the First Congress. The *Myers* case is not unique in treating the First Congress very much as a postadjournment session of the constitutional convention.[25] Reliance on the First Congress is a natural consequence of accepting history as intent as a valid principle of constitutional adjudication.

Argument against the Court's position with respect to using the First Congress goes in three directions. First, it is pointed out that Congress bears no legal responsibility for the Constitution but is itself a creature of it. This is so — the First Congress was not legally responsible for the Constitution. Indeed, the Constitutional Convention itself did not bear legal responsibility for the Constitution; this lay in the hands of the state ratifying conventions. More importantly, legality lies in the text adopted, not in the debates on it. Nevertheless, the search for constitutional intent is a search for historical understanding, not for legal responsibility, and in this search the records of the First Congress may be of aid.

Second, it is claimed that the fundamental tasks of the Constitutional Convention and the First Congress were so different that the two bodies cannot be compared in ascertaining constitutional intent. This is only partially true. Either because the members of the Convention could not agree among themselves or because they feared ratification could not be secured for a more explicitly worded constitution, they deliberately left issues they considered important to the establishment of the new government for determination at a later day. The First Congress recognized that it was determining the meaning of the Constitution in this spirit.

The third argument against the use of the First Congress for constitutional interpretation is the most general one. It is that any evidence of the late eighteenth century — Constitutional Convention, First Congress, *The Federalist*, or anything else — should have no influence over contemporary constitutional law. The strength of this argument lies not merely in the claim that the past should not bind the present, but also in the fact behind that claim, that the past is different from the present. This, for instance, is how Chief Justice Hughes attempted to overcome the historical argument of the dis-

---

25. For several examples see Myers v. United States, 272 U.S. 52, 175 (1926); and the discussion in Jacobus ten Broek, "Use by the United States Supreme Court of Extrinsic Aids in Constitutional Construction," *California Law Review*, 27 (1939), 171–79.

senters in the mortgage moratorium case. But the problem of changing circumstances does not arise in the *Myers* situation. The issues and values surrounding presidential control over executive officers are today not essentially different from those at the time of the founders, and the dissents did not argue that they were.[26] The conclusion is that, if the Court's view of the issue in *Myers* is accepted — that all executive officers, not just postmasters, are involved — and if the evidence of history as intent is a valid principle of constitutional adjudication, then the Court is justified in organizing its *Myers* opinion around the arguments on the removal power as presented in the First Congress.

The First Congress: its debate over the presidential removal power. Whether the Court's decision to rely on the debates of 1789 is ultimately justified depends on whether it correctly perceived what happened in the First Congress, and it is to this that the discussion now turns.[27]

The First Congress' consideration of the bill to establish a department of foreign affairs is difficult to unravel. The debates make it clear that the votes must be seen in the context of parliamentary tactics and not merely as expressions of constitutional — or congressional — construction. From Tuesday through Friday, June 16–19, 1789, the House of Representatives debated a motion to strike from the bill as introduced a clause which permitted the secretary of foreign affairs "to be removable from office by the President of the United States." Near the end of business on Friday the motion to delete the clause was defeated 34–20, without a roll-call vote.[28] The clause remained in the bill, but only for the weekend. On the follow-

26. The differences that do exist are real: increased patronage in the appointments, the development of the civil service system, greater power of the President and the government in the society, more public employees, and the establishment of independent commissions. But the debates of the First Congress show that the problems arising from each of these were considered, though in different terminology, at the time. The theoretical problem of the right of the President to remove officials of the government without first obtaining the approval of the Senate remains unchanged.

27. This account relies on the proceedings of the House of Representatives as reported in *Annals*, I, 455–591. The Senate also considered the issue of presidential removal, but no record of its debates exists. We know only that the Senate ultimately agreed to the House version of the bill to establish a department of foreign affairs by a vote of eleven to ten, Vice-President Adams breaking a tie. See Myers v. United States, 272 U.S. 52, 115, 195, 284 (1926).

28. *Annals*, I, 576.

ing Monday two roll-call votes were taken. The first, by the count of 30–18, amended the provision for the chief clerk of the proposed department by entrusting him with departmental records "whenever the said principal officer shall be removed from office by the President of the United States, or in any other case of vacancy." [29] The second, 31–19, struck out the "to be removable clause" that had been left in the previous Friday.[30] The consequence was that the only words left in the bill pertaining to removal of the secretary of foreign affairs from office was the passive-voiced "whenever [he] shall be removed" clause. These parliamentary maneuvers were well understood by the members of the House of Representatives. The "to be removable" clause had appeared to be a legislative grant to the President from Congress. But "whenever [he] shall be removed" appeared to be an admission of constitutional power over which the legislature had no control.

James Madison, on whom Chief Justice Taft principally relies in the *Myers* case, desired a declaration of constitutional meaning rather than a legislative grant, and he ultimately had his way. But he had to contend with two groups of opponents: those who thought that Congress rather than the Constitution determined the issue (the "Congressionalists"); and those who thought that the Constitution determined the issue, not in favor of the President's right of removal by himself ("Presidential Constitutionalists" — Madison's group), but in favor of the Senate's participation in removing an officer as incident to its constitutional participation in appointing him ("Senatorial Constitutionalists").[31] To deal with his two groups of

29. *Ibid.,* 580.
30. *Ibid.,* 585.
31. There was also a view, held by two or three Congressmen, that removal could take place constitutionally only by impeachment. A myopically textual construction supports this view, but the vast majority of the House did not read the Constitution this way, or, if they did, found it impractical. Logically, the categories appear this way:

Congressionalists
Constitutionalists
  Presidential
  Senatorial
  Impeachment

The terms are adapted from Corwin, "Tenure of Office," 361–62. Conceivably, the Congressionalists could have split into Senatorial and Presidential factions. But apparently they all agreed, out of deference to George Washington and for the purpose of this bill, that the power should be granted to the President — so long as it was ultimately controllable by Congress.

opponents, Madison, through his colleague Egbert Benson of New York, first introduced the "whenever [he] shall be removed" clause, forcing the Congressionalists to vote in its favor (since its implication was neutral with regard to their position, so long as the other clause, "to be removable by the President," remained in the bill to confirm their views on congressional power); and forcing the Senatorial Constitutionalists to vote against it (since the amendment, considered independently, by implication conferred the constitutional power of removal on the President, and, considered in conjunction with the "to be removable" clause, enhanced the policy with which they disagreed). Having divided his opposition one way to add the "whenever [he] shall be removed" clause, Madison now proceeded to divide them the other way. He proposed, again through Benson, to delete the original "who shall be removable" clause, thus leaving in the bill the clause favored only by his own group, the Presidential Constitutionalists. The new motion forced the Senatorial Constitutionalists to vote for the deletion (since they did not favor Presidential removal under any circumstances), and the Congressionalists to vote against it (since purposefully striking "shall be removable" plainly implied that the Constitution, rather than Congress, had the final say on the removal power).

Madison's opponents, in a word, had been had.[32] As a member of the Congressionalists put it: "I am embarrassed in this question . . . because the vote is taken in such a manner as not to express the principles upon which I vote."[33] "A side blow," said an Impeachment Constitutionalist.[34] And a Senatorial Constitutionalist correctly pointed out that Madison's group "had changed their ground," having first fought to maintain "who shall be removable" (in the non-roll-call vote the previous Friday), and now voting to delete the same clause. "It was now left to be inferred from the Constitution," this Congressman continued, "that the President had the power of removal without even a legislative declaration on that point, which they [Madison's Presidential Constitutionalists] had heretofore so strongly insisted upon."[35]

This was indeed the inference that Madison desired, and the one

32. More decorously put by Justice Brandeis: "the success of this endeavor was due to the strategy of dividing the opposition and not to unanimity of constitutional conceptions." 272 U.S. at 287 n. 75.
33. Thomas L. Tucker, in *Annals,* I, 584.
34. William L. Smith, *ibid.,* 579.
35. John Page, *ibid.,* 580.

that Chief Justice Taft obligingly made in the postmaster removal case. A vote on the bill as amended was taken on Wednesday, June 24. To the final plea of the Congressman just quoted that a "respectable minority" disapprove establishing the department of foreign affairs because of the removal issue, the measure passed by a 31–19 roll-call vote.[36] So was enacted the "decision of 1789." [37]

Interpretation of the decision of 1789 prior to the Myers *case.* In deciding *Myers*, Chief Justice Taft relies heavily, but not exclusively, on the debates of the First Congress. The reliance on the eighteenth century is qualified as follows: "This Court has repeatedly laid down the principle that a contemporaneous legislative exposition of the Constitution when the founders of our Government and the framers of our Constitution were actively participating in public affairs, acquiesced in for a long term of years, fixes the construction to be given its provision." [38] Ongoing history, in other words, supplements history as intent.

In its use of ongoing history the Court contends that, with the exception of the egregious and soon recognized error of the Tenure of Office Act in the 1860's, the decision of 1789 had been continuously acquiesced in and that this therefore "fixe[d] the construction" of the Constitution. The materials offered in proof of this contention are Joseph Story's *Commentaries on the Constitution,* the views of Webster, Clay, and Calhoun, a political interpretation of the origins of the Tenure of Office Act, and judicial precedent. At each step in this demonstration the Court's conclusions are challenged by the dissenting opinions, and with considerable success. By the end, the superstructure of the acquiescence theory, the use of ongoing history, appears even weaker than the foundation of the work of the First Congress, the use of history as intent.

The opinion of the Court quotes this passage from Justice Story's *Commentaries on the Constitution:* "The public . . . acquiesced in [the] decision [of 1789]; and it constitutes, perhaps, the most extraordinary case in the history of the government of a power, conferred by implication on the executive by the assent of a bare majority of Congress . . ." [39] The first clause of this sentence is a statement of the acquiescence in the decision of the First Congress as

36. *Ibid.,* 591.
37. The voting pattern of the House of Representatives with regard to the "decision of 1789" is analyzed in detail in the Appendix.
38. 272 U.S. at 175.
39. 272 U.S. at 149, quoting from Story, *Commentaries,* Sec. 1543.

Chief Justice Taft understood it. But in the second clause the Court is compelled to reveal that Story believed the removal power was "conferred . . . on the executive by . . . Congress" — in other words a Congressionalist interpretation of the debates and an interpretation at variance with the one adopted by Taft, namely, that the removal power of the executive was merely recognized by Congress as inhering in the Constitution.[40] Even more damaging to the Court's position, however, is the statement of Story, quoted at the outset of Justice Brandeis' dissent, that "at all events, it will be a consolation to those who love the Union, and honor a devotion to the patriotic discharge of duty, that in regard to 'inferior officers' . . . the remedy for any permanent abuse is still within the power of Congress, by the simple expedient of requiring the consent of the Senate to removals in such cases." [41] This is directly contrary to the only necessary justification for relying on the debates of Congress in the first place, that its decision about a cabinet officer is relevant to a decision about inferior officers, in this case a postmaster.

The views of Webster, Clay, and Calhoun are manifestly in opposition to the decision of 1789, even on a cabinet level. The opinion of the Court grudgingly concedes this point but insists that these men were speaking "in the heat of political differences between the Executive and the Senate," by implication suggesting that the calm of Congress in 1789 permitted a more legitimate statement of the removal power.[42]

The acquiescence theory of the Court reaches its nadir at the critical juncture of the Tenure of Office Act, when Congress "reversed" the decision of 1789. The Court writes that the "construction [of 1789] was followed by the legislative department and executive department continuously for seventy-three years." [43] But if this theory of legislative acquiescence leads up to the Tenure of

40. In addition, Story holds that the act of Congress only "by implication" gave the power to the President. But the Chief Justice believed that the Constitution "expressly and by implication withholds from Congress power to determine who shall appoint and who shall remove except as to inferior offices." 272 U.S. at 129. What Taft had in mind when he used "expressly" is impossible to determine.

41. 272 U.S. at 240, quoting from Story, *Commentaries,* Sec. 1544. The passage is also quoted by Justice McReynolds, 272 U.S. at 202, and, inexplicably, by the Court, 272 U.S. at 150.

42. 272 U.S. at 175. The views of the men are discussed by the Court at 150–52.

43. 272 U.S. at 175.

Office Act, the dissent's view leads away from it. Justice Brandeis declares on the other side: "The historical data submitted present a legislative practice . . . [which] has existed, without interruption, continuously for the last fifty-eight years." [44]

The Court attempts to bypass the episode of the Tenure of Office Act by contrasting the "political calm" of the First Congress with the "heated political difference of opinion" that characterized the Reconstruction Congress.[45] As the Chief Justice surely recognized, however, the damage — reversal of the decision of 1789 — existed in the legislation, not in the politics behind it. (This, at any rate, was the practice Taft had followed when it helped rather than harmed his cause: he accepted the legislation of the First Congress as a positive good but ignored the detailed politics of passage of the removal clause in that legislation.)

When the two sides in the postmaster removal case turned to previous decisions of the Court, the result was a dialogue equally at cross-purposes. In only one case, but that one Marbury v. Madison, had the Supreme Court ever claimed that a fixed-term appointment, which Mr. Myers' postmastership was, vested an irrevocable legal right to the office for the duration of the appointment.[46] Chief Justice Taft, expressing the highest respect for the case and for the Chief Justice responsible for establishing the power he was then using to declare an act of Congress unconstitutional, says that this element of John Marshall's *Marbury* opinion "was certainly *obiter dictum*." [47] The dissents denied this vehemently.[48]

All of the remaining cases considered by the Court in *Myers* had discussed the debates of 1789, admitted the controversial nature of

44. 272 U.S. at 283. It is difficult to explain why Taft's figure apparently covers 1789–1862 and Brandeis' 1868–1926, leaving a gap of six years. The gap results, however, in each justice giving the other a one-year leeway on the matter of governmental practice. Justice Brandeis points out that a removal clause requiring the consent of the Senate was first enacted in 1863, "show[ing] that it did not originate in the contest of Congress with President Johnson, as has sometimes been stated." 272 U.S. at 279. Chief Justice Taft, on the other hand, is concerned almost exclusively with the Tenure of Office Act of 1867, regardless of whether it was the first law of its kind.

45. 272 U.S. at 176, 175. Justice McReynolds, in contrast, characterizes Madison's speeches of 1789 as "polemic" delivered during a "heated debate." 272 U.S. at 239, 218.

46. 1 Cr. 137, 167 (1803).

47. 272 U.S. at 141.

48. See Justice McReynolds, 272 U.S. at 215–19, and Justice Brandeis, 272 U.S. at 242–44.

the conclusion of the First Congress, and consistently refused to interfere with the executive's removal of inferior officials.[49] None of these cases, however, involved a statute requiring the Senate's concurrence in the removal of an official, and none of them said, even by way of dictum, that such a statute would be void. What they held was that, in the absence of such a statute, the decision of 1789 bound the Court to consider the right of removal vested in the executive officer (not always the President) who had been responsible for the appointment.

Both sides of the Court in *Myers* could, and did, read out of these cases just what they read into them. The majority insisted that the previous decisions favored "a statutory construction not inconsistent with the legislative decision of 1789 [and indicated] a trend of view that we should not and can not ignore." [50] Justice Brandeis, with equal accuracy, stated: "In no case, has this Court determined that the President's power of removal is beyond control, limitation, or regulation by Congress." [51]

History, the First Congress, and the decision in Myers. The constitutional basis of the Court's reliance in *Myers* on the debates of the First Congress is that with respect to the removal power there can be no constitutional distinction among executive officers appointed with the consent of the Senate. Either they are all subject to unlimited presidential removal, from department head to postmaster, or they are all subject to removal only with the consent of the Senate. The nature of the office makes no difference.[52] Less than a week after the passage of the act to establish a department of foreign affairs, James Madison, the guiding spirit of Chief Justice Taft's opinion, exploded this basis completely. Speaking to the House of Representatives with regard to a removal clause applicable to the controller in

49. The most important of these were Ex parte Hennan, 13 Pet. 230 (1839); United States v. Guthrie, 17 How. 284 (1854); Bigler v. Avery, 24 Fed. Cas. 902 (1867); United States v. Perkins, 116 U.S. 483 (1886); Parsons v. United States, 176 U.S. 324 (1897); Shurtleff v. United States, 189 U.S. 311 (1903). All of the cases heard in the Supreme Court were unanimous except the *Guthrie* case, in which the Court did not reach the merits of the President's removal of the Chief Justice of the Territory of Minnesota, and Justice McLean dissented. The *Hennen* and *Parsons* cases contain particularly good discussions of the decision of 1789.

50. 272 U.S. at 176.

51. 272 U.S. at 242–43.

52. This is implied throughout the opinion of the Court. The only express statement of it, however, is not a very clear one. 272 U.S. at 134.

the Treasury Department, he said: "It will be necessary . . . to consider the nature of this office, to enable us to come to a right decision on the subject [of tenure] . . . The principal duty seems to be deciding upon the lawfulness and justice of the claims and accounts subsisting between the United States and particular citizens: this partakes strongly of the judicial character, and there may be strong reason why an officer of this kind should not hold his office at the pleasure of the executive branch of the Government."[53]

To construct his opinion, therefore, Chief Justice Taft had to claim that Madison's arguments over the removal of a cabinet officer (the secretary of foreign affairs) were valid, but that his arguments concerning the removal of an inferior officer (the controller in the Treasury Department) were invalid; and that Madison's first arguments, although not directed towards them, were relevant to inferior officers, but that his second, although expressly directed towards them, were irrelevant.[54] The Chief Justice also claimed that the First Congress was not binding authority in constitutional interpretation, but that it had so fixed that interpretation that the 39th Congress did not have the right to alter it. He claimed further that the First Congress had made a decision which an analysis of its votes demonstrates that it did not make. And he claimed finally that subsequent history supported acquiescence in that interpretation, when what it principally showed was that the decision of 1789 had been objected to by legal commentators and politicians, questioned by the courts, and ignored in hundreds of statutes applicable to officers such as the one who gave his name to the *Myers* case.

The *Myers* case is not alone in utilizing history that is neither right nor relevant. But the pounding insistence on the validity and arguments of the decision of 1789 for seventy pages of Court opinion calls attention to two possibilities, both of which unfortunately turn out to be true: that the Court's argument is largely an insubstantial shield for political values, and that other appropriate vehicles of interpretation for reaching its conclusion are largely lacking.

Yet the values of the Court majority are not senseless. The trouble lies in the unrefined premise used to uphold them, namely, that the

53. *Annals,* I, 611–12.

54. This is the implication of the Chief Justice's opinion. Madison's remarks on the controller's office were brought to light by Edward S. Corwin, who severely criticized the *Myers* decision. "Tenure of Office and the Removal Power under the Constitution," *Columbia Law Review,* 27 (1927), 353–99. They are not mentioned in any of the opinions in the case.

nature of the particular executive office involved was unimportant in considering the circumstances under which the officeholder could be displaced. A more sophisticated view of the situation would have preserved the essential value of the Court, that the President must have ultimate control over certain of his subordinates, and would never have led the Court into an historical quagmire. When the *Myers* holding was drastically limited several years after it was announced, a unanimous Court (which included four of the six justices who had joined Chief Justice Taft) revised the premise: "Whether the power of the President to remove an officer shall prevail over the authority of Congress to condition the power by fixing a definite term and precluding a removal except for cause, will depend upon the character of the office." [55]

Viewed as an exercise in the use of history, the *Myers* decision offers an instructive comparison to the mortgage moratorium case. In *Blaisdell*, it may be recalled, the Court majority had much less historical support for its decision than it did in *Myers*, for a particular constitutional clause was shown to have been expressly designed to prevent the legislation which the Court upheld. It was not a question of constitutional silence. Yet Chief Justice Hughes wrote a convincing opinion while Chief Justice Taft did not.

From one perspective the difference in the opinions is attributable to the dissimilar capabilities and temperaments of the opinion-writers. It is generally recognized that Hughes had the more powerful and discriminating judicial mind and was more careful how he used it. In addition, Hughes's premise — an evolving Constitution — fitted the situation in *Blaisdell*. Taft's premise — the need for executive control of subordinates — did not fit the situation in *Myers*. Apart from these differences, however, the distinguishing factor in the two opinions is how the two jurists handled history. In *Blaisdell* the damaging history was frankly acknowledged, only to be discarded for other principles of adjudication. In *Myers*, history was warmly embraced and became the germ which infected the entire endeavor of the Court. There are sound reasons for the majority's view that the President should have control over executive officers. But what is the context in which these reasons are stated? "It is convenient in

55. Humphrey's Executor v. United States, 295 U.S. 602, 631 (1935). The Court in *Humphrey* did not overrule the earlier case. *Myers* was distinguished as a case about first class postmasters; the decision of 1789 was held to be a debate about the Secretary of State. But the short of it was that Chief Justice Taft's masterpiece was wrecked.

the course of our discussion of this case to review the reasons advanced by Mr. Madison and his associates for their conclusion, supplementing them, so far as may be, by additional considerations which lead this Court to concur therein." [56] And sixty pages later what is the consequence? "When, on the merits, we find our conclusion strongly favoring the view which prevailed in the First Congress, we have no hesitation in holding that conclusion to be correct." [57]

The postmaster removal case was flawed by history in two ways. First, the history related by the Court was poor history. Second and more important, history — in the form of a single congressional debate 140 years prior to the decision — was really the Court's only principle of adjudication. The failure to offer additional justification for the *Myers* holding brought into question its constitutional adequacy from the time it was announced. The historical discussion so weighed down the opinion that it was in constant danger of disappearing from the surface of contemporary constitutional law — which it soon did.

56. Myers v. United States, 272 U.S. 52, 115 (1926).
57. 272 U.S. at 176.

CHAPTER V

POLITICAL EXPRESSION:

ESTABLISHING A HERITAGE

FOR THE FIRST AMENDMENT

In constitutional law as in national life generally, the concept of freedom is central to the image of American history. A language of freedom has developed, beginning with the Declaration of Independence and the Preamble to the Constitution and continuing to the most important decisions of the Supreme Court in the 1960's. This chapter is an examination of the Supreme Court's use of history as a part of the language of freedom in American life. Its focus is on the freedom of speech and press guaranteed by the first amendment, and particularly on political expression, the kind of speech and press the framers of that amendment were most intent on preserving. The Court's use of history in political expression cases will be grouped under three heads: prior restraint, newspaper taxes, and picketing; seditious libel; and the rhetoric of the history of freedom.

Prior Restraint, Newspaper Taxes, and Picketing

The modern history of the right to a free press begins with the protest against British censorship in the seventeenth century. The license required for the publication of books and pamphlets was the chief object of John Milton's attack in *Areopagitica* (1644). By the end of the seventeenth century the licensing system had been ended in Great Britain and the colonies. William Blackstone, writing in the 1760's, believed this to be the final achievement in the field. Liberty of the press, he felt, was indeed essential. But it consisted "in laying no *previous* restraints upon publications, and not in freedom from censure for criminal matter when published." [1]

1. *Commentaries on the Laws of England* IV, *151 (emphasis in original).

Although more was usually claimed for freedom of the press in America than in England, this minimum, the absence of prior restraint, was never in doubt. In 1931 the Supreme Court for the first time decided a case in which previous restraint was an issue. Though the justices divided five to four in the case, all agreed that in principle the first amendment prohibited prior restraint on publication. In this case a Minnesota statute authorized a permanent injunction against the future publication of any "malicious, scandalous and defamatory newspaper, magazine or other periodical." [2] A Minneapolis weekly, the *Saturday Press*, had accused the mayor, the police chief, and the county attorney of official misconduct for having condoned the activities of Jewish gangsters said to be responsible for gambling, bootlegging, and racketeering in the city. The Supreme Court held that "the operation and effect of the statute . . . imposes an unconstitutional restraint upon publication." [3]

The opinion of the Court, written by Chief Justice Hughes and concurred in by Justices Holmes, Brandeis, Stone, and Roberts, devotes over a quarter of its twenty-two pages to the facts of the case. Then it turns to the constitutional issue: "The question is whether a statute authorizing such proceedings in restraint of publication is consistent with the conception of liberty of the press as historically conceived and guaranteed." [4]

In search of the historical conception of liberty of the press Chief Justice Hughes consults several authorities on English and American constitutional history.[5] His inquiry contains extensive quotation from the "Report" on the Virginia Resolutions by James Madison ("the leading spirit in the preparation of the 1st Amendment of the Federal Constitution") in opposition to the Alien and Sedition Acts of 1798.[6] And it quotes from the "Letter to the Inhabitants of Quebec" sent by the Continental Congress in 1774 to persuade that colony to join in protest against Great Britain.[7] The legal significance of Madison's "Report" is that it is premised on the validity

2. Quoted in Near v. Minnesota, 283 U.S. 697, 702 (1931).

3. 283 U.S. at 723.

4. 283 U.S. at 713; the issue is similarly expressed at 708.

5. These include Thomas Erskine May, *Constitutional History of England* (1880); Jean Louis DeLolme, *Commentaries on the Constitution of England* (1840 ed.); Zechariah Chafee, Jr., *Freedom of Speech* (1920); and Clyde Augustus Duniway, *The Development of Freedom of Press in Massachusetts* (1906).

6. 283 U.S. at 717, Madison's "Report" is quoted at 714, 718, and 722.

7. The "Letter" is quoted in 283 U.S. at 717.

of Blackstone's statement that liberty of the press consists in laying no prior restraint on publication. The political and historical significance of both the "Report" and the "Letter" is that they express the founders' views that great public benefit is to be derived from the right to criticize public officials.

After presenting the evidence as to the history of free political expression, Chief Justice Hughes turns to a form of argument that plays a similar role in his opinion in the mortgage moratorium case. It is not enough, says the Chief Justice in both instances, to recount the past. The validity of the Court's decision must be demonstrated in terms of the present, and particularly in terms of any differences between past and present. In the mortgage moratorium case this difference is the increased "interrelation of the activities of our people and the complexity of our economic interests." [8] In the free press case, although the substantive logic is different (since the purpose is to reinforce rather than to deviate from the framers' specific constitutional intentions) the manner of argument is the same:

> The importance of this immunity [from previous restraint on publication] has not lessened. While reckless assaults upon public men, and efforts to bring obloquy upon those who are endeavoring faithfully to discharge official duties, exert a baleful influence and deserve the severest condemnation in public opinion, it cannot be said that this abuse is greater, and it is believed to be less, than that which characterized the period in which our institutions took shape. Meanwhile, the administration of government has become more complex, the opportunities for malfeasance and corruption have multiplied, crime has grown to most serious proportions, and the danger of its protection by unfaithful officials and of the impairment of the fundamental security of life and property by criminal alliances and official neglect, emphasizes the primary need of a vigilant and courageous press, especially in great cities.[9]

In other words, if the abuse of the press is less today than earlier and the need for a vigilant press is greater, then the arguments of Blackstone, Madison, and the others are all the more valid today.

8. Home Building and Loan Ass'n. v. Blaisdell, 290 U.S. 398, 442 (1934). The full passage is quoted above, pp. 48–49.
9. Near v. Minnesota, 283 U.S. 697, 719–20 (1931).

Ongoing history thus adds to the force of history as intent and strengthens the argument against previous restraint on publication.

Since the majority opinion nowhere suggests any sympathy with the sentiments of the magazine whose right to publish it affirms, it may be assumed that for Chief Justice Hughes and his associates a strong preference for a free press was the only guiding political value in the case. The minority, on the other hand, operated on a quite different premise: "It is of the greatest importance that the States shall be untrammeled and free to employ all just and appropriate measures to prevent abuses of the liberty of the press . . ." [10] The defendants' regular business, says the dissent in a statement uncontested by the Court, "was the publication of malicious, scandalous and defamatory articles concerning the principal public officers, leading newspapers of the city, many private persons and the Jewish race." [11] It was "fanciful to suggest similarity," the dissent continued, between this case "and the *previous restraint* upon the press by licensers as referred to by Blackstone and described in the history of the times to which he alludes." [12]

If what was historically relevant in this case was legal procedures restraining the press, then the dissenters had the better argument. The eighteenth century was concerned with confirming freedom from administrative censorship and protecting the legal rights of persons charged with libel. It was not concerned with postpublication injunction. But to the majority of the Supreme Court, Minnesota's action was an example of previous restraint in the classical sense. A court had determined that future articles of the paper would be as scandalous as past ones and had ordered the paper to cease publishing. This permanent suppression, said Chief Justice Hughes, was "the essence of censorship." [13] To the majority of the Court, eighteenth-century British procedures were not so important as the expanded colonial conception of the effect that press restraint, no matter how accomplished, would have on political expression and therefore on governmental affairs. In a narrowly decided case in which the publication at issue was admitted by all to be without

10. 283 U.S. at 732.
11. 283 U.S. at 724. A number of articles from the *Saturday Press* are printed in the dissent. They deny "launching [an] attack on the Jewish people AS A RACE," but their tone fully supports the dissent's characterization of them. *Ibid*.
12. 283 U.S. at 736 (emphasis in the original). Justice Butler's historical sources are comparable to those used in the majority opinion.
13. 283 U.S. at 713.

value, it was the historic conception of liberty of the press which was decisive in the opinion of the Court.

In 1936 the Supreme Court turned from previous restraint to another aspect of government control over political expression, the power of taxation. The legislature of Louisiana had imposed a 2 per cent gross receipts "license tax" on all publications which sold advertising and had a circulation in excess of 20,000 per week. The unabashed reason for this law was that all such papers opposed the Huey Long regime of the state, while the smaller papers supported it.[14]

The two constitutional grounds for attacking the Louisiana statute were that by discriminating against large newspapers the law violated the equal protection clause of the fourteenth amendment, and that by taxing newspapers of any description with the clear intent to limit circulation it violated the guaranty of a free press. The first of these arguments seems the more straightforward since it does not require any assumption concerning the intent of the legislature and it leaves untouched the general right to levy taxes on businesses. Also, this argument would appear to appeal to the more conservative justices on the Court. Despite this reasoning, however, Justice Sutherland wrote an opinion for a unanimous Court which ignored the equal protection argument and held the Louisiana newspaper tax a violation of the first-amendment right to freedom of the press.[15] The main vehicle of the opinion is history: "A determination of the question whether the tax is valid . . . requires an examination of the history and circumstances which antedated and attended the adoption of the abridgement clause of the First Amendment." [16]

The Court's history begins, expectedly, with *Areopagitica*. But, says the Court, Milton's ultimate victory over licensing "was soon recognized as too narrow a view of the liberty of the press," and the struggle continued in the early eighteenth century against a tax on newspapers and advertisements.[17] The newspaper and advertisement

14. Grosjean v. American Press Co., 297 U.S. 233 (1936). The case involved nine publishers of thirteen newspapers. According to the opinion of the Court there were 120 weekly newspapers in Louisiana. The background of the case is described in Zechariah Chafee, Jr., *Free Speech in the United States* (Cambridge, Mass.: Harvard University Press, 1941), p. 382.

15. For background on the strategy of counsel for the newspapers, see Paul A. Freund, "The Challenge of the Law," *Tulane Law Review,* 40 (1966), 481–82.

16. 297 U.S. at 245.

17. 297 U.S. at 246.

tax, says the Court, was designed "to suppress the publication of comments and criticisms objectionable to the Crown . . ." [18] The Court's story then jumps to the American Revolution, which, according to Justice Sutherland, "really began when, in 1765, that government sent stamps for newspaper duties to the American colonies." [19] This history, says Sutherland, "is enough to demonstrate beyond peradventure that in the adoption of the English newspaper stamp tax and the tax on advertisements, revenue was of subordinate concern; and that the dominant and controlling aim was to prevent or curtail the opportunity for the acquisition of knowledge by the people in respect of their governmental affairs . . . In the ultimate, an informed and enlightened public opinion was the thing at stake." [20]

The history the Court was dealing with is briefly this. Taxes on British newspapers, dating from an act of 1712 which applied only to Great Britain, were indeed designed to restrict circulation and hence freedom of the press. But the Stamp Act of 1765, directed only towards "the British colonies and plantations in America," was not.[21] Passed in March 1765 and repealed one year later, the act taxed legal documents (including contracts, court pleas, land grants, college diplomas, and liquor licenses), publications and advertisements, and gambling items (dice and playing cards). The stated purpose of the law was to defray "the expense of defending, protecting, and securing" the colonies. This purpose was real. A large public debt had been incurred during the Seven Years War, just ended, and the Stamp Act was only one of several measures designed to increase British revenue.

The American colonists saw these measures first as a blow to their economy and only afterwards — particularly with the Stamp Act, the first direct tax levied — as affecting their "rights as Englishmen." These rights, however, were summed up by "taxation without representation" and had nothing to do with freedom of the press. The colonial press, whether it complied with or evaded the requirements of the act, became, if anything, more free in its criticism of the royal government and more widespread in its circulation. The Stamp Act Resolutions passed by the Virginia House of Burgesses in May 1765

18. *Ibid.*
19. *Ibid.*
20. 297 U.S. at 247.
21. The relevant portions of the Stamp Act are printed in Henry Steele Commager (ed.), *Documents of American History* (2 vols.; New York: Appleton-Century-Crofts, 1949), I, 53–55.

emphasized that taxation through representation was "the distinguishing characteristick of British freedom" and said nothing about freedom of the press. The resolutions passed by delegates from nine colonies at the Stamp Act Congress later in the year were of the same character, except that several particular grievances were mentioned — but not restrictions on the press.[22]

Despite Justice Sutherland's belief, James Kent was accurate when he stated in the early nineteenth century that the Stamp Act was adopted "for the mere purpose of revenue." [23] A standard modern account of the Stamp Act crisis leaves a similar impression.[24] In his extensive study of freedom of speech and press in early America, Leonard Levy presents nothing to corroborate Justice Sutherland's opinion.[25] In defending the absence of a bill of rights in the original Constitution, Alexander Hamilton argued that a clause guaranteeing freedom of the press would be useless to prevent the taxation of newspapers, as that must "depend on legislative discretion, regulated by public opinion." "We know," he continued, "that newspapers are taxed in Great Britain, and yet it is notorious that the press nowhere enjoys greater liberty than in that country." [26] In short, there is no substantial evidence that opposition to the Stamp Act was related to freedom of expression, or that the first amendment was designed with the example of taxes on newspapers in mind.

The Supreme Court concluded, nevertheless, that in the light of its background "the First Amendment . . . was meant to preclude the national government . . . from adopting any form of previous restraint upon printed publications, or their circulation, including that which had theretofore been effected by [newspaper and ad-

22. The Virginia Stamp Act Resolutions, the Resolutions of the Stamp Act Congress, and other protests of the colonists against the Stamp Act are printed in Commager, 55–59.

23. *Commentaries on American Law,* ed. Charles M. Barnes (Boston: Little, Brown, 1884), II, *5.

24. Edmund S. and Helen M. Morgan, *Stamp Act Crisis* (Chapel Hill: University of North Carolina Press, 1953). See also Arthur M. Schlesinger, Sr., "The Colonial Newspapers and the Stamp Act," *New England Quarterly,* 8 (1935), 63–83.

25. *Freedom of Speech and Press in Early American History: Legacy of Suppression* (New York: Harper Torchbooks, 1963). The only relevant passage in this book (p. 86) tells of a publisher who suspended publication as an act of opposition to the tax but resumed publication when the Sons of Liberty, by threat of physical harm, persuaded him that opposition was better expressed by publishing and not paying.

26. *The Federalist,* No. 84 (Wright ed., p. 536, note).

vertisement taxes]." [27] Applying this principle to the states under the due process clause of the fourteenth amendment, the Louisiana tax was invalid as "a deliberate and calculated device in the guise of a tax to limit the circulation of information to which the public is entitled in virtue of the constitutional guaranties." [28] The Court noted further that the Louisiana tax was the only one of its kind in American national history, although a comparable tax had been maintained in England until after the middle of the nineteenth century.[29]

It is evident that the Court's chief historical supports in this case, that early Americans valued their press as a vehicle for criticism of British policies and that the colonists were furious at the stamp tax (which included fees on newspapers), have no historical relationship to each other. Although these two cherished uprights were used in constructing the story of American freedom, it was the Court, not history, that built a crossbeam between them.

Yet it is just this innovated historical relationship between liberty of the press and opposition to the Stamp Act that gives to the opinion of a unanimous Court its strength as a statement of liberty of the press. Seven years later, when the Court took a second look at taxes on the press, the earlier ingenious political history came under attack, but too late.[30] A majority of the Court held unconstitutional, as applied to the distribution of religious literature, a municipal ordinance requiring a license and fees for the solicitation of orders for, or the delivery of, merchandise. Although the ordinance was directed at traveling salesmen and was held invalid with respect to religious activities, the Court insisted the case concerned freedom of the press.[31] For the four dissenting members of the Court in this case, Justice Reed recalled that newspapers had never been held immune from "the ordinary forms of taxation." [32] Citing a number of historical sources he sought to undermine the earlier argument of the Court:

27. Grosjean v. American Press Co., 297 U.S. 233, 249 (1936).

28. 297 U.S. at 250.

29. 297 U.S. at 248, 250–51.

30. Murdock v. Pennsylvania, 319 U.S. 105 (1943).

31. A later case throws into doubt how much the Court really believed the case involved freedom of the press rather than the free exercise of religion. Breard v. Alexandria, 341 U.S. 622 (1951).

32. Murdock v. Pennsylvania, 319 U.S. 105, 128 (1943), quoting from Grosjean v. American Press Co., 297 U.S. 233, 250 (1936).

Is subjection to nondiscriminatory, nonexcessive taxation in the distribution of religious literature, a prohibition of the exercise of religion or an abridgment of the freedom of the press? Nothing has been brought to our attention which would lead to the conclusion that contemporary advocates of the adoption of a Bill of Rights intended such an exemption . . . The available evidence of Congressional action shows clearly that the draftsmen of the amendments had in mind the practice of religion and the right to be heard, rather than any abridgment or interference with either by taxation in any form.

There have been suggestions that the English taxes on newspapers, springing from the tax act [of 1712], influenced the adoption of the First Amendment. These taxes were obnoxious but an examination of the sources of the suggestion is convincing that there is nothing to support it except the fact that the tax on newspapers was in existence in England and was disliked . . . If there had been any purpose of Congress to prohibit any kind of taxes on the press, its knowledge of the abominated English taxes would have led it to ban them unequivocally.[33]

This is a fair correction of the historical record. But by pointing to the deficiency in the earlier historical reasoning without suggesting that it had led to the wrong conclusion in the Louisiana case, the dissent could hardly be persuasive to the majority of the Court. By this time history was not in point. The Court was less interested in the newspaper tax opinion as argument than in the decision as precedent. Indeed, the weakness of the history, combined with the sharp split of the Court on the occasion of the first application of the Louisiana newspaper tax case to different circumstances, suggests that the free press argument — and the historical symbolism behind it — had not been the true basis of decision in the earlier case. Rather, the Court had apparently decided the Louisiana case on the basis of the equal protection clause — unfair discrimination against large newspapers — and on the basis of the political motivation of the Huey Long regime in enacting it, but had taken the case as an excellent opportunity to anchor more firmly the principle of liberty of the press in constitutional law.

The cases of the 1930's, in which political expression had been inhibited by previous restraint on publication or by taxation, were

33. Murdock v. Pennsylvania, 319 U.S. 105, 121–26 (1943) (notes omitted).

decided in large part by reference to eighteenth-century history. This history provided adequate, though not determinative, analogies. In the 1940's, however, the Supreme Court began to hear a series of free expression cases which were without close historic parallel and which therefore had to be decided on a different basis. These cases concerned picketing by labor unions in order to express economic grievances. Until the picketing became entwined with violence, instances later termed "free speech plus," the union activities afforded the Court the opportunity to apply historically established principles of free expression to a novel situation and to justify this in terms of an evolving or adaptable Constitution.

In the first and leading case on picketing, Thornhill v. Alabama, a state statute forbade picketing "without a just cause . . . for the purpose of hindering, delaying, or interfering with or injuring any lawful business or enterprise of another." [34] The Supreme Court found the statute unconstitutional on its face because of the "pervasive threat" of such legislation to stifle constitutionally protected speech.[35] "The power of the licensor against which John Milton directed his assault by his 'Appeal for the Liberty of Unlicensed Printing,'" wrote Justice Murphy, using the sanctified reference, "is pernicious not merely by reason of the censure of particular comments but by reason of the threat to censure comments on matters of public concern." [36] Labor unions in the twentieth century had the same right to express their opinions as merchants in the eighteenth century. In a manner reminiscent of Chief Justice Hughes's opinions in the mortgage moratorium and prior restraint cases, Justice Murphy constructed a bridge between the beliefs of the Founding Fathers and contemporary needs. Referring to a number of historical sources at the outset of his argument, he discussed the present application of the traditional principles of free expression:

> The exigencies of the colonial period and the efforts to secure freedom from oppressive administration developed a broadened conception of these liberties as adequate to supply the public need for information and education with respect to significant issues of the times . . . Freedom of discussion, if it would fulfill its historical function in this nation, must embrace all issues about

34. 310 U.S. 88, 91 (1940), from Sec. 3448 of the Alabama State Code of 1923.
35. 310 U.S. at 97.
36. *Ibid.*

which information is needed or appropriate to enable the members of society to cope with the exigencies of their period.

In the circumstances of our times the discussion of information concerning the facts of a labor dispute must be regarded as within that area of free discussion that is guaranteed by the Constitution . . . Free discussion concerning the conditions in industry and the causes of labor disputes appears to us indispensable to the effective and intelligent use of the processes of popular government to shape the destiny of modern industrial society.[37]

In the circumstances of peaceful picketing which *Thornhill* presented the Court, it was not difficult to make the leap from the eighteenth to the twentieth century. As the Court said, free expression was related to the "public need for information" and the "intelligent use of the processes of popular government." But what about picketing that became enmeshed in violence? Did it serve these same purposes? In a six-to-three decision a year after *Thornhill* the Court decided that it did not. Upholding a state court injunction against such picketing, Justice Frankfurter wrote for the Court: "It must never be forgotten . . . that the Bill of Rights was the child of the Enlightenment. Back of the guaranty of free speech lay faith in the power of an appeal to reason by all the peaceful means for gaining access to the mind."[38] Picketing as free speech could be justified initially as a modern extension of an historically grounded principle, and it could be modified on the same basis.

In the picketing cases, as in the previous restraint and taxation cases, the Court used history both to substantiate its decisions and to plead the cause of freedom of political expression. To the degree that history was used to substantiate the decision, the lesson from the cases discussed appears to be that the more detailed the history, the weaker its support for contemporary circumstances. To apply the

37. 310 U.S. at 102–03 (notes omitted). The historical sources cited by Justice Murphy include the "Letter to the Inhabitants of Quebec" of the Continental Congress, Madison's "Report" on the Virginia Resolutions, and Duniway, *The Development of Freedom of Press in Massachusetts.*

38. Drivers Union v. Meadowmoor Dairies, 312 U.S. 287, 293 (1941). Justice Murphy, author of the *Thornhill* opinion, agreed with the Court. The two dissents in the case also invoked history on their side. Justice Black, with whom Justice Douglas concurred, cited Thomas Jefferson. 312 U.S. at 301. Justice Reed argued generally that "our whole history teaches that adjustment of social relations through reason is possible while free speech is maintained." 312 U.S. at 320.

eighteenth-century strictures against prior restraint, Chief Justice Hughes was required to claim that the procedure against which Blackstone and others had objected, administrative censorship, was not central to the views of the framers of the first amendment. In declaring the Louisiana newspaper tax unconstitutional the Court offered a unique interpretation of the Stamp Act crisis in order to relate early eighteenth-century British taxes on newspapers to late eighteenth-century principles of freedom of speech. Only in the picketing cases, where no detailed history was to the point, was the Court able to find — and phrase — a covering principle that explained how the intentions of the framers applied to the twentieth century.

But the three types of political expression cases used history for another reason — to plead the cause of free speech. And in this they were uniformly successful. The Court recognized that political values are a product of tradition and that tradition is therefore one of the most certain sources of argument in their favor. In the prior restraint case the history of free expression was the soundest choice in constructing an appealing argument. To defend the publication in the case without it would have left the opinion both too abstract and too susceptible to the charge that the majority justices found value in the particular scandal sheet at issue. In the taxation case, the Court could have used a much more conventional constitutional approach, the equal protection clause. Its choice of free press and history was apparently a deliberate attempt to reinforce a political value in a case whose outcome was in no dispute. In the picketing cases the Court reminded the public that its historically grounded principle of free expression was painlessly adaptable to modern circumstances, that the present and the past were in essential harmony. In all three types of cases history was used to secure more firmly a generally held political value.

Seditious Libel

The central historical and theoretical problem of freedom of political expression in America has been that of seditious libel. Seditious libel is an archetypical political, as contrasted to legal, crime, and it therefore has no precise definition. But it amounts to any criticism of the government which subjects its author to criminal prosecution. The common law of seditious libel, however defined or circumscribed by requirements for proof or the process of trial, was accepted by Blackstone: "To punish as the law does at present any dangerous or offensive writings, which, when published, shall on a fair and impartial trial be adjudged of a pernicious tendency, is necessary for the preservation of peace and good order, of government and religion, the only solid foundations of civil liberty." [39] One of the most important questions in the debate over seditious libel in American history has been whether the society which revered Blackstone and the common law in many respects regarded this statement as compatible with the first amendment. The Declaration of Independence, proclaimed within a decade of the publication of Blackstone's *Commentaries*, was the most monumental seditious libel in British history. But because the Declaration was treated as an act of political secession to be met with military rather than legal force, it adds little to the debate over the acceptance of seditious libel in the colonies.[40] With regard to postrevolutionary America, the problem is even more complex and, because of the scantiness of relevant legal materials, perhaps ultimately beyond a satisfactory solution.[41]

The debate over colonial acceptance of seditious libel would be entirely academic and historical except for the fact that its solution would help determine the right of Congress to make seditious libel a statutory crime. That would shed light on the Sedition Act of 1798, whose constitutionality has been questioned ever since it was first proposed. And that in turn would give a much clearer constitutional perspective on several efforts to suppress criticism of the government in the twentieth century.

39. *Commentaries*, IV, *151.
40. For a discussion of the development of seditious libel in England, emphasizing its ignoble ancestry, see Irving Brant, "Seditious Libel: Myth and Reality," *New York University Law Review*, 39 (1964), 1–19.
41. In general, see Alfred H. Kelly, "Constitutional Liberty and the Law of Libel: A Historian's View," *American Historical Review*, 74 (1968), 429–52. For contrasting discussions of seditious libel see Irving Brant, *The Bill of Rights: Its Origin and Meaning* (Indianapolis: Bobbs-Merrill, 1965), and Levy, *Freedom of Speech and Press in Early American History*. It is Mr. Levy's thesis that the first amendment was not designed to abolish the common law of seditious libel, in spite of what members of the Supreme Court such as Justices Holmes, Brandeis, Black, and Douglas have said on the subject. A close reading of Levy's evidence suggests that his narrow legal-theoretical approach does not do justice to the spirit and practices of the time. Colonial Americans did not devise a clear theoretical statement against the concept of seditious libel, but they also refused to succumb to the legal or political consequences of the British theory that accepted seditious libel as a crime.

The Sedition Act of 1798 provided for the punishment of "any person who shall write, print, utter or publish . . . any false, scandalous and malicious writings against the government of the United States . . . with intent to defame or to bring it into contempt or disrepute . . ." [42] Expiring of its own force at the end of the administration of John Adams, the act was never tested in the Supreme Court. But Americans generally looked back on it as unwise if not unconstitutional. Thomas Jefferson pardoned every person convicted under the act on the ground that the law was a "nullity," and Congress eventually repaid fines collected in its prosecution.[43]

In the nineteenth-century legal commentaries there were various reactions to the Sedition Act. St. George Tucker, a Virginia jurist who had fought in the Revolution and was a friend of Jefferson, excoriated it in an appendix to the first American edition of Blackstone's *Commentaries* in 1803.[44] But in this era he was an exception. William Rawle in his *View of the Constitution* (1825) maintained a completely Blackstonian position with respect to seditious libel, although he did not mention the Sedition Act itself.[45] James Kent, also a Blackstonian, did not even distinguish political expression from private defamation and thereby avoided the entire topic.[46] The matter was taken up in detail, however, by Joseph Story. Acknowledging disagreement over the issue, he contended strongly for the constitutionality of the Sedition Act. But he concluded that the law had left "no permanent traces in the constitutional jurisprudence of the country" and was "not likely to be renewed." [47] It was Thomas Cooley, emphasizing constitutional limitations rather than constitutional powers, who, for the first time since St. George Tucker's day, claimed that the Sedition Act had been unconstitutional. In the late 1860's Cooley elaborated a theory of free expression considerably wider than Blackstone: "The English common-law rule which made libels on the constitution or the government indictable, as it was administered by the courts, seems to us unsuited to the condition and

42. 1 Stat. 596. The act is contained in Commager, *Documents*, I, 177–78.

43. A convenient summary of the history of the act is found in the opinion of the Court in New York Times Co. v. Sullivan, 376 U.S. 254, 273–77 (1964).

44. Vol. II, Appendix, Note G.

45. *A View of the Constitution of the United States of America* (Philadelphia, 1825), pp. 119–20.

46. *Commentaries on American Law*, II, *16–26.

47. *Commentaries on the Constitution of the United States* (2 vols.; Boston: Little, Brown, 1858), Secs. 1293–94, 1880–92. The quotations are from Secs. 1293 and 1294.

circumstances of the people of America, and therefore never to have been adopted by the several States. If we are correct in this, it would not be in the power of the State legislatures to pass laws which should make mere criticism of the constitution or of the measures of government a crime, however sharp, unreasonable, and intemperate it might be." [48]

When the Supreme Court eventually began to hear free speech cases, nineteenth-century commentaries supplied an uncertain tradition with respect to the constitutionality of seditious libel. This, with the uncertain eighteenth-century history, has allowed the justices considerable latitude in using and molding the historical background to fit their own outlooks and the variety of situations presented by the free expression cases. The trend has been for the Court slowly to free itself from the specifically legal view, that is, from the common law tradition, and to accept the more liberal American contribution as a guide to the first-amendment rights. In this evolution the Court has found history both relevant and adaptable as a vehicle of judicial reasoning and a source for contemporary values.

Just as seditious libel was a highly political offense under the common law, the chief opportunities for the Supreme Court to pronounce on comparable statutory law in modern America have also been in politically charged circumstances. In emphasizing the historical portions of the Court's opinions in the cases to be discussed, this context of decision must not be forgotten. It is, in fact, the political context, in conjunction with the outcomes of the cases and one's views on the judicial mind, that determines whether the history in the opinions of the Court appears as a foil for personal beliefs or as a thread in the fabric of constitutional law.

Like the Sedition Act of 1798, modern legislation involving the concept of seditious libel has stemmed largely from American fears of foreign political doctrines. In particular, the cases heard by the Supreme Court are the outgrowth of World War I and the Cold War. Three cases set the background. The first is a decision of 1897 in which the Court denied habeas corpus to several sailors who had jumped ship in California and claimed that their contracts as seamen no more deprived them of personal liberty than did other agreements for employment. Justice Brown, for eight members of the Court,

48. *A Treatise on the Constitutional Limitations which rest upon the legislative power of the states of the American Union* (Boston: Little, Brown, 1878), *429.

rejected the claim. He concluded, after a survey of the legal status of sailors from ancient Rhodes to modern England, that if all other legal codes in western history had treated seamen as an exception to general rules, then so did the American. The sailors stayed in jail, and the Bill of Rights was circumscribed as follows:

> The law is perfectly well settled that the first ten amendments to the Constitution, commonly known as the Bill of Rights, were not intended to lay down any novel principles of government, but simply to embody certain guaranties and immunities which we had inherited from our English ancestors, and which had from time immemorial been subject to certain well-recognized exceptions arising from the necessities of the case. In incorporating these principles into the fundamental law there was no intention of disregarding the exceptions, which continued to be recognized as if they had been formally expressed. Thus, the freedom of speech and of the press (art. 1) does not permit the publications of libels, blasphemous or indecent articles, or other publications injurious to public morals or private reputation.[49]

In view of what was subsequently made of this passage, it should be noted: first, it was hardly accurate to say the law was "perfectly well settled" that the Bill of Rights did not intend to lay down any "novel principles of government" — this is what the fight over the Sedition Act of 1798 was all about; second, the statement on freedom of expression was obiter dictum — the case had to do with the traditional powers of a captain over his sailors; and third, the description of speech that the Court agreed could be forbidden did not explicitly include seditious libel — in fact, by speaking of "public morals" rather than of public order, the opinion seemed to skirt the issue of political expression entirely. In spite of these qualifications, however, Justice Brown's statement became the Court's initial position on both history and law. The United States had adopted the British heritage in the Bill of Rights, and the Bill of Rights did not protect expression deemed harmful to the government.

The first evidence that this was the position of the Court came a

---

49. Robertson v. Baldwin, 165 U.S. 275, 281 (1897). The single dissent was by Justice Harlan, who thought the history of other times and places sprang from cultural and legal systems so dissimilar to the American that it was irrelevant to a decision in the case.

decade after the decision on the sailors. In 1907 the Supreme Court refused to overturn a state contempt-of-court conviction based on newspaper criticism of court action in a pending case.[50] The necessary argument in the opinion of Justice Holmes for the Court was that there is no constitutional protection for those whose activities tend to obstruct the fair administration of justice, whether in the press, in the courtroom, or elsewhere. But, quoting from Blackstone, Holmes, the Court's greatest historian of the common law and the editor of Kent's *Commentaries*, added: "The main purpose of such constitutional provisions [insuring free speech and press] is 'to prevent all such *previous* restraints as had been practiced by other governments,' and they do not prevent the subsequent punishment of such as may be deemed contrary to the public welfare." [51] If there is a real distinction between the "public morals" used in the sailors' case and the "public welfare" used here, then Justice Holmes's opinion made even more restrictive the right of free expression. Dissenting, Justice Harlan took direct issue with the notion: "I cannot assent to that view, if it be meant that the legislature may impair or abridge the rights of a free press and of free speech whenever it thinks that the public welfare requires that to be done." [52]

In 1915, before the anxieties of war broke over the country and before Louis Brandeis took his seat on the bench, the Supreme Court had one more occasion to pronounce on the meaning of the first amendment, again in a field different from the traditional concerns of seditious libel. A statute of the state of Washington provided for the punishment of persons whose publications had "a tendency to encourage or incite the commission of any crime." [53] Its constitutionality was challenged in a case over a publication which was said to encourage violation of the state's indecent exposure law. The statute was unanimously upheld. The reason, said the Court through Justice Holmes, was that the statute must be construed as applying only to publications that encouraged "an actual breach of law." [54] This was a qualification that was soon to be elaborated.

Under the stress of the early months of America's participation in World War I, Congress passed the Espionage Act of 1917, the first

50. Patterson v. Colorado, 205 U.S. 454 (1907).
51. 205 U.S. at 462.
52. 205 U.S. at 465. Justice Brewer also dissented in the case, but on a different ground.
53. Fox v. Washington, 236 U.S. 273, 275 (1915).
54. 236 U.S. at 277.

federal seditious libel legislation since 1798. As amended, this act provided for the heavy punishment of persons attempting to obstruct the draft and of those who, "when the United States is at war, shall willfully utter, print, write, or publish any disloyal, profane, scurrilous, or abusive language about the form of government of the United States, or of the Constitution of the United States . . . or any language intended to bring [these] into contempt, scorn, contumely or disrepute." [55]

Within a year and a half of the 1918 Armistice, the Supreme Court had upheld the Espionage Act in six cases.[56] The first three were decided unanimously, with the opinions, as had become customary in free expression cases, written by Justice Holmes. Holmes upheld the act's prohibition of speech advocating the commission of crimes by reference to the Court's statement (quoted above) in the sailors' case of 1897. And in the same spirit as his own recent opinion in the case from Washington state, he wrote: "The 1st Amendment while prohibiting legislation against free speech as such, cannot have been, and obviously was not, intended to give immunity for every possible use of language . . . We venture to believe that neither Hamilton nor Madison, nor any other competent person then or later, ever supposed that to make criminal the counselling of a murder within the jurisdiction of Congress would be an unconstitutional interference with free speech." [57] As no one had remotely counseled murder in this case, the name-dropping that ties the validity of the Espionage Act to the Founding Fathers takes on a defensive tone uncommon for Justice Holmes. But, however explained, the act was upheld.

Yet in a companion case, while admitting the constitutionality of the act, Holmes was more expansive and constructive. He qualified his statement in the 1907 contempt-of-court opinion that the main purpose of the first amendment was simply to adopt Blackstone's views against previous restraint. This qualification liberated the constitutional issue of free expression from its common law background. At the same time, Justice Holmes proposed a standard derived from the common law for determining when the bounds of constitu-

---

55. 40 Stat. 553. The relevant portions are printed in Commager, *Documents,* II, 325–26.

56. Schenck v. United States, 249 U.S. 47 (1919); Frohwerk v. United States, 249 U.S. 204 (1919); Debs v. United States, 249 U.S. 211 (1919); Abrams v. United States, 250 U.S. 616 (1919); Schaefer v. United States, 251 U.S. 466 (1920); and Pierce v. United States, 252 U.S. 239 (1920).

57. Frohwerk v. United States, 249 U.S. 204, 206 (1919).

tionally guaranteed speech had been passed. The standard was the clear and present danger doctrine:

> It well may be that the prohibition of laws abridging the freedom of speech is not confined to previous restraints, although to prevent them may have been the main purpose, as intimated [by Holmes for the Court] in Patterson v. Colorado . . . We admit that in many places and in ordinary times the defendants, in saying all that was said in the circular, would have been within their constitutional rights. But the character of every act depends upon the circumstances in which it is done . . . The question in every case is whether the words used are used in such circumstances and are of such a nature as to create a clear and present danger that they will bring about the substantive evils that Congress has a right to prevent. It is a question of proximity and degree.[58]

Applying this principle in the next case arising under the Espionage Act, Justice Holmes broke away not only from the Court but also from his own earlier position on the intent of the first amendment with respect to seditious libel. The Court had been urged by both parties to the case to decide the issue on the basis of history. The government, citing among its sources a committee report of the House of Representatives recommending passage of the Alien and Sedition Acts, claimed that the first amendment "clearly refers us back to the law prior to the adoption of the Constitution, and intends to fix the liberty of the press by that law. What such liberty was at the time of adoption of the Constitution, that it shall continue to be, no more, no less." [59] In opposition, the plaintiffs-on-appeal referred to Milton, Jefferson, and the libertarian sentiments of St. George Tucker in his 1803 edition of Blackstone.[60] The majority of the Court ignored the invitation to settle the historical question of seditious libel. But not Justice Holmes. With Justice Brandeis concurring, he finally and firmly adopted an anti-Blackstonian view of early constitutional history, very much like that of Justice Harlan, who had dissented against his (Holmes's) opinion for the Court in the 1907 contempt-of-court case. Holmes declared: "I wholly dis-

58. Schenck v. United States, 249 U.S. 47, 51–52 (1919).
59. Brief on behalf of the United States, p. 19, Abrams v. United States, 250 U.S. 616 (1919).
60. See Brief for Plaintiffs-in-Error, e.g., p. 43, Abrams v. United States, 250 U.S. 616 (1919).

agree with the argument of the Government that the 1st Amendment left the common law as to seditious libel in force. History seems to me against the notion. I had conceived that the United States through many years had shown its repentance for the Sedition Act of July 14, 1798, by repaying fines that it imposed." [61]

Whether historical reflection, the different social and legal context of the later cases, or the persuasiveness of Justice Brandeis and others played the greatest role in the evolution of Holmes's outlook on the history of political expression in America, it is not possible to say. But whatever the cause, Holmes not only redirected his own thought but eventually that of the Court also. Yet until the Court as a whole finally adopted the anti-Blackstonian position on seditious libel, the whole range of Holmes's prestigious remarks on the historical background of freedom of expression was cited by various justices in support of their views in different cases.

The early views of Holmes appear in the cases of prior restraint, cases in which it was unexceptionable to appeal to Blackstone and his followers. Chief Justice Hughes, for instance, more than once referred to Holmes's statement that the "main purpose" of the first amendment was to prevent previous restraint on publication.[62] The early Holmesian views appeared also in the opinions of Justice Frankfurter when he wished to emphasize the nonabsolute nature of the first-amendment freedoms. Concurring in the leading case construing the Alien Registration Act of 1940 (the Smith Act), Justice Frankfurter wrote: "The historic antecedents of the First Amend-

61. Abrams v. United States, 250 U.S. 616, 630 (1919). In a free speech case decided several years later the Court was asked again to consider the constitutionality of the Sedition Act of 1798. The issue, said the defendant's counsel, "was whether freedom of speech and press was to be construed in the light of Blackstone and the common law, or in that of the Declaration of Independence." Brief for Plaintiff-in-Error, p. 81, Gitlow v. New York, 268 U.S. 652 (1925). This time the Court explicitly declined the invitation, apparently as conscious of the odious place of the Sedition Act in American history as it was intent on upholding the state criminal anarchy law at issue in the case: "We need not enter upon a consideration of the English common-law rule of seditious libel or the Federal Sedition Act of 1798, to which reference is made in the defendant's brief. These are so unlike the present statute that we think the decisions under them cast no helpful light upon the questions here." Gitlow v. New York, 268 U.S. 652, 672 (1925) (note omitted). Justice Holmes, dissenting with Justice Brandeis, did not reiterate his conclusion on seditious libel and the law of 1798.

62. Near v. Minnesota, 283 U.S. 697, 714 (1931); Lovell v. Griffin, 303 U.S. 444, 452 (1938).

ment preclude the notion that its purpose was to give unqualified immunity to every expression that touched on matters within the range of political interest." [63] But this same case, and others involving communist doctrine and similarly alleged un-American political expression or activities, also brought out, on the part of Justices Black and Douglas, the later Holmesian view — that the first amendment had outlawed the concept of seditious libel in America.[64]

On two further occasions the Supreme Court has been faced with the problem of seditious libel in history, but under less direct circumstances than in the cases involving statutes aimed at protecting the government from criticism. The first illustrates how the angle of judicial perspective may determine the use of history; the second seems finally to settle the judicial dispute over the history of seditious libel. In the first case the Court upheld the constitutionality of a state "group libel" law.[65] The purpose of such a law is to prevent dangers to public peace caused by racial or religious agitators by prohibiting, in the words of the Illinois statute at issue in the case, the publication of material portraying "depravity, criminality, unchastity, or lack of virtue of a class of citizens, of any race, color, creed, or religion . . . [or exposing them to] contempt, derision, or obloquy or which is productive of breach of the peace or riots." [66]

The wording of the law immediately brings to mind seditious libel, except that "class of citizens" is substituted for government. But in his opinion for the Court, Justice Frankfurter's analogy went in a different direction, to personal libel. He premised the constitutionality of the state law on the view that in the first decades after the Constitution was adopted, "nowhere was there any suggestion that

---

63. Dennis v. United States, 341 U.S. 494, 521 (1951). The Alien Registration Act provides in part: "It shall be unlawful for any person . . . to knowingly or willfully advocate, abet, advise, or teach the duty, necessity, desirability, or propriety of overthrowing any government in the United States by force or violence; [or with that intent] to print . . . circulate . . . or publicly display any written or printed matter advocating [such goals; or] to organize . . . any society, group, or assembly of persons who teach [this doctrine]." 54 Stat. 670, 671. Relevant portions are printed in Commager, *Documents,* II, 613.

64. The best example is Justice Black's dissent in Communist Party v. Control Board, 367 U.S. 1, 137 (1961), in which over half of the 22-page opinion is devoted to the British and American history of the suppression of political dissent. Justice Holmes's later views are quoted with approval, 367 U.S. at 159. See also Justice Douglas' dissenting opinion in Scales v. United States, 367 U.S. 203, 262 (1961).

65. Beauharnais v. Illinois, 343 U.S. 250 (1952).

66. 343 U.S. at 251, from 111. Rev. Stat. 1949, ch. 38, sec. 471.

the crime of libel be abolished." [67] In dissent, Justice Black argued that the Court's logic ran the wrong way. Instead of comparing group libel to private libel, it should be compared to seditious libel: "Prior efforts to expand the scope of criminal libel beyond its traditional boundaries have not usually met with widespread popular acclaim. 'Seditious libel' was such an expansion and it did have its day, particularly in the English Court of Star Chamber. But the First Amendment repudiated seditious libel for this country . . . Whatever the danger, if any, in such public discussions [as in this case], it is a danger the Founders deemed outweighed by the danger incident to the stifling of thought and speech." [68] But Justice Frankfurter's analogy — and the evidence of racial disturbances in Illinois — carried the day.

In the second case indirectly dealing with seditious libel the Court unanimously reversed a civil libel judgment in which the basis of a damage award had been the publication of false statements about an official's performance of his public duties.[69] This case, New York Times Co. v. Sullivan, has resulted in the apparently permanent establishment of the anti-seditious-libel doctrine as authentic constitutional history. The later Holmesian view has become constitutional law. The Supreme Court, through Justice Brennan, based its historical discussion in the *New York Times* case on the proposition that "what a State may not constitutionally bring about by means of a criminal statute is likewise beyond the reach of its civil law of libel." [70] Behind this legal proposition lay the libertarian theory of Madison, Jefferson, and St. George Tucker of the "right of freely examining public characters and measures, and of free communications among the people thereon . . ." [71] The Court opinion in the *Times* libel case contains an essay on the history and philosophy of freedom of political expression. It concludes that although the

67. 343 U.S. at 254–55. Justice Frankfurter's historical sources include Charles Warren, *The Supreme Court in United States History* (1922), letters of Jefferson and John Adams, and a manuscript draft of Jefferson's 1801 State of the Union Message.

68. 343 U.S. at 272, 275.

69. New York Times Co. v. Sullivan, 376 U.S. 254 (1964). The Court's actual holding was that "the Constitution delimits a State's power to award damages for libel in actions brought by public officials against critics of their official conduct" by requiring "proof of actual malice" — which had not been shown in this case. 376 U.S. at 283.

70. 376 U.S. at 277 (note omitted).

71. From The Virginia Resolutions (Madison), quoted in 376 U.S. at 274.

Sedition Act of 1798 "was never tested in this Court, the attack upon its validity has carried the day in the court of history." [72] Justice Black, in a concurring opinion joined by Justice Douglas, agreed: "As the Court's opinion correctly points out . . . [the] Act came to an ignominious end and by common consent has generally been treated as having been a wholly unjustifiable and much to be regretted violation of the First Amendment." [73] Justice Goldberg, with whom Justice Douglas also concurred, spoke of the "impressive array of history . . . marshalled by the Court." [74] He fully agreed "that the attack upon the validity of the Sedition Act of 1798 . . . 'has carried the day in the court of history' . . . and that the Act would today be declared unconstitutional." [75] With the *Times* libel case the constitutional and historical uncertainty of seditious libel was judicially laid to rest.

The Rhetoric of the History of Freedom

The "court of history" which the Supreme Court invoked — or convoked — to set at rest the question of the constitutionality of the Sedition Act and the historical meaning of freedom of political expression under the first amendment is a novel tribunal from the point of view of both historian and judge. To the historian, the constitutionality of the Sedition Act ought to depend on evidence of the time, not on the reaction of subsequent generations. To the judge, the practice of determining constitutionality retrospectively creates the appearance of attempting to halt the process of constitutional development: for while it is justifiable to argue that what might have been valid a century ago is void today because of the nature of ongoing history, it is a baffling and literal anachronism to remove an uncontested law from the stream of history just long enough to declare it unconstitutional by modern standards, and then replace it

72. 376 U.S. at 276 (note omitted). Madison is cited by the Court at 271, 274, 275, and 282; Milton at 279; and John Stuart Mill at 272 and 279. The Sedition Act is discussed at 273–77.

73. 376 U.S. at 296. This historical portion of Justice Black's opinion relies particularly on St. George Tucker, whose views are cited at 296 and 297.

74. 376 U.S. at 298.

75. *Ibid.*, n. 1. Justice Goldberg would have gone further than the Court in undoing the Sedition Act. Both the Court and the eighteenth-century law included malice as an element of legal libel. Justice Goldberg felt that the right of free speech "should not depend upon a probing by the jury of the motivation of the citizen or press." 376 U.S. at 298 (note omitted).

in order to enjoy the illusory satisfaction that the act had been notoriously invalid all the time.

Yet despite the sense of these propositions the Court's unusual use of history in the *Times* case and in other political expression cases has an explanation, and one that does not lie in the province of law or history but in that of political sociology. In essence, the reason for this special use of history is that the Court is securing the "blessings of liberty" to the posterity of the founders. It does so by stressing the historical and constitutional continuity of freedom of expression as central to American society and government. The Court is not acting here as historian or as judge but as instructor in political values. The medium of instruction that appeals strongly to the teacher, and seems effective for the students, is history. History becomes a means of education in political philosophy. In the political expression cases history is an important principle of adjudication in the standard sense: it is one of several vehicles leading to the outcome of the case, and in this sense it functions as it did in the mortgage moratorium and presidential removal power cases. What distinguishes the political expression cases from the others in the use of history is the tone, the style, and the fervency of presenting it, as well as the confidence that the meaning of the first amendment is both clarified and sanctified by referring to its history.

The special educational function of history in these cases would be no surprise to the framers of the first amendment. The framers considered a bill of rights valuable largely as a touchstone of political philosophy, rather than as a text of legally enforceable rights, and they thought history the best mode of inculcating civic virtue. History as much as law contributed to the meaning of the Bill of Rights, and history and political practice as much as law would determine its future. One of Alexander Hamilton's unpersuasive arguments that a bill of rights was not necessary for the Constitution was that there was no firm definition for freedom of the press, that it was "impracticable" to define. Further, its security depended "altogether . . . on public opinion, and on the general spirit of the people and of the government." [76] Contemplating the proposed bill of rights demanded by the states as the price of ratification, Madison agreed. He wrote to Jefferson in the fall of 1788 that bills of rights served to protect the people from themselves by instilling "political truths" in a "solemn manner"; and that they served to protect the people from

76. *The Federalist,* No. 84 (Wright ed., p. 535).

their government by presenting "the sense of the community" for all to see.[77] In the days before the development of constitutional law, it was this quality of moral admonition and civic education, not legal safeguard, that a bill of rights was expected to serve.[78]

The Supreme Court has overcome any qualms about the legal enforceability of the Bill of Rights, but it has not because of this lost touch with the expectations of the framers that the Bill of Rights and its background can and should contribute to the molding of fundamental political principles. In the political expression cases the Court has used history for just this purpose. Three identifiable techniques have been developed for the use of history in the instruction of the values of free expression. The first is the typical historical essay, found in the political expression cases concerned with the events surrounding the adoption of the first amendment. This was the technique of Chief Justice Hughes in the prior restraint case, of Justice Sutherland in the newspaper taxation case, and of Justice Brennan for the Court in the *Times* libel suit. The other techniques for using history in political expression cases appear to be reserved for the occasions when the Court is giving the public instruction in the value of first-amendment freedoms. The first is a "parade of horribles" from British history; its master is Justice Black. The second is a special method of rhetoric perfected by Justice Brandeis. It succinctly states a coherent modern doctrine of free expression as if it came from the mouths of the framers.

The "parade of horribles" approach consists of recounting reprehensive practices of English history from the sixteenth century on, and claiming that the American colonists revolted in large part to be rid of this legacy, finally adopting the Bill of Rights to prevent anything comparable from ever occurring in the United States. A typical example may be found in Justice Black's opinion for the Court holding unconstitutional a municipal ordinance that prohibited the distribution of handbills failing to contain the names and addresses of the persons responsible:

> Anonymous pamphlets, leaflets, brochures and even books have played an important role in the progress of mankind. Persecuted

77. Letter of Oct. 17, 1788, in *The Writings of James Madison,* ed. Gaillard Hunt (9 vols.; New York: Putnam's Sons, 1900–1910), V, 273.

78. The genesis of the idea of judicial enforceability of the Bill of Rights was nevertheless evident in the 1780's. See the discussion of Jefferson and Madison in Edmond Cahn, "The Parchment Barriers," *American Scholar,* 32 (1962), 32–34.

groups and sects from time to time throughout history have been able to criticize oppressive practices and laws anonymously or not at all. The obnoxious press licensing law of England, which was also enforced in the Colonies, was due in part to the knowledge that exposures of the names of printers, writers and distributors would lessen the circulation of literature critical of the government. The old seditious libel cases in England show the length to which government had to go to find out who was responsible for books that were obnoxious to the rulers. John Lilburne was whipped, pilloried and fined for refusing to answer questions designed to get evidence to convict him or someone else for the secret distribution of books in England. Two Puritan Ministers, John Penry and John Udal, were sentenced to death on charges that they were responsible for writing, printing or publishing books. Before the Revolutionary War colonial patriots frequently had to conceal their authorship or distribution of literature that easily could have brought down on them prosecutions by English-controlled courts. Along about that time the Letters of Junius were written and the identity of their author is unknown to this day. Even the Federalist Papers, written in favor of the adoption of our Constitution, were published under fictitious names. It is plain that anonymity has sometimes been assumed for the most constructive purposes.[79]

Justice Black, in fact, can scarcely write an opinion in the entire area of civil liberties without adverting unfavorably to British history and favorably to the beliefs of the Founding Fathers, particularly Madison and Jefferson.[80] History, in sum, tells us what to avoid and whom to accept.

The influence of Justice Black on the impact of Court opinions or on the law of the first amendment in general is certainly greater for his constant reminder of the antecedents to today's constitutional rights than it would be if his opinions were composed solely of legal

79. Talley v. California, 362 U.S. 60, 64–65 (1960) (notes omitted). The references: John Lilburne, c. 1614–1657; John Penry, 1559–1593; John Udal, 1560–1592; and the "Letters of Junius," published in a London newspaper from 1769 to 1772, critical of George III and the current British ministry.

80. See, e.g., Justice Black's dissents in Noto v. United States, 367 U.S. 290, 300 (1961); and Communist Party v. Control Board, 367 U.S. 1, 137 (1961). For examples from Justice Douglas, see his dissents in Scales v. United States, 367 U.S. 203, 270–74 (1961); and Dennis v. United States, 341 U.S. 494, 590 (1951).

or contemporary references. This cannot be measured, of course; it must be taken on the common sense of the matter. What the courts can do in the area of free expression by their decisions must be augmented by what is said in the opinions, for freedom of speech and press means nothing if vindicated only in courts of law. Not only is legal action normally too late to be of real aid in the cases that are heard, but freedom of expression as a whole serves no purpose unless it is embedded in the social and political mores of the nation. Justice Black and others who cite history as a means of instruction in contemporary civic virtue agree with Madison and Hamilton that it is the public and its government rather than legal definition that determines the status of free expression, and they consciously incorporate this belief in their opinions.

The special rhetorical technique that Justice Brandeis has contributed to the use of history for instruction in political values stands in marked contrast to the method of Justice Black. While Justice Black asks us to draw lessons from history, Justice Brandeis asks the Founding Fathers to speak directly to us. No passage better illustrates this than the following from Justice Brandeis' concurring opinion in the free speech case of Whitney v. California:

> Those who won our independence believed that the final end of the state was to make men free to develop their faculties; and that in its government the deliberative forces should prevail over the arbitrary. They valued liberty both as an end and as a means. They believed liberty to be the secret of happiness and courage to be the secret of liberty. They believed that freedom to think as you will and speak as you think are means indispensable to the discovery and spread of political truth; that without free speech and assembly discussion would be futile; that with them, discussion affords ordinarily adequate protection against the dissemination of noxious doctrine; that the greatest menace to freedom is an inert people; that public discussion is a political duty; and that this should be a fundamental principle of the American government. They recognized the risks to which all human institutions are subject. But they knew that order cannot be secured merely through fear of punishment for its infraction; that it is hazardous to discourage thought, hope and imagination; that fear breeds repression; that repression breeds hate; that hate menaces stable government; that the path of safety lies in the

opportunity to discuss freely supposed grievances and proposed remedies; and that the fitting remedy for evil counsels is good ones. Believing in the power of reason as applied through public discussion, they eschewed silence coerced by law — the argument of force in its worst form. Recognizing the occasional tyrannies of governing majorities, they amended the Constitution so that free speech and assembly should be guaranteed . . .

Those who won our independence by revolution were not cowards. They did not fear political change. They did not exalt order at the cost of liberty. To courageous, self-reliant men, with confidence in the power of free and fearless popular government, no danger flowing from speech can be deemed clear and present, unless the incidence of the evil apprehended is so imminent that it may befall before there is opportunity for full discussion.[81]

Although Justice Brandeis supported these words with footnote references to Harold Laski, Zechariah Chafee, Jr., and Thomas Jefferson, it is plain that his words depend entirely on their own style and merit. And if authority had to be cited it would have been at least appropriate to acknowledge aid from a renowned democratic leader who had told his audience that, "unlike any other nation, we regard him who takes no part in public affairs not as unambitious but as useless; and we Athenians decide public questions for ourselves, or at least endeavor to arrive at a sound understanding of them, in the belief that debate is not a hindrance in the way of action but rather an indispensable preliminary to any wise action at all." [82] "These [heroes]," continued Pericles, "take as your model, and judging happiness to be the fruit of freedom and freedom of valour, never decline the dangers of war." Those who won our independence, says Justice Brandeis, "believed liberty to be the secret of happiness and courage to be the secret of liberty." [83]

81. Whitney v. California, 274 U.S. 357, 375–77 (1927) (notes omitted). A comparable passage appears in Justice Brandeis' dissent in Olmstead v. United States, 277 U.S. 438, 478–79 (1928).

82. Pericles' "Funeral Oration," in Thucydides, *The Peloponnesian War,* Book II, Chap. 40; adapted from the translations of Crawley (Modern Library edition) and C. F. Smith (Loeb edition).

83. The Periclean sentence is the Crawley translation (Modern Library edition, p. 108). The Greek is "to eudaimon to eleutheron, to d'eleutheron to eupsychon kriantes" (Book II, Chap. 43), which Smith, in the Loeb edition, translates literally as "judging freedom to be happiness and courage to be freedom."

The similarity of thought and language between the American and the Athenian, even if unconscious on the part of Justice Brandeis, is not accidental, for the virtues of the societies praised by the two men are the same. Periclean Athens, the Funeral Oration in particular, is a traditional source of inspiration for the rhetoric of democracy. To both Pericles and Brandeis, civic virtue for the individual and political value for the society consisted in the exercise of freedom. Participation in the formation of public policy through freedom of expression was the high duty as well as the sacred right of citizens in a democracy. This was the freedom both Athenian and American heroes fought to defend.

A second reading of Justice Brandeis' concurrence in *Whitney* serves to remind us that history can be used without specific historical references. The lack of specific event and person in the passage quoted emphasizes the general philosophical message. Political principles are conveyed as part of value-laden historical allusion. The Supreme Court has justifiably said that Justice Brandeis' words "gave the principle [of freedom of expression] its classic formulation." [84] What is classic about the opinion, however, lies not alone in its philosophy or its history, but in the perfect marriage of the two. Though rhetoric may often be ornament, in this case it has become art, art in the service of politics and of law, and art whose authenticity we do not question.[85]

84. New York Times Co. v. Sullivan, 376 U.S. 254, 270 (1964).

85. The Court has cited and quoted Justice Brandeis' *Whitney* opinion on scores of occasions. Among those in which it is quoted at length are Justice Brennan's opinion for the Court in New York Times Co. v. Sullivan, 376 U.S. 254, 270 (1964); Justice Douglas dissenting in Dennis v. United States, 341 U.S. 494, 585–86 (1951); and Justice Black dissenting in Wilkinson v. United States, 365 U.S. 399, 422 (1961). Unmistakable echoes of the *Whitney* style have also appeared in Court opinions. See, e.g., Justice Douglas dissenting in Beauharnais v. Illinois, 343 U.S. 259, 287 (1952).

CHAPTER VI

THE SIT-IN CASES OF 1964:

THE FOURTEENTH AMENDMENT

AND THE GAP IN HISTORY

In 1964 the Supreme Court decided the case of Bell v. Maryland.[1] Several protesters had been prosecuted for trespass after "sitting-in" at a Baltimore restaurant. The Court was asked to determine whether the fourteenth amendment directly guaranteed to Negroes the right to nondiscriminatory service at restaurants, lunch counters, and similar facilities. Although a majority of the Court did not resolve the constitutional issue, concurring and dissenting opinions dealt with it at length. Like other attempts to deal with this American dilemma, the justices' opinions faced the tragic history of race in America, especially as it was reflected in constitutional law from the Civil War amendments to the school segregation cases of 1954.[2] The school cases had been followed by a decade of virtual unanimity on the Court in civil rights litigation. But in the sit-in cases the Court fell apart.

The course that *Bell* and its companion cases took in the Supreme Court is intertwined with the consideration by Congress, during the same months, of the Civil Rights Act of 1964.[3] In the light of the split on the Court, the justices would certainly have been grateful for congressional legislation to refer to in reaching a decision. Many members of Congress, on the other hand, would have welcomed a clear-cut constitutional decision to refer to in their own debate — although, whichever way the decision went, it would have entangled even more the legislative maneuvering. Caught in the middle was the Department of Justice, which had argued originally that the cases

1. 378 U.S. 226.
2. Brown v. Board of Education, 347 U.S. 483.
3. 78 Stat. 241.

could "properly be decided . . . on the basis of relatively narrow and well settled principles of constitutional adjudication," [4] but which later complied with the Court's request to express "the views of the United States [on the] broader constitutional issues." [5]

The invitation of the Court for the government's broader constitutional views yielded a heavily documented Supplemental Brief that emphasized the history of Negro rights in America from the framing of the Constitution to the present, with particular focus on the Reconstruction Era and the return to rigid segregation practices afterwards. In the sit-in cases, as in much other civil rights litigation, the government found the concept of "state action" central. State action, a term that embraces very much what its user wishes, is any action legally attributable to the state. In the school segregation cases, for instance, it was clear that the state was legally responsible for the existence of separate white and Negro schools. In the sit-in cases, however, the role of the state was not so evident. The two principal methods of demonstrating state action in the circumstances of previous sit-ins had been to point to state enforcement (by police, prosecutors, or judges) of trespass or breach-of-the-peace ordinances, and to administrative regulations concerning licensing, zoning, safety, wages, or health.[6]

The state action argument of the Supplemental Brief of the gov-

4. Brief for the United States as Amicus Curiae, p. 5, Bell v. Maryland, 378 U.S. 226 (1964). The brief was filed in September 1963 and the cases were argued on October 14 and 15.

5. Miscellaneous Order of Nov. 18, 1963, 375 U.S. 918. The Solicitor General had said earlier that if the Court disagreed with the Justice Department's narrow constitutional claim "we would be prepared to make a full statement." Brief, p. 5. The Court's order for a supplemental brief by the United States also stated that Justices Black, Clark, Harlan, and White were "of the opinion that the Court should not request the Department of Justice to file a brief concerning its views upon the basic constitutional issues on which the Department chose not to take a position in its original brief and in its oral argument." 375 U.S. 918 (1963). In view of their later dissent on constitutional grounds it is not clear what this position indicates on the part of Justices Black, Harlan, and White. (Justice Clark agreed with the opinion of the Court in *Bell*, deciding the case on narrow nonconstitutional grounds.) Perhaps these justices were not yet convinced that the constitutional issue had to be faced by the Court. Or perhaps they wanted to avoid embarrassing the executive in its efforts in behalf of civil rights legislation.

6. Justice Douglas in particular has employed these methods on the Court. For an example of the first, see his concurring opinion in Bell v. Maryland, 378 U.S. 226, 259 (1964); for an example of the second, see his concurring opinion in Lombard v. Louisiana, 373 U.S. 267, 282–83 (1963).

ernment, however, was utterly different from these. It was the argument of historical nexus:

> History and an appreciation of current institutions (whose meaning is partly a product of history) show that racial segregation in places of public accommodation cannot be viewed as merely a series of isolated private decisions . . . or even as a wide-spread private custom unrelated to governmental action . . . The custom is infused with official action both in its origin and implementation . . . State responsibility does not end with the bare repeal of laws commanding segregation . . . The very history of the caste system belies the claim of legal innocence . . . The State is responsible for the momentum its action has generated . . . Until time and events have attenuated the connection, the respondents continue to bear responsibility . . . They have not wiped the slate clean.[7]

The mayhem this approach works on the traditional concept of state action is obvious. Under the government's proposal the distinction between public and private action, an axiomatic distinction in American thought, would disappear. Socially, of course, a state cannot escape its history, including the history of its official actions. But to be unable legally to cut ties with the past is a novel concept in America.[8] In addition, as used by the Justice Department, the state-action-through-history argument is applicable only in civil rights cases originating in the South; it is an ad hoc position that would be worse than useless if applied nationally.[9]

7. Supplemental Brief of the United States as Amicus Curiae, pp. 11, 12, 18, Bell v. Maryland, 378 U.S. 226 (1964).

8. In another form, the Constitution recognizes this in the treason clause (Art. iii, sec. 3): "The Congress shall have power to declare the punishment of treason, but no attainder of treason shall work corruption of blood, or forfeiture except during the life of the person attainted."

9. The usefulness of the argument for political, in contrast to legal, purposes is just the reverse. In the legislative battle for the Civil Rights Act of 1964, then going on, the notion of state-action-through-history would only confirm the opposition of southern Congressmen, but it would not alienate the uncommitted middle group of Congressmen who did not represent the South. Not all discriminatory practices were confined to the South, of course, but in 1964 these were what was on the public's mind. For the Court's later recognition of the nationwide historical pattern of discrimination in the sale and rental of housing, see the majority opinion of Justice Stewart and the concurring opinion of Justice Douglas in Jones v. Alfred H. Mayer Co., 392 U.S. 409 (1968).

Although the historical nexus argument makes sense as social explanation, the government recognized that the Court might not be willing to adopt it as a constitutional principle. The more standard historical approach was therefore also presented in the sit-in cases, with the expected conclusion: "It is an inescapable inference that Congress, in recommending the Fourteenth Amendment, expected to remove the disabilities barring Negroes from the public conveyances and places of public accommodations with which they were familiar . . ." [10]

With the historical and other constitutional arguments before it, the Supreme Court considered the cases and strove mightily to lose the race with Congress in elucidating the Constitution with respect to sit-ins. Still it won. On the last day of the term, June 22, 1964, the Court announced its decision in Bell v. Maryland on nonconstitutional grounds. Ten days later, on July 2, Congress passed and the President signed the Civil Rights Act of 1964, a law which gave explicit federal sanction to the behavior of the Negro defendants in the sit-in cases.[11]

Four opinions were written in Bell v. Maryland. Five members of the Court concurred in Justice Brennan's opinion reversing and remanding the decision of the Maryland Court of Appeals on a

10. Supplemental Brief, p. 136.

11. 78 Stat. 241. The relevant portions of the act were unanimously upheld under the commerce clause in Atlanta Motel v. United States, 379 U.S. 241 (1964), and Katzenbach v. McClung, 379 U.S. 294 (1964). In concurring opinions Justices Douglas and Goldberg added that the fourteenth amendment also gave support to the act's constitutionality.

In a case decided on the same day as *Atlanta Motel* and *McClung,* the Court dismissed, by a vote of five to four, all state prosecutions for all demonstrations engaged in to secure the civil rights that had been made legal under the act. Hamm v. Rock Hill, 379 U.S. 306 (1964). This decision was certainly more politics than law. Not only was there no solid evidence that Congress intended the pending cases to be dismissed, but the principal historical foundation of the majority opinion was subsequently shown to be based on a false chronological relationship between a Supreme Court case and the passage of a federal law in 1871. See John P. MacKenzie, "*Hamm* v. *City of Rock Hill* and the Federal Savings Statute," *Georgetown Law Journal,* 54 (1965), 173–82.

A parallel civil rights race between the Court and Congress came in the spring of 1968, but this time Congress won. Federal open housing legislation was signed into law on April 12, 1968; the Supreme Court revived the Civil Rights Act of 1866 to accomplish essentially the same purposes in a decision of June 17. Jones v. Alfred H. Mayer Co., 392 U.S. 409 (1968). Justices Harlan and White argued in dissent in this case that the new legislation had so diminished the public importance of the litigation that the Court should have dismissed the certiorari writ under which it was heard.

nonconstitutional ground.[12] Justice Douglas, joined by Justice Goldberg, wrote an opinion that would have reversed and dismissed the case on constitutional grounds.[13] Justice Goldberg, joined by Chief Justice Warren and Justice Douglas, delivered an opinion to the same effect.[14] And Justice Black, joined by Justices Harlan and White, dissented from the Court's disposition but argued also that there was no direct constitutional right to be served in the restaurants and other businesses subject to sit-in demonstrations. The outlook of the three constitutional opinions is captured immediately in the words chosen to represent the practices and facilities at issue. Justice Douglas refers throughout his opinion to "apartheid," Justice Goldberg to "places of public accommodation," and Justice Black to "privately owned establishments."

The constitutional argument of Justice Douglas revives the privileges or immunities clause of the fourteenth amendment from the coma that began with the Slaughter-House Cases in 1873.[15] Against the nationally protected rights of citizens to nondiscriminatory service in places of public accommodation, Justice Douglas argues, neither the power of the states nor the rights of private business can

12. Chief Justice Warren and Justices Clark, Stewart, and Goldberg joined the opinion. The technical ground chosen by the Court was that there had been a "significant change" in Maryland law subsequent to the decision of the highest state court which had heard *Bell* on appeal below. The Court felt that this change, the passage of certain antidiscrimination legislation by Maryland, might require abatement of the case under state law. The argument was exceedingly weak since the case was no longer pending in the state courts; since the antidiscrimination legislation, by revising state trespass laws, probably fell under the language of the state savings (i.e., nonabatement) law; and since "considerations of policy," as Justices Douglas and Black said in their constitutional opinions, amounted to an evasion of a ripe and justiciable constitutional issue that was before the Court.

13. Justice Goldberg did not concur in Part I of Douglas' opinion. This Part excoriated the Court for its evasion of the question: "Why . . . should a minority prevent a resolution of the differing views? . . . At the argument and at our conferences we were not concerned with [the state law] question, the issue being deemed frivolous. Now it is resurrected to avoid facing the constitutional question . . . We stand mute, avoiding decision of the basic issue by an obvious pretense . . . The people should know that when filibusters occupy other forums, when oppressions are great, when the clash of authority between the individual and the State is severe, they can still get justice in the courts. When we default, as we do today, the prestige of law in the life of the Nation is weakened." Bell v. Maryland, 378 U.S. 226, 242–45 (1964).

14. Justice Douglas did not concur in Part I of this opinion, in which Justice Goldberg stated that if it were not for the constitutionally grounded dissent, he would not have felt impelled to concur for constitutional reasons.

15. 16 Wall. 36.

prevail. As to the power of the states, affirmance of the state court judgments "would remit [these] Negroes to their old status [prior to the Civil War amendments] and allow the States to keep them there by force of their police and their judiciary." [16] As to the rights of businessmen, "affirmance would make corporate management the arbiter of one of the deepest conflicts in our society." [17] The real issue, says Douglas, is not racial prejudice but corporate profits. If the Court held that state courts could not constitutionally uphold the claims of segregated restaurants, then "all restaurants would be on an equal footing and the [economic] reasons given in this and most of the companion cases for refusing service to Negroes would evaporate." [18]

The concurring opinion of Justice Goldberg in *Bell* is devoted to history, not economics. As an attempt to prove that it was the contemporary understanding of the fourteenth amendment that Negroes were to be guaranteed nondiscriminatory service at places of public accommodation, Justice Goldberg's historical essay is very similar to that part of the Supplemental Brief of the United States which treats the purposes of the framers of the Civil War amendments.[19] It is the Justice's purpose to show that among the rights accompanying the citizenship conferred on Negroes by the fourteenth amendment was that of service at all places of public accom-

16. Bell v. Maryland, 378 U.S. 226, 247 (1964).

17. 378 U.S. at 264. The sentence is italicized in the original.

18. 378 U.S. at 246. Justice Douglas carries out his economic argument elaborately, supplementing his opinion with twenty-five pages of appendixes to demonstrate how corporate organization and policy can influence and control the social life of a section of the country. At one point he argues his case in this fashion: "Charles A. Beard had the theory that the Constitution was 'an economic document drawn with superb skill by men whose property interests were immediately at stake.' An Economic Interpretation of the Constitution of the United States (1939), p. 188. That school of thought would receive new impetus from an affirmance of these judgments. Seldom have modern cases (cf. the ill-starred *Dred Scott* decision, 19 How. 393) so exalted property in suppression of individual rights." 378 U.S. at 253. The manner of Justice Douglas' expression is completely unwarranted when it suggests that Beard and his "school of thought" intended to exalt property over individual rights as a political value. And the substantive objection, a charge of impudence for questioning the political idealism of the founders, makes the statement even more peculiar, for Justice Douglas' own sociological argument is essentially the same as Beard's, that politics follows economics.

19. Three quarters of Justice Goldberg's thirty-two-page opinion is concerned with history as intent. The government's historical nexus argument, that state action may take the form of an historical incubus, plays no role whatever.

modation, and that the framers of the amendment intended these rights to be enforced by direct constitutional command. The numerous historical sources from which Goldberg constructs his opinion, however, are not equal to the task.[20] In the first place, almost all the references in the 39th Congress to the specific civil rights acquired by Negroes occur in the context of debates on legislation anticipating or implementing the fourteenth amendment, not on the amendment itself. This, as Justice Black points out in dissent, causes most of Justice Goldberg's historical search to miss the point. In the second place, there was never any court interpretation of the direct applicability of the fourteenth amendment. Both the federal and state court opinions cited by Justice Goldberg are concerned with legislation presumably passed in pursuance of the Constitution, not with the Constitution itself. Third, Justice Goldberg demonstrates no regular pattern of the rights of white citizens litigated and upheld under the common law (or statutes) to secure access to places of public accommodation. Without this pattern it is difficult to formulate a specific standard for the rights of the new Negro citizens.

In tangling with the original understanding of the fourteenth amendment Justice Goldberg is careful to refrain from attaching his general conclusion, that the amendment of its own force outlawed segregation in places of public accommodation, to specific statements of the time, in or out of Congress. In addition, there is typically an alternative explanation to his own more specific conclusions. For instance, Justice Goldberg writes: "contemporary understanding of the general public was that freedom of discrimination in places of public accommodation was part of the Fourteenth Amendment's promise of equal protection." [21] But did the "general public" view this promise as one to be carried out through legislation, as the Reconstruction Congresses always seemed to feel, or was it a promise of the amendment by itself? [22] Further, in dealing

20. The sources, drawn mostly from the government's Supplemental Brief, though reshaped and undoubtedly researched anew, include over two dozen federal cases, nine state court cases, a British case of 1701, sixteen books and articles, and citations to over thirty passages in congressional debates of the Reconstruction era. The Supplemental Brief is quoted directly in two places: 378 U.S. at 290, quoting from the Brief, pp. 122 and 136. And two other points derive from the Brief. Compare 378 U.S. at 291 n. 6, with Brief, pp. 129-30; and 378 U.S. at 309-11 and nn. 29-31 with Brief, pp. 75-76.

21. 378 U.S. at 290.

22. The conclusions of the United States, in its Supplemental Brief, are

with the congressional origins of the fourteenth amendment Justice Goldberg refers to the Civil Rights Act of 1866 and the Freedmans Bureau Bill of the same year. But since quotations from Congressmen which say precisely what the Justice has in mind are evidently lacking, and the laws themselves are not specific as to the rights to public accommodations, the conclusion must be formed by the opinion-writer: "the critical fact is that it was generally understood that 'civil rights' certainly included the right of access to places of public accommodation for these were most clearly places and areas of life where the relations of men were traditionally regulated by governments." [23] This unspecific use of the state action argument and the juxtaposition of "generally" and "certainly" in the sentence suggest that the matter was not actually settled at the time.[24] "At the heart of the Fourteenth Amendment's guarantee of equal protection," the Justice finally writes, was the assumption that there was a common law duty, or at least a "customary expectation" on the part of white citizens, and therefore a privilege guaranteed the new Negro citizens, of access to places of public accommodation.[25] But the validity of this argument in constitutional history was even more difficult to demonstrate than that of the others.[26]

---

also ambiguously worded. Justice Goldberg adopts the one quoted in the text: "it is an inescapable inference that Congress, in recommending the Fourteenth Amendment, expected to remove the disabilities barring Negroes from . . . places of public accommodation." 378 U.S. at 290. But this sentence does not say that Congress expected to remove the disabilities by force of the amendment alone, which is the essential subject of dispute. The government is quoted further to the effect that members of Congress in 1868 "would have answered affirmatively" when asked "whether the Civil Rights Act of 1866 *and* the Fourteenth Amendment would have the effect of securing" nondiscriminatory service. 378 U.S. at 290 n. 5 (emphasis added). What does the word "and" imply? If the act and the amendment are taken together, there is no way of determining what the amendment means alone; if they are taken separately, it is still impossible, since the amendment never existed when the act was not in force.

23. 378 U.S. at 294.

24. A footnote referring to a law review article, John P. Frank and Robert F. Munro, "The Original Understanding of 'Equal Protection of the Laws,'" *Columbia Law Review,* 50 (1950), 131–69, candidly confirms this. 378 U.S. at 294.

25. 378 U.S. at 296.

26. The common law duties and definitions were taken from sources such as Chief Justice Holt (1642–1710), Blackstone, Story, and Tidswell, *The Innkeeper's Legal Guide* (1864). The only nineteenth-century case cited by Justice Goldberg which states that Negroes had the right to nondiscriminatory service at common law suggests it as obiter dictum. Ferguson v. Gies, 82

The difficulties Justice Goldberg encountered in the use of historical materials to prove his argument occur at several levels, from the interpretation of a specific document to a generalization about the development of segregated practices in the South after the Civil War. Two instances will serve as illustrations.

Shortly after he was appointed to the Supreme Court in 1870, Justice Joseph P. Bradley engaged in correspondence with Judge William B. Woods, who was hearing a case under the Enforcement [Ku Klux Klan] Act of 1870. In 1883 Justice Bradley wrote the opinion for the Court (which then included Woods) in the Civil Rights Cases. In Bell v. Maryland, Justice Goldberg refers to the Bradley-Woods correspondence of 1871 as support for his thesis that the 1883 Civil Rights Cases stand for the assumption that a state denying the right of access to public accommodations under its common law denied the constitutional right of equal protection of the laws.[27]

Justice Goldberg first writes that "it is significant that Mr. Justice Bradley . . . expressed the view [to Judge Woods] that the Fourteenth Amendment 'not only prohibits the making or enforcing of laws which shall abridge the privileges of the citizen; but prohibits the states from denying to all persons within its jurisdiction the equal protection of the laws.' "[28] This is such a close paraphrase of the words of the fourteenth amendment that it is difficult to see what is significant about it.

Justice Goldberg writes next: "In taking this position, which is consistent with his opinion and the assumption in the *Civil Rights Cases* [Justice Bradley] concluded that: 'Denying includes inaction as well as action. And denying the equal protection of the laws includes the omission to protect as well as the omission to pass laws for protection.' "[29] This is indeed a radical view, and one which the Court did not adopt in the Civil Rights Cases or later.[30]

Mich. 358, 365 (1890), quoted in 378 U.S. at 302. A modern Canadian case has held that there is no such common law duty. King v. Barclay, 31 Western Wkly. Repts. 451 (Alberta Dist. Ct. 1960), affirmed on other grounds, 35 Western Repts. 240 (Alberta App. Div. 1961). The "expectation of service" theory was advanced by Thomas P. Lewis in "The Sit-In Cases: Great Expectations," *Supreme Court Review* (1963), 101–51. Justice Goldberg mentions this article in another connection. 378 U.S. at 290 n. 5.

27. The correspondence is discussed by Justice Goldberg, 378 U.S. at 308–11.
28. 378 U.S. at 309.
29. *Ibid.*
30. Justice Goldberg says the "omission to pass laws for protection" is

Finally, in a footnote to these sentences Justice Goldberg writes: "A comparison of the 1871 Bradley-Woods correspondence . . . with Justice Bradley's 1883 opinion in the *Civil Rights Cases* indicates that in some respects the Justice modified his views. Attached to a draft of a letter to Judge Woods was a note, apparently written subsequently, by Justice Bradley stating that: 'The views expressed in the foregoing letters were much modified by subsequent reflection, so far as relates to the power of Congress to pass laws for enforcing social equality between the races.' The careful wording of this note . . . supports the conclusion that Justice Bradley had only modified, not abandoned, his fundamental views . . ."[31] In the first place, there is no reason to evaluate the earlier rather than the later views as "fundamental." Second, what Justice Goldberg describes as "in some respects . . . modified" and "only modified, not abandoned," Justice Bradley describes as "much modified." Should the author or the interpreter of the views be given more credence? Third, Justice Bradley, by speaking of "social equality" but having in mind the "civil" rights of the Civil Rights Act, evidently saw no distinction between social and civil rights. (Or if he did, then the note does not pertain to any rights guaranteed by the Civil Rights Act or at issue in the Civil Rights Cases, and therefore it would be a useless piece of evidence for Justice Goldberg.) It is Justice Goldberg's contention elsewhere in his opinion, however, that the framers of the fourteenth amendment saw an important distinction between civil and social rights and included access to places of public accommodation among the former.[32] Therefore, either Justice Bradley's note does not contain the "careful wording" that Justice Goldberg claims for it, or, more likely, Justice Bradley is more accurate than Justice Goldberg in describing the views as "much modified."

Justice Goldberg's argument concerning Bradley's note ultimately depends on contrasting the "explicit assumption [of the Civil Rights Cases] as to the legal rights which the States were affirmatively protecting" (by virtue of the fourteenth amendment alone) with the

---

the equivalent of the state "inaction" condemned by the Court in such cases as Shelley v. Kraemer, 334, U.S. 1 (1948), which held unenforceable racially restrictive real estate covenants. This is a dubious equivalence. Nothing in *Shelley* suggests that the state had violated the Constitution by failing to pass a fair housing law.

31. 378 U.S. at 309 n. 30.

32. 378 U.S. at 294.

contention that Bradley's views were modified only "so far as relates to the power of Congress." Justice Goldberg offers nothing to show the significance of this contrast to Justice Bradley personally. And it is scarcely credible, in the light of the opinion in the Civil Rights Cases, the dissent of Justice Harlan in those cases, and the social and political context of the 1880's, that the point was of any material significance to the decision of the Court.

More generally, Justice Goldberg's difficulties with historical material are illustrated by his use of a well-known study, *The Strange Career of Jim Crow*, by C. Vann Woodward.[33] Justice Goldberg writes: "Although reconstruction ended in 1877, six years before the *Civil Rights Cases*, there was little immediate action in the South to establish segregation, in law or in fact, in places of public accommodation." [34] The implication that such places were racially integrated is clear from the supporting footnote to this sentence, which begins: "Woodward, *The Strange Career of Jim Crow* (1955), 15–26, points out that segregation in its modern and pervasive form is a relatively recent phenomenon." [35] This accurately states one of Woodward's principal points. But is was phrased by the historian himself rather differently in a foreword to the 1961 edition of his book — as if to prevent the interpretation of his argument given by Justice Goldberg in 1964: "There is plenty of evidence to indicate that *from the first* the freedmen were often denied their civil rights and subjected to discrimination, exclusion, and mistreatment by railroads, hotels, inns, and places of entertainment generally." [36] Most of Woodward's evidence of exceptions to discriminatory practices is concerned with transportation, not public accommodations, and is therefore not to the point in *Bell*. In addition, it is also clear from Woodward that the custom of Jim Crow generally preceded its enactment into law, despite Justice Goldberg's intimation that the two occurred simultaneously. The absence of legislation did not at all mean the widespread acceptance of Negroes at places of public accommodation. And if nondiscrimi-

33. New York: Oxford University Press, 1955.
34. 378 U.S. at 307–08.
35. 378 U.S. at 308 n. 26.
36. Woodward, *Strange Career* (1961 ed.), p. xvii (emphasis added). In the second revised edition, published in 1966, Woodward made even more emphatic his disagreement with such an interpretation of his book as Justice Goldberg's (see pp. ix and 102).

natory service was required by state common law, as Justice Goldberg believed, it was not generally recognized or obeyed.

Although Justice Goldberg's historical essay says much that is
true and almost nothing that is demonstrably false, it is ultimately
unconvincing.[37] The basic reason, of course, is that sufficient evidence
for his historical position does not exist. Apart from this, however,
the methodological assumptions employed in the essay, while standard for lawyers, are dubious for historians. The most important of
these assumptions is the belief that historical research is bound to
yield a definitive result. The lawyer accepts this as true because he
works backwards from the answer. The historian, working forward
from the question, does not. Further, the historian has more freedom
than the lawyer in formulating both question and answer and can
therefore present a more persuasive argument. A second assumption
by Justice Goldberg is that historical sources should be interpreted
liberally. This is a legitimate assumption when tangible evidence
for a conclusion is lacking but the truth of the matter is plain. In
such a situation the use of specific references which do not quite
meet the point at issue can still fortify the conclusion. But when
the truth of the matter is not so clear, the use of these references,
as in Justice Goldberg's opinion, only emphasizes the weakness of
the conclusion because of their failure to deal directly with the
issue under discussion. A third procedural deficiency in the opinion
is its failure to consider alternative explanations for the historical
data presented. This is perhaps to be expected in an opinion directed
at an outcome known in advance. But as Chief Justice Hughes's
treatment of the historical background of the contract clause in the
mortgage moratorium case demonstrates, bad history can be admitted
without fatally flawing the opinion. Even where it is not admitted
explicitly, devoting 75 per cent of an opinion to such inconclusive
material can only weaken the force of the argument.

If Justice Goldberg did not acknowledge the specific methodological weaknesses of his historical essay, he did understand its substantive liabilities. More than that, he recognized the limitations of

37. For concurring opinions see Alfred Avins, "The Civil Rights Act of
1875: Some Reflected Light on the Fourteenth Amendment and Public Accommodations," *Columbia Law Review*, 66 (1966), 873–915; Alexander M.
Bickel, *Politics and the Warren Court* (New York: Harper and Row, 1965),
p. 170; and Monrad G. Paulsen, "The Sit-In Cases of 1964: 'But Answer
Came There None,'" *Supreme Court Review* (1964), 137–70, esp. 155.

the entire approach of history as intent, no matter what it showed. Near the end of his opinion he invoked a variety of ongoing history, the principle of adjudication that best supported his position. In a page and a half which rather awkwardly begins "Even if the historical evidence were not as convincing as I believe it to be" and which consists largely of quotation from other cases, Justice Goldberg ultimately grounds his opinion "on the fundamental principle of constitutional interpretation proclaimed by Chief Justice Marshall." [38] This principle, not actually stated, means in the *Bell* situation that places of public accommodation, like the public schools a decade earlier, must be considered "in the light of [their] full development and present place in American life throughout the Nation." [39] Here was certainly a socially more persuasive argument, and the one that the school segregation cases had relied on. It was also, implicitly, the approach of Justice Douglas' concurring opinion, in which Justice Goldberg joined. But history as intent was the safer legal principle. In charting a new constitutional path the Justice hoped that the familiar means would suffice.

The final opinion in Bell v. Maryland is the dissent of Justice Black, joined by Justices Harlan and White. Justice Black's position, felt by some of his colleagues to be a defection from his judicial liberalism, is based on the constitutional rights of the owners of the business establishments subject to sit-in demonstrations.[40] In his constitutional discussion Justice Black takes up the two chief historical arguments presented in the case, the government's and Justice Goldberg's. The government had argued that a state's record of discriminatory legislation in the past involved it in discriminatory state action today, even if the old laws were no longer in force. This argument, Justice Black writes, "rests on a long narrative of historical events, both before and since the Civil War, to show that in Maryland, and indeed in the whole South, state laws and state actions have

38. 378 U.S. at 316 (note omitted).

39. Brown v. Board of Education, 347 U.S. 483, 492–93 (1954), quoted in 378 U.S. at 316.

40. Justices Douglas and Goldberg quote Justice Black by name in their concurring opinions — perhaps to chide their colleague, perhaps to convince readers that Black had in fact defected from a cause he had formerly espoused, perhaps even to buttress their own views with those of a respected liberal jurist. See the opinion of Justice Douglas, 378 U.S. at 262, and the opinion of Justice Goldberg, 378 U.S. at 293. In a series of public lectures Justice Black vigorously denied changing his constitutional views. See Black, *A Constitutional Faith* (New York: Knopf, 1968).

been a part of a pattern of racial segregation in the conduct of business, social, religious, and other activities. This pattern of segregation hardly needs historical references to prove it . . . [But we cannot] appreciate the fairness or justice of holding the present generation of Marylanders responsible for what their ancestors did in other days . . ." [41]

The two defects in the government's argument, as Justice Black points out, are that it is ad hoc for the South and no true principle of state action; and that it attempts to bind the present to the past with the force of law. Coming from Justice Black the second defect may sound less than authentic, for Black more than any other member of the modern Court believed that the nation is bound to its past as reflected in the designs and purposes of those who framed and ratified the Constitution and the amendments. Yet Justice Black's position is consistent from the point of view of his jurisprudence, since he carefully distinguishes the national Constitution from ordinary law. We are bound by the Constitution from generation to generation, he says, until it is properly amended. But laws have no legal effect beyond their explicit terms. Further, the social patterns of one state, caught in a moment of time, should be distinguished from the legal meaning of the Constitution. Although a distinction between Constitution and custom is difficult to accept from a social standpoint, since the Constitution is largely what is practiced in its name, as legal theory Justice Black's argument does make sense.

When he turns to Justice Goldberg's historical argument on the intent of the framers of the fourteenth amendment, Justice Black is also on fairly solid ground.[42] Justice Goldberg's argument, says Black, "runs something like this: (1) Congress understood the 'Anglo-American' common law, as it then existed in the several States, to prohibit owners of inns and other establishments open to the public

41. 378 U.S. at 334.
42. The chronology of the Black-Goldberg dispute would appear to be as follows: (a) Justice Black did not expect to deal with the constitutional issues of the sit-in case at all (see above, n. 5); (b) Justice Douglas was convinced that the constitutional issues should be dealt with; (c) in the face of this, Justice Black prepared a dissent; (d) Justice Goldberg felt the dissent should be answered in a more traditional form than Justice Douglas' concurring opinion; (e) Justice Black expanded the historical section of his dissent to meet Justice Goldberg's arguments; (f) Justice Goldberg emphasized his reliance on the constitutional principle of deciding in the light of "what this nation has become" by prefacing his statement with the acknowledgment quoted in the text above.

from discriminating on account of race; (2) in passing the Civil Rights Act of 1866 and other civil rights legislation, Congress meant access to such establishments to be among the 'civil rights' protected; (3) finally, those who framed and passed the Fourteenth Amendment intended it, of its own force, to assure persons of all races equal access to privately owned inns and other accommodations." [43] Justice Black deals with these three points in turn, showing that there is scant, contradictory, or no evidence in support of each proposition. He does not feel he must show that the common law did *not* require nondiscriminatory service, but only that the common law was either unclear or ineffective on the subject. His examples therefore do not come from treatises on common law, such as Justice Goldberg used, for these were intended to be authoritative, not to raise questions about the law's uncertainty. Justice Black points instead to congressional debate (on an antidiscrimination law for District of Columbia street railways) which shows that there was doubt in Congress as to what the common law required. As to the civil rights statutes, Justice Black says — and Justice Goldberg's opinion does not contradict him — that privately owned accommodations were never a subject for discussion in the House's consideration of the Civil Rights Act of 1866. If it was a civil right to be treated without discrimination in such places, the act itself does not say so. Turning finally to the problem of the fourteenth amendment itself, Justice Black states that there is no evidence from the debates on that amendment to show a purpose of securing nondiscriminatory access to restaurants, inns, and similar places;[44] that the omission of the right to equal access to public accommodations in the detailed list of rights in the Civil Rights Act of 1866 suggests even more that there was no intent to place the omitted right in the Constitution by way of the fourteenth amendment; and that the inclusion of the right of equal access in the Civil Rights Act of 1875 shows that

43. 378 U.S. at 335.

44. Justice Black reviews virtually every reference to the *Congressional Globe* cited by Justice Goldberg to show that the debates referred to either were irrelevant to the issue of the sit-in case or pertained to legislation rather than to the proposed amendment. 378 U.S. at 336–40. Justice Black concludes: "We have confined ourselves entirely to those debates cited in Brother Goldberg's opinion the better to show how, even on its own evidence, the opinion's argument that the Fourteenth Amendment without more prohibits discrimination by restaurants and other such places rests on a wholly inadequate historical foundation." 378 U.S. at 340.

Congress believed the Constitution authorized this only through the enforcement clause of the fourteenth amendment.[45]

Justice Black's opinion, like the opinions of Justices Douglas and Goldberg, did not determine the outcome of the sit-in cases. Bell v. Maryland is the case that did not decide the constitutionality of the sit-ins and is a case of no lasting legal consequence. In its nonprevailing constitutional opinions, however, *Bell* brings out clearly the problem that constitutional law faces in dealing with a chasm in history.

Constitutional tradition is notable for its continuity and is incomprehensible without it. The Civil War itself was the only significant interruption in the course of American history, and perhaps some return afterwards to antebellum patterns was inevitable. This meant, however, the debilitation of the fourteenth amendment. A legal chasm in the interpretation of the amendment opened between 1873, when the Slaughter-House Cases held that civil rights for Negroes rather than economic issues were at the center of the amendment's purpose,[46] and 1883, when the Civil Rights Act of 1875 was declared unconstitutional.[47] Between the two decisions came the Compromise of 1877, the withdrawal of federal troops from the South, and the end of Reconstruction. With the energies of the country directed elsewhere, the political and social gap dividing the radical Republican spirit of the postwar decade from late nineteenth-century America grew wider. In the South, where any change would be most evident, the tentatively planted practices of Jim Crow developed a tenacious root-system to which few whites objected.

In the middle of the twentieth century, when social concerns

---

45. This clause reads: "The Congress shall have power to enforce, by appropriate legislation, the provisions of this article." In his opinion concurring in the Court's upholding of the constitutionality of the Civil Rights Act of 1964, however, Justice Black declined to rely on the enforcement clause. But he did agree that "in view of the Thirteenth, Fourteenth, and Fifteenth Amendments, it is not possible to deny that the aim of protecting Negroes from discrimination is . . . a legitimate end." 379 U.S. at 276. He also agreed with the Court in upholding the constitutionality — under the thirteenth amendment — of the Civil Rights Act of 1866, and in interpreting that act as having been intended to outlaw racial discrimination in the sale and rental of housing. Jones v. Alfred H. Mayer Co., 392 U.S. 409 (1968).

46. 16 Wall. 36.

47. Civil Rights Cases, 109 U.S. 3.

about the race question were revived, seventy-five years of ethical torpor had to be crossed to find a genesis for that social spirit in American history. When the issues reached the Supreme Court, neither constitutional law nor constitutional theory was prepared to cope with the gap.[48] Despite a panoply of scholarly and ingenious methods of attack, the Supreme Court was unable to overcome the gap either in the school segregation cases or during the decade that followed. The attempts to reconstruct the reconstructionists foundered each time on the facts of social and constitutional history.

Bell v. Maryland, one of the last civil rights cases in which major attempts to deal with the gap in constitutional history were made, presents four methods of handling the problem.[49] Two of these are varieties of history as intent, and two are varieties of ongoing history. Justice Goldberg's essay on the intent of the framers of the fourteenth amendment is the traditional approach. It failed, however, and not merely because it was rebuttable history. Even if the Justice's essay was conclusive as to the 1860's, it remained unpersuasive in the 1960's. Too much of intervening history worked against it to let it float into the mainstream of constitutional law.[50]

The second variety of history as intent is related to the first but is also an independent and substantial method of its own. It is the theory of broad purpose, or open-ended intent. Under this theory one searches not so much for the particular purposes of the framers as for their attitude towards the freedom they intended later generations to have in interpreting their constitutional handiwork. It is this theory that formed a basis of the reargument in the school

48. For a discussion of the legal unpreparedness for the sit-in issue, see John Silard, "A Constitutional Forecast: Demise of the 'State Action' Limit on the Equal Protection Guarantee," *Columbia Law Review,* 66 (1966), 855–72, esp. 859.

49. The very last attempt, possibly, is Jones v. Alfred H. Mayer Co., 392 U.S. 409 (1968), dealing with open housing. Issues that might lead the Court on future historical excursions, however, include real estate "blockbusting," de facto school segregation, and racial discrimination by private social clubs. For the use of history in the open housing case see Gerhard Casper, "Jones v. Mayer: Clio, Bemused and Confused Muse," *Supreme Court Review* (1968), 89–132; and Robert L. Kohl, "The Civil Rights Act of 1866, Its Hour Come Round at Last: *Jones v. Alfred H. Mayer Co.*," *Virginia Law Review,* 55 (1969), 272-300.

50. The same approach, meeting the same failures — a rebuttable intent history followed by a discontinuous ongoing history — was attempted by the Court with regard to the Civil Rights Act of 1866 in the open housing case. *Ibid.*

segregation cases.[51] And it is the basis for the answer to the problem of a specific "original understanding" of the fourteenth amendment given in a substantial article on the segregation cases and constitutional history by Alexander Bickel: "Should not the search for congressional purpose . . . properly be twofold? One inquiry should be directed at the congressional understanding of the immediate effect of the enactment on conditions then present. Another should aim to discover what if any thought was given to the long-range effect, under future circumstances, of provisions necessarily intended for permanence." [52] In the school segregation cases the Court agreed that there was open-ended intent in the fourteenth amendment. Justice Goldberg refers to the Bickel article in *Bell*, but a majority of the Court did not accept its thesis in coming to a decision in the sit-ins.[53]

The third method of bridging the historical gap in the *Bell* case is a variety of ongoing history. It is the government's theory of inherited state action. This is an attempt to match the legal significance of racial discrimination with its pervasiveness, both past and present. In its special use in the sit-in cases the method required also the application of original intent, for unless it was intended that certain state actions be unconstitutional, their remote progeny could not be declared void. Of all the legal arguments that concern the fourteenth amendment and rely on history, the government's is by

51. The Court asked attorneys to discuss this question: "If neither the Congress in submitting nor the States in ratifying the Fourteenth Amendment understood that compliance with it would require the immediate abolition of segregation in public schools, was it nevertheless the understanding of the framers of the Amendment (a) that future Congresses might, in the exercise of their power under section 5 of the Amendment, abolish such segregation, or (b) that it would be within the judicial power, in light of future conditions, to construe the Amendment as abolishing such segregation of its own force?" Brown v. Board of Education, 345 U.S. 972 (1953).

52. Alexander M. Bickel, "The Original Understanding and the Segregation Decision," *Harvard Law Review*, 69 (1955), 59. Mr. Bickel was law clerk to Justice Frankfurter in the October 1952 Term of the Court when the order for reargument in the school segregation cases was issued. William W. Van Alstyne, examining the fourteenth amendment in another connection, concludes, "In retrospect Professor Bickel's analysis is even more attractive than when he first offered it." "The Fourteenth Amendment, the 'Right' to Vote, and the Understanding of the Thirty-Ninth Congress," *Supreme Court Review* (1965), 78.

53. Bell v. Maryland, 378 U.S. 226, 316 n. 36 (1964). For a discussion of open-ended intent as one of several "two-clause" theories of constitutional interpretation, see below, pp. 162–67.

far the simplest and most conclusive from the historian's point of view. But if the method is a relief to the historian, it is a vexation to the lawyer and a quite disagreeable proposition to the political and constitutional theorist. It cannot carry the day.

The final employment of history in the sit-ins is a generalized use of ongoing history — "what this nation has become." This is the central feature of the school cases and, despite the limited and perfunctory treatment of it, it is a central principle of Justice Goldberg's opinion in Bell v. Maryland. The use of ongoing history permits the Court to cut loose from specific intentions and embrace without apology the maxim, "We ought never forget that it is *a constitution* we are expounding." [54] At the extreme, the acceptance of this principle leaves the constitutional document itself completely empty. Standards for its valid use must therefore be devised. And where do these standards come from? In Justice Goldberg's opinion in *Bell*, as in most cases, they are drawn from and phrased in terms of the American experience. Justice Goldberg's standard is the freedom and equality of the Declaration of Independence and the Civil War amendments. These are verities that are timeless yet historically sanctioned: "In the light of this American commitment to equality and the history of that commitment, [the Civil War] Amendments must be read . . . 'as the revelation of the great purposes which were intended to be achieved by the Constitution as a continuing instrument of government.' " [55]

But to speak in the same breath of revelation and of a continuing instrument of government is to back away, in both directions at once, from the traditional notions of history used in constitutional law, both history as intent and, in its more detailed form, ongoing history. Only by escaping both the uncertain intentions of 1868 and the certain practices of the dark ages of post-Reconstruction could the racial discrimination of the sit-ins be held unconstitutional. Justice Goldberg, like the twentieth-century civil rights movement, had encountered a unique phenomenon in the American experience, a discontinuous history. And he proposed for the law what the civil rights movement proposed for society, to overcome it by an appeal to ancient truths and contemporary needs.

54. McCulloch v. Maryland, 4 Wheat. 316, 407 (1819).
55. 378 U.S. at 287; the internal quotation is from United States v. Classic, 313 U.S. 299, 316 (1941).

CHAPTER VII

REAPPORTIONMENT: HISTORICAL

INTENT, HISTORICAL TENDENCY,

AND THE POLITICAL

VALUES OF THE JUDICIARY

Between March 1962 and June 1964 the Supreme Court literally and figuratively changed the map of American politics. In those two years the Court held that legislative apportionment was a justiciable issue; that all votes must count equally in elections for statewide offices; and that, so far as practicable, there must be equally populated election districts within a state for members of Congress and for both houses of the state legislature.[1] Breathtaking in their reversal of the Court's previous position on these issues, the apportionment cases have generally been recognized as "politics in search of law."[2] But because the effects of the new rulings cannot be criticized on any theory except one which a majority of Americans either do not hold or are not vocal about — some variety of minority rule — the apportionment decisions, no matter how political, have been accepted as law in a way that other momentous exercises of judicial review have not been. "One person, one vote," the popular simplification of the Court's holding, has come to sound almost as indigenous as one of its ancestors, "No taxation without representation."

In the Supreme Court the apportionment cases comprise a score

1. The leading cases are Baker v. Carr, 369 U.S. 186 (1962); Gray v. Sanders, 372 U.S. 368 (1963); Wesberry v. Sanders, 376 U.S. 1 (1964); and Reynolds v. Sims, 377 U.S. 533 (1964), and four companion cases. The rule of equally populated election districts has been extended, after some delay, to local governmental units. Avery v. Midland County, 390 U.S. 474 (1968).

2. The phrase comes from an article analyzing the first of the cases. Phil C. Neal, "Baker v. Carr: Politics in Search of Law," *Supreme Court Review* (1962), 252–327.

of opinions covering over 450 pages in the official reports. In them, the Court deals with two issues central to American democracy: the role of the judiciary, and the basis of representative government. These issues forced the Court into a most complex confrontation with American history. Although the historical arguments and considerations were uniformly ineffective in the apportionment cases, due either to inherent weakness or the misfortune of being presented by justices in the minority, they gather into a single focus the varieties of history employed as a vehicle and as a value of constitutional adjudication. This chapter treats the Supreme Court's use of history in the apportionment cases under the following headings: history and political questions; ongoing history as a "cause" of malapportionment; apportionment and the intent of the framers; historical trends and the political values of the judiciary; and history as a guide to a standard of apportionment.

History and Political Questions

The initial obstacle to the judicial determination of the apportionment issue was the doctrine of "political questions." This doctrine is a political value held by judges about the judiciary. It maintains that, for the benefit of the courts and the governmental system as a whole, certain subjects that may appear in the form of litigation are more properly treated by another branch of government. They should not be handled by the judiciary because they are too "political." In terms of their outcome, if not always their wording, all apportionment cases previous to Baker v. Carr, the first of the modern series, were disposed of under the political-question doctrine. In the words of Justice Frankfurter for the Court in the most significant of these early cases, "The one stark fact that emerges from a study of the history of Congressional apportionment is its embroilment in politics, in the sense of party contests and party interests . . . To sustain this action would cut very deep into the very being of Congress. Courts ought not to enter this political thicket." [3] In the *Baker* case, however, the Court did enter the thicket, but only after insisting that it was not political. Justice Brennan managed to mold all the precedents into a new theory, according to which political

3. Colegrove v. Green, 328 U.S. 549, 554, 556 (1946). The fact that *Colegrove* concerned congressional rather than state apportionment was of no consequence in the opinions in *Colegrove* or in the treatment of the case in Baker v. Carr. See 369 U.S. at 202.

questions involved only those cases which infringed on the separation of powers doctrine, or those for which there were no peculiarly judicial criteria for decision. These two points were held not involved in *Baker*, and apportionment became a justiciable issue.[4]

In arriving at the new definition of political questions, Justice Brennan nowhere suggested that the legal precedents reflected any historical pattern, or indeed any political reality which would justify the Court's abstaining from decision in apportionment cases. His treatment of the cases exemplified a legal historian's judgment in another context: "drained of historical significance . . . constitutional cases may the more easily be manipulated as so many capsules of legal essence."[5] As Justice Brennan remarked in his discussion, deference to the political departments of government, the main support of the political-question doctrine, "rests on reason, not habit."[6] By use of reason Justice Brennan was able to present an abstract and timeless analysis of political questions which left history — which he called "habit" — completely out of account.

The approach of Justice Frankfurter, dissenting in the *Baker* case, was strikingly different. Enhanced by cascades of judicial rhetoric, the 63-page opinion was the Justice's last great essay. It shows a range of considerations, a political awareness, and an authoritative scholarship that none of the other opinions remotely challenges. Unlike the Court, which emerges safely at the haven of justiciability from its self-constructed maze of precedents, Justice Frankfurter

4. Justice Brennan's summation of the political-question doctrine reads: "Prominent on the surface of any case held to involve a political question is found [1] a textually demonstrable constitutional commitment of the issue to a coordinate political department; or [2] a lack of judicially discoverable and manageable standards for resolving it; or [3] the impossibility of deciding without an initial policy determination of a kind clearly for nonjudicial discretion; or [4] the impossibility of a court's undertaking independent resolution without expressing lack of the respect due coordinate branches of government; or [5] an unusual need for unquestioning adherence to a political decision already made; or [6] the potentiality of embarrassment from multifarious pronouncements by various departments on one question." Baker v. Carr, 369 U.S. 186, 217 (1962).

Of the six elements, the first, fourth, fifth, and sixth pertain by their own words to a conflict between the judiciary and another branch of the federal government and therefore involve the separation of powers. The second and third pertain to the problem of formulating judicial standards in the area of policy-making.

5. Julius Goebel, Jr., "Constitutional History and Constitutional Law," *Columbia Law Review*, 38 (1938), 556.

6. Baker v. Carr, 369 U.S. 186, 213 (1962).

points to the natural conclusion that in previous apportionment litigation "of decisive significance is whether in each situation the ultimate decision has been to intervene or not to intervene." [7]

Justice Frankfurter plants the earlier cases firmly in their political and historical contexts. His *Baker* opinion is suffused with evocative phrases which the majority of the Court apparently considered symbolic of habit rather than reason: ". . . long judicial thought and experience . . . this Court has consistently recognized . . . policy being traditionally committed not to courts . . . settled judicial experience . . . policy traditionally fought out in non-judicial forums . . . broad issues of political organization historically committed to other institutions . . . settled line of cases reaching back more than a century . . ." [8] The decision in Baker v. Carr, says the Court's most history-minded justice, brings "destructively novel judicial power . . . [to bear] in the essentially political conflict of forces by which the relation between population and representation has time out of mind been and now is determined." [9] The decision is a "massive repudiation of the experience of our whole past." [10] This contrast between the "habit" of Justice Frankfurter and the "reason" of Justice Brennan for the Court is nowhere sharper than in their discussions of the leading political-question case, Luther v. Borden, decided in 1849.[11] Justice Brennan presents the background of the case in a few rather stiff legal sentences, while the comparable passage in Justice Frankfurter's opinion is a concise history of Rhode Island's Dorr Rebellion, in which the case originated, with emphasis on its popular grievances concerning suffrage and legislative apportionment.[12]

One of the unusual features of Justice Frankfurter's dissent is his discussion of apportionment practices in Great Britain. Although he does not state directly what the relevance of the English experience is to America, he brings out several points that show comparative political history to be both as illuminating and as deceptive as analysis of America's own past. First the Justice notes that, in spite of the fact that the Founding Fathers considered the British experience "in its most salient aspects of numerical inequality . . . a model to be

7. 369 U.S. at 285.
8. 369 U.S. at 280, 282, 287, 289.
9. 369 U.S. at 267.
10. *Ibid.*
11. 7 How. 1.
12. Compare 369 U.S. at 218–22 with 369 U.S. at 292–97.

avoided," American representation by political units has its roots in the British practice.[13] Second, contemporary British practice, regulated by Boundary Commissions, does not rely exclusively on a population principle for apportionment. In fact, even a 25 per cent deviation from a mathematically determined electoral quota was found too restrictive for sound legislative districting. Third, until placed in the hands of the Boundary Commissions, apportionment had been a fiercely political matter in England. And it had never been handled by the judiciary.

In view of Justice Frankfurter's well-known Anglophilia it would not be surprising if the British experience did not yield very helpful conclusions for his argument concerning apportionment in America. As far as his analysis goes, it is certainly correct; but once comparative analysis is admitted as a legitimate principle of adjudication, the other side must also be heard from. In the first place, national apportionment in a small unified country such as Great Britain would seem, without explanation, to involve very different problems from those of a large federal country. From the point of view of governmental structure, Canada and Australia, devoted to and influenced by British legal and political practices, would have provided more apt comparative studies with the United States than did England.

Secondly, the present permissible population disparity among British electoral districts can be explained in part on social and political grounds peculiar to Great Britain. Strong party control in Parliament makes individual electoral constituencies less significant in Great Britain than in America. The cabinet form of government makes a party majority in Parliament more important than in Congress or in the state legislatures. British urban voters had not been so neglected by Parliament as American urban voters were by state legislatures. Moreover, geographical and community ties are stronger in less mobile and more tradition-bound England than they are in America. In sum, if Great Britain finds it proper to deviate from a population basis in apportionment, this may be for reasons which do not apply to America at all.[14]

Finally, one may question the relevance of, or at least the support to be drawn from, the British experience in terms of the political

13. 369 U.S. at 307.
14. For a convenient survey of theory and practice see Vincent E. Starzinger, "The British Pattern of Apportionment," *Virginia Quarterly Review*, 41 (1965), 321–41.

nature of determining the legislative districts. Except for ultimate parliamentary control, Great Britain has taken apportionment out of politics completely by placing decisions in the hands of the Boundary Commissions. If such "depoliticalization" is unfeasible in America by way of the federal courts, as Justice Frankfurter would insist, an independent regulatory commission, a type of agency with which Americans have long been familiar, might formulate and abide by known and objective standards of judgment, just as in Great Britain.

The argument from comparative political history, as the example of apportionment demonstrates, is subject to one of the major weaknesses suffered by many of the Court's arguments from American history. For purposes of adjudication a problem before the Court may be fruitfully compared to a similar problem occurring at another time or place only to the extent that the contexts from which the problems arise are also comparable. In the case of apportionment there are sufficient contextual differences between the United States and Great Britain to bring into question the validity of Justice Frankfurter's discussion.

Returning to America, Justice Frankfurter's ultimate argument from history is essentially that the Supreme Court, not having acted in the past in the field of apportionment, cannot act in this field now. To make this proposition persuasive, however, it must be more than self-fulfilling. It must be accompanied by the force of reason. But Justice Frankfurter's use of reason — reliance on the "presuppositions of the Constitution" and the nature of the judicial process — like his use of history, forecloses an evolving future.[15] What is then most unfortunate about the discussion of political questions is that the Court majority, which asked for "reason, not habit" in support of its conclusions, offered largely rationalization, not reason.[16] If the Court

15. Richard G. Stevens shows that reason and history are the keys to Justice Frankfurter's method of adjudication in general, and that in the area of due process they do not at all prevent change. "Reason and History in Judicial Judgment: Mr. Justice Frankfurter's Treatment of Due Process" (unpub. diss. University of Chicago, 1963).

16. Justice Douglas, one of the least history-conscious members of the Court when it comes to adjudication (as distinguished from his popular writing and some of his Court rhetoric), suggested as much in his concurrence in *Baker*: "I feel strongly that many of the cases cited by the Court and involving so-called 'political' questions were wrongly decided. In joining the opinion, I do not approve those decisions but only construe the Court's opinion in this case as stating an accurate historical account of what the prior cases have held." Baker v. Carr, 369 U.S. 186, 241 n. 1 (1962). After surveying other voting rights cases, particularly those relating to racial dis-

had only admitted to some repudiation of its past, it might have argued more convincingly for the present. The history of the political-question doctrine cannot be wiped out, but perhaps there are reasons why part or all of it ought not to continue. So far, the Court has not said.

Ongoing History as a "Cause" of Malapportionment

In the two leading state reapportionment cases, Baker v. Carr and Reynolds v. Sims, the state constitution or statute at issue provided for decennial reapportionment of the legislature on a population basis. For sixty years, in both cases, these laws had been ignored. Assuming that the apportionment provisions were legitimate if adhered to, it was only the passage of time, a form of ongoing history, that resulted in the states' invalid pattern of districting in the 1960's. There had been no unconstitutional action — only unconstitutional inaction. This situation, often called the "silent gerrymander," is not a necessary element to prove malapportionment to the Court. When present, however, the Court makes the most of the effect of the passage of time on the constitutionality of the resulting pattern of apportionment.[17] The matter raises several interesting problems.

First, what would be the constitutional status of an apportionment pattern that, although not violating "federal constitutional requisites,"[18] had existed unchanged for decades in disregard of a state constitutional command to reapportion decennially? Presumably it would not present a federal question, since there is — or was in the

crimination and fraud, Justice Douglas returned to the apportionment cases previously rejected by the Court under the political question doctrine: "With the exceptions of Colegrove v. Green . . . MacDougall v. Green . . . South v. Peters [the three leading apportionment cases], and the decisions they spawned, the Court has never thought that protection of voting rights was beyond judicial cognizance. Today's treatment of those cases removes the only impediment to judicial cognizance of the claims stated in the present complaint." 369 U.S. at 249–50. As Justice Douglas admits and Justice Frankfurter proves, the Court had indeed given the earlier cases a "treatment."

17. "It is primarily the continued application of the 1901 Apportionment Act to this shifted and enlarged voting population which gives rise to the present controversy." Baker v. Carr, 369 U.S. 186, 192 (1962). See also Justice Clark concurring, 369 U.S. at 254. In the series of state legislature cases of 1964 see Reynolds v. Sims, 377 U.S. 533, 540, 542, 570, 584; WMCA, Inc. v. Lomenzo, 377 U.S. 633, 643; Davis v. Mann, 377 U.S. 678, 691; Roman v. Sincock, 377 U.S. 695, 700–01.

18. Davis v. Mann, 377 U.S. 678, 691 (1964).

early 1960's — no federal requirement that reapportionment take place regularly. But the only adequate defense to the charge of unconstitutional districting would be a showing by the state that the alleged silent gerrymander had come to pass after an apportionment determined on the basis of the most recent decennial census.[19]

Second, if a state has become malapportioned due both to passage of time and to the provisions of a constitution or statute that, under the *Reynolds* standard of one person, one vote, would be declared unconstitutional if enacted today, should the Court reach back into the past to declare the law invalid as of the date of its passage? This is comparable to asking the Court to overrule the Civil Rights Cases of 1883 or Plessy v. Ferguson when announcing new law in the field of civil rights; or it is like expecting the Court to declare the Sedition Act of 1798 unconstitutional when formulating doctrine in contemporary political-expression cases. In the reapportionment situation, however, this practice would appear to have little legal and even less political justification. Nevertheless, according to the Court, the original complaint in the New York case "asserted that the legislative apportionment provisions of the 1894 New York Constitution, as amended, are not only presently unconstitutional, but also were invalid and violative of the Fourteenth Amendment at the time of their adoption . . ."[20]

The Court does not deal with this claim explicitly. Yet, if the claim of retrospective invalidity was made in order to insure that the New York apportionment plan would be rendered defective for reasons other than accumulated invalidity (ongoing history), which the only precedent then existing, Baker v. Carr, suggested was the primary reason for an unconstitutional apportionment scheme, then the general discussion of the Court vindicated the plaintiffs' argument. On the other hand, the Court might have taken the opportunity expressly to reject the claim that the New York constitution was invalid when adopted. It could have relied on the principle of the school segregation case that "we cannot turn the clock back." Since the Court's entire treatment of apportionment was a completely new development in constitutional law, the claim of the New York voters would have provided an excellent chance for integrating the apportionment

---

19. The decennial basis is strongly urged by the Court: "if apportionment were accomplished with less frequency, it would assuredly be constitutionally suspect." Reynolds v. Sims, 377 U.S. 533, 584 (1964).

20. WMCA, Inc. v. Lomenzo, 377 U.S. 633, 636–37 (1964).

cases into the theory of an evolving and adaptable constitution. But by the time of the New York case, one of the last in the series of apportionment decisions, it was too late. The Court had made so many claims of its own — that it was merely following precedent in accepting the justiciability of the complaints, or that the Founding Fathers had intended in the 1780's that the Constitution require equally populated congressional districts — and the dissenters had spread on the record so many corrective facts of judicial and political history, that it would have been as difficult for the Court to admit that the apportionment decisions were an innovation designed to keep the Constitution viable as it had earlier seemed difficult to deny it. What could not be handled without embarrassment had to be ignored.[21]

Justice Frankfurter raises a third point relative to malapportionment as the result of continued state inaction. In Baker v. Carr the appellants had suggested that, to the extent the fourteenth amendment lacked a clear standard for determining a constitutional plan of apportionment, this could be provided by the Tennessee Constitution of 1871, which contained a population-based rule. When the legislature abridges rights granted by its own constitution, according to this argument, it violates the federal equal protection clause. Justice Frankfurter's reply comes from an opinion he had written for the Court over twenty years earlier:

"Here, according to petitioner's own claim, all the organs of the state are conforming to a practice, systematic and unbroken for more than forty years, and now questioned for the first time. It would be a narrow conception of jurisprudence to confine the notion of 'laws' to what is found written on the statute books, and to disregard the gloss which life has written upon it. Settled state practice cannot supplant constitutional guarantees, but it can establish what is state law. The Equal Protection Clause did not write an empty formalism into the Constitution. Deeply embedded traditional ways of carrying out state policy such as those

21. The district court had excluded evidence offered by the plaintiffs in the New York case to show "intentional discrimination against the citizens of New York City in the designing of the legislative apportionment provisions of the 1894 Constitution." As the New York apportionment scheme was held invalid at present, the Supreme Court said it would "express no view on the correctness of the District Court's exclusion of this evidence." 377 U.S. at 639 n. 4.

of which the petitioner complains, are often tougher and truer
law than the dead words of the written text." [22]

In the present case, "Tennessee's law and its policy respecting apportionment are what 60 years of practice show them to be, not what
appellants cull from the unenforced and, according to its own judiciary, unenforceable words of its Constitution." [23]

This is just the reverse of the assumption of the Court. Instead of a
previously constitutional apportionment plan becoming unconstitutional due to the passage of time, time (by hypothesis) has changed
an unconstitutional policy into a constitutional one, or at least into a
policy which could not be invoked as a standard for determining unconstitutionality. Whatever may have been the case earlier, according
to Justice Frankfurter, the continued practice of the state validates
itself. Law is evolutionary, and it is the living law that matters.[24] The
Court's reply to this argument is that it is the Constitution which is
the living law, evolutionary or not, and that state apportionment
schemes must be judged as they are found, not as they have developed.[25]

Apportionment and the Intent of the Framers

The Supreme Court announced the principle of "one person, one
vote" for congressional apportionment in Wesberry v. Sanders.[26] In
Reynolds v. Sims, decided four months later, the same principle was

22. Baker v. Carr, 369 U.S. 186, 326 (1962), quoting from Nashville, C.
& St. L. R. Co. v. Browning, 310 U.S. 362, 369 (1940).

23. 369 U.S. at 327.

24. Justice Frankfurter is consistent in this belief, even to the extent of
following it backwards. In an opinion for the Court in one of the early
birth-control cases he held that just as a law may acquire validity by the
passage of time, it may also acquire invalidity as the result of desuetude, at
least enough so that the Court will not decide on its merits a case brought
under a statute that the state never attempts to enforce. Poe v. Ullman, 367
U.S. 497 (1961).

25. Concurring in Baker v. Carr, Justice Clark wrote: "It is suggested that
the districting is not unconstitutional since it was established by a statute
that was constitutional when passed some 60 years ago. But many Assembly
Sessions since that time have deliberately refused to change the original act,
and in any event 'a statute [constitutionally] valid when enacted may become
invalid by change in the conditions to which it is applied.' Nashville, C. &
St. L. R. Co. v. Walters, 294 U.S. 405, 415 (1935)." 369 U.S. at 254 n. 6.

26. 376 U.S. 1 (1964).

applied to apportionment for state legislatures.[27] In *Wesberry* the Court fully exercised its traditional option of relying in detail on the intent of the framers to support its holding. In *Reynolds*, history as intent was ignored completely. In view of this difference it is ironic that the Court was less justified by the facts when it did resort to history than when it did not.[28]

One of the reasons why the framers were paid such respect in the first case and not in the second is that the original Constitution, which was at issue in the congressional districting dispute, was drafted by the unassailable Founding Fathers, while the fourteenth amendment, at issue in the state apportionment cases, was formulated by the fallible members of the hyper-partisan 39th Congress. The Court cannot be criticized for its choice of heroes. In addition, one must look at the authors of the Court opinions in the two cases in order to understand why history was employed as it was. In the first case, on congressional apportionment, the opinion was written by Justice Black, whose constitutional jurisprudence is absolutist in nature and wedded to the Constitution as a document, and whose attitude towards the past is that of the period he regards most highly and interprets most often, the era of the Founding Fathers — namely, that a prime purpose of history is to instruct in civic virtue.[29] Conversely, the author of the second opinion was Chief Justice Warren, whose opinions, though containing historical excursions, show especial attachment to explaining the Constitution in conformity with institutional and political realities, rather than to expounding a particular theory of jurisprudence or an attitude towards the past.

In *Wesberry*, the congressional apportionment case, the history

27. 377 U.S. 533 (1964).
28. In *Wesberry* the Court's history was pulverized in the dissent of Justice Harlan and was viewed by most commentators with such disdain that it was not even accorded serious treatment. See, e.g., Alfred H. Kelly, "Clio and the Court: An Illicit Love Affair," *Supreme Court Review* (1965), 135–36. A detailed refutation of the Court's history in *Wesberry* appears in L. Brent Bozell, *The Warren Revolution: Reflections on the Consensus Society* (New Rochelle, N.Y.: Arlington House, 1966), pp. 80–112, 341–50. In the *Reynolds* case, where the Court did not use history, Justice Harlan's essay in dissent has been shown to be less than conclusive. Edward M. Goldberg, "Mr. Justice Harlan, the Uses of History, and the Congressional Globe," *Journal of Public Law*, 15 (1966), 181–86; and William W. Van Alstyne, "The Fourteenth Amendment, the 'Right' to Vote, and the Understanding of the Thirty-Ninth Congress," *Supreme Court Review* (1965), 33–86.
29. Compare Justice Black's use of history in the freedom of expression cases, above, pp. 95–97.

involved is that of article 1, sections 2 and 4. The relevant words are that the House of Representatives shall be elected "by the People," and that the "times, places and manner of holding elections" shall be prescribed by the state legislatures but may "at any time by law" be altered by Congress. In *Reynolds*, the state apportionment case, the history involved is that of the fourteenth amendment, sections 1 and 2. The relevant provisions are the equal protection clause and the reduction in representatives in Congress proportional to the denial by states, to male citizens over the age of twenty-one, of the right to vote in federal and state elections. In order to understand the potential, as well as the central deficiency, in the arguments in the two cases based on the history of the constitutional provisions at the time of their framing, the question must be asked: "What kind of equality are we searching for in the history of suffrage in America?"

In the Constitutional Convention of 1787 the basic question about representation did not concern equality among people but among states: were the states to be represented equally in respect to their sovereign status or in respect to their populations? The "Great Compromise," establishing the Senate on one principle and the House of Representatives on the other, determined that within Congress as a whole both states and population would be permanently represented. Only after this basic question of representation had been disposed of could the Constitution makers, whether at the Convention or in later Congresses proposing amendments, turn to equality among people. In light of the apportionment cases, equality among people must be separated into two sets of factors, personal and locational. The personal factors are voting qualifications determined by civil status (slave or free, citizen or alien, resident or nonresident), sex, race, and property. Locational factors refer to the boundaries and population sizes of the election districts.

Whatever may have been assumed about locational factors with respect to voting rights, both the Constitutional Convention and subsequent Congresses in proposing amendments (until the 1960's) have been concerned explicitly with the personal factors only. Since the apportionment cases are concerned with locational factors only, constitutional history, as the intent of the framers, provides analogy at best, and almost nothing directly to the point. This is the essential weakness of Justice Black's opinion for the Court in *Wesberry* and of Justice Harlan's dissents in both *Wesberry* and *Reynolds*. Yet the Court, at least, could have made up for this weakness. The silence of

the Constitutional Convention and the concern of the fifteenth, nineteenth, and twenty-fourth amendments with the personal factors of
voting could have permitted the Court to follow the principle of
open-ended intent or of an evolving Constitution. Locational factors
could have been added to personal ones in setting constitutional
standards concerning the franchise. But Justice Black, believing in
neither open-ended intent nor constitutional evolution, offers an in-
novative interpretation of the Great Compromise in an attempt to
show that from the beginning the Constitution has commanded
equally populated congressional election districts. And Justice Harlan, who would accept both doctrines, finds that the intent of the
framers was not as indefinite as might be claimed, or that the evolution desired by the Court majority is contradicted by the facts and
trends of American history.

Justice Black's only constitutional argument in Wesberry v. Sanders
concerns the intent of the framers.[30] No argument is presented from
the constitutional text.[31] The Justice concludes that, "construed in
its historical context, the command of Art. 1, Sec. 2, that Representatives be chosen 'by the People of the several States' means that as
nearly as practicable one man's vote in a congressional election is to
be worth as much as another's." [32] With the artlessness of a devoted
school teacher, Justice Black tells the story of the formation of the
federal union and of the importance of the Great Compromise that
established representation in the House and Senate on the basis of
two different principles. (This story is told with the blessing of James
Madison, "who took careful and complete notes during the Convention, [and] believed that in interpreting the Constitution later
generations should consider the history of its adoption . . ." [33])
Confident of its relevance to the case at hand, the Justice writes:
"The debates at the Convention make at least one fact abundantly
clear: that when the delegates agreed that the House should represent 'people' they intended that in allocating Congressmen the num-

30. The 16-page opinion contains a short introduction describing the case
and two pages asserting that the issue is justiciable. The remainder of the
opinion is devoted to history.
31. Justice Black had written in dissent in a similar case eighteen years
earlier that "the Constitution contains no express provision requiring that
congressional election districts established by the states must contain approximately equal populations." Colegrove v. Green, 328 U.S. 549, 570 (1946).
He did not admit this much again, however.
32. Wesberry v. Sanders, 376 U.S. 1, 7–8 (1964) (note omitted).
33. 376 U.S. at 9 n. 12.

ber assigned to each State should be determined solely by the number of the State's inhabitants." [34]

But the debates could not make clear, because the subject never came up, that the determination of congressional districts within the states should be based solely on the number of inhabitants. Inserted in the middle of Justice Black's opinion, therefore, is a statement of faith and a great historical leap: "It would defeat the principle solemnly embodied in the Great Compromise — equal representation in the House for equal numbers of people — for us to hold that, within the States, legislatures may draw the lines of congressional districts in such a way as to give some voters a greater voice in choosing a Congressman than others." [35] The faith is a justified one, since the founders no doubt thought equal election districts most in conformity with their new plan of government. And the leap might even be plausible if it were not surrounded by so much detailed historical distortion. But analogy cannot perform in the mask of proof.

The chief fault of Justice Black's history is its implication that the various remarks cited from the Philadelphia Convention, the state ratifying conventions, and contemporaneous writings referred to the "by the People" clause and related that clause to the districting of Congressmen within the states. The fact is that the remarks cited by Justice Black referred to the Great Compromise in general or to the "times, places and manner" clause in particular, or else they were taken out of context.

Two examples taken from James Madison and James Wilson illustrate this. These two men were the most influential and articulate political theorists at the Convention. Both had fought — and lost — the battle to have both houses of Congress based on population. Wilson definitely and Madison very likely believed that electoral districts should contain equal numbers of people. But what can be made of their remarks by Justice Black? The Justice writes: "Wilson urged [in the Convention] that people must be represented as individuals, so that America would escape the evils of the English system under which one man could send two members to Parliament to represent the borough of Old Sarum while London's million people sent but four." [36] The entire speech referred to, as reported in Madison's *Notes*, reads:

34. 376 U.S. at 13 (note omitted).
35. 376 U.S. at 14. Justice Harlan in dissent calls this a slide rather than a leap. 376 U.S. at 26.
36. 376 U.S. at 14–15 (note omitted).

The leading argument of those who contend for equality of votes among the States [in the Senate] is that the States as such being equal, and being represented not as districts of individuals, but in their political and corporate capacities, are entitled to an equality of suffrage. According to this mode of reasoning the representation of the boroughs in England which has been allowed on all hands to be the rotten part of the Constitution, is perfectly right and proper. They are like the States represented in their corporate capacity like the States therefore they are entitled to equal voices, old Sarum to as many as London. And instead of the injury supposed hitherto to be done to London, the true ground of complaint lies with old Sarum; for London instead of two which is her proper share, sends four representatives to Parliament.[37]

The speech does not contradict Justice Black's account of it. But it likewise suggests nothing about congressional districting or, indeed, about the House of Representatives. It is simply one of Wilson's losing arguments against a Senate in which states were to be equally represented.

Justice Black writes next: "Madison in *The Federalist* described the system of division of States into congressional districts, the method which he and others assumed States probably would adopt: 'The city of Philadelphia is supposed to contain between fifty and sixty thousand souls. It will therefore form nearly two districts for the choice of Federal Representatives.'"[38] In the number of *The Federalist* from which Madison is quoted, the discussion is directed against those who claimed that 30,000 people were too large a number for a single man to represent in Congress. Madison continues: "[Philadelphia] forms, however, but one county, in which every elector votes for each of its representatives in the State legislature. And what may appear to be still more directly to our purpose, the whole city actually elects a *single member* for the executive council."[39] If an inference concerning districting must be drawn from this passage, it is that states, like Pennsylvania counties, would elect their representatives at large. Single-member districts were not the practice at the time, and Madison himself would only say that under

---

37. Max Farrand (ed.), *The Records of the Federal Convention of 1787* (3 vols.; New Haven: Yale University Press, 1911), I, 449–50.
38. 376 U.S. at 15 (notes omitted).
39. *The Federalist*, No. 57 (Wright ed., p. 387) (emphasis in original).

the "times, places and manner" clause the legislatures would control "whether the electors . . . should all vote for all the representatives; or all in a district vote for a number allotted to the district." [40]

In a lengthy dissent Justice Harlan replied to the history offered by the Court, supplying the original constitutional context omitted by Justice Black. In particular, Justice Harlan demonstrates that under the "times, places and manner" clause the framers of the Constitution deliberately left to the states the matter of legislative apportionment unless Congress should intervene.[41] Yet as to the framers' personal beliefs about equally populated districts, the question which was uppermost in Justice Black's mind, Justice Harlan seems ambiguous. At one point he writes that "many, perhaps most, of [the delegates] . . . believed generally — but assuredly not in the precise, formalistic way of the majority of the Court — that within the States representation should be based on population . . ." [42] Yet several pages later he declares: "Whatever the dominant political philosophy at the Convention, one thing seems clear: it is in the last degree unlikely that most or even many of the delegates would have subscribed to the principle of 'one person, one vote' . . ." [43] The apparent inconsistency between these two statements can be resolved only by letting the first refer to locational and the second to personal factors concerning the issue of voting. But when this is done, the accuracy of Justice Harlan's history of the "by the People" clause and of the intent of the "times, places and manner" clause topples everything in Justice Black's opinion except its central thesis, that the framers believed that "one man's vote in a congressional election is to be worth as much as another's." [44]

40. Quoted by Justice Harlan, 376 U.S. at 32, from Farrand, *Records,* II, 240.

41. 376 U.S. at 30–42.

42. 376 U.S. at 27 (note omitted).

43. 376 U.S. at 30–31 (note omitted).

44. Much of Justice Harlan's evidence to show the falsity of Justice Black's contention misses the distinction between personal factors (which *Wesberry* was not about) and locational factors (which it was about). Thus Harlan italicizes a passage from *The Federalist,* No. 54, stating that "the right of choosing this allotted number [of Congressmen] in each State is to be exercised by such part of the inhabitants, as the State itself may designate." Quoted in 376 U.S. at 31 n. 15. But "such part of the inhabitants" clearly refers to personal qualifications for the vote. No one imagined that an entire area of the state would be denied the franchise. On the other hand, the passage does support Justice Harlan's reading of the "times, places and manner" clause, his strongest and quite irrefutable historical argument.

A striking quotation on this latter point is a statement of Madison to

With all its potential and qualifications, the large truth about equality of votes for the House of Representatives at the Constitutional Convention is nevertheless obscured by what amounts to a big lie, for the framers certainly did not believe that the text of the Constitution required equally populated districts within the states. More discouraging than the use of this shoddy means of adjudication is its acceptance — not only by the people and states affected by the apportionment decisions who may, after all, view the outcome as just, but by five members of the Court majority other than Justice Black. To the extent the promulgation of the Court's history is not attributable to the particular juristic traits of Justice Black, it must be the consequence of what Mark DeWolfe Howe, referring to the apportionment cases, termed a lack of "judicial honesty and intellectual morality," [45] plus — equally important — the need on the part of the justices and the expectation on the part of the people that contemporary constitutional law would be related to the nation's past.

When one turns to Reynolds v. Sims and the other decisions on state legislative apportionment, the situation is not so dire. Chief Justice Warren did not present an historical interpretation of the origins of the fourteenth amendment. Justice Harlan's dissent in these cases, therefore, argues against a void. In addition, although his argument is good history, it is rebuttable history. With respect to apportionment, the congressional debate over the fourteenth amendment suffers the same difficulties as the Convention debate over article 1, namely, that the only suffrage problems discussed with any specificity related to personal rather than to locational factors. Explaining why he proposed "to rake the history of the Fourteenth Amendment still another time," Justice Harlan's most thorough academic critic said that the surfeit of fourteenth amendment his-

the Virginia ratification convention: ". . . it was thought that the regulation of time, place, and manner, of electing the representatives, should be uniform throughout the continent. Some states might regulate the elections on the principles of equality, and others might regulate them otherwise. This diversity would be obviously unjust. Elections are regulated now unequally in some states, particularly South Carolina, with respect to Charleston, which is represented by thirty members [in the state legislature]. Should the people of any state by any means be deprived of the right of suffrage, it was judged proper that it should be remedied by the general government." 376 U.S. at 37–38, quoting from Jonathan Elliot (ed.), *The Debates in the Several State Conventions on the Adoption of the Federal Constitution* (5 vols.; Washington, 1836–1845), III, 367

45. *The Garden and the Wilderness: Religion and Government in American Constitutional History* (Chicago: University of Chicago Press, 1965), p. 145.

tories had focused on different issues — predominantly, of course, on Negro rights.[46] These histories do not deceive. When the 39th Congress debated the voting aspects of the various proposals that became the fourteenth amendment, the issue was the Negro franchise, not legislative districting. It is not surprising, therefore, that almost every one of the two dozen passages quoted by Justice Harlan from the *Congressional Globe* refers explicitly to the freedman's vote, which was indeed to be left in the hands of the states.

This is illustrated by the Justice's treatment of section 2 of the fourteenth amendment and a statement in Congress on it by Senator Howard of Michigan, a member of the Joint Committee of Fifteen on Reconstruction and a principal figure in the legislative history of the amendment. Justice Harlan italicizes a portion of Senator Howard's explanation of the proposed amendment: "The second section leaves the right to regulate the elective franchise still with the States, and does not meddle with that right." [47] This seems to meet the point. But when the preceding sentence of Senator Howard is read, quoted by Justice Harlan but without italics, it proves too much: "It was our opinion that three fourths of the States of this Union could not be induced to vote to grant the right of suffrage, even in any degree or under any restriction, to the colored race . . ." [48] Section 2 of the fourteenth amendment reduces the congressional representation of states "when the right to vote at any election . . . is denied . . . or in any way abridged . . ." When Senator Howard pointed out that this meant the amendment did "not meddle" with the states' authority over the franchise, he was not talking about apportionment but about Negroes. Section 2 was a compromise necessitated by the refusal of the states to agree at the time with any constitutional "meddling" with Negro suffrage. Of the franchise in general or of apportionment in particular there is not a word, either in the amendment or in the speech of Senator Howard. All talk is directed towards Negro suffrage. And even Senator Howard's argument fell away two and a half years later with the adoption of the fifteenth amendment flatly enfranchising all Negroes. If the significant historical context of the fourteenth amendment is relevant to constitutional adjudication a century later, then the Su-

---

46. Van Alstyne, "The Fourteenth Amendment," p. 37.
47. Reynolds v. Sims, 377 U.S. 533, 601 (1964), quoting from *Congressional Globe*, 39th Cong., 1st Sess. (1866), p. 2766.
48. *Ibid.*

preme Court should be free to ignore section 2 in deciding the state apportionment cases and to argue, as it did, on the basis of the equal protection clause.

From the congressional debates, however, Justice Harlan concludes that powers over voting in general were retained by the states; and from this it is only a logical deduction that apportionment questions — which had not been raised at all — likewise remained exclusively in state control.[49] Next the Justice turns to the "practices of the time," which often play an important role in the search for historical intent. In the case of the fourteenth amendment and state apportionment these practices offer Justice Harlan strong support.[50] The state apportionment patterns at the time of the adoption of the amendment and in the years immediately following offer indisputable evidence that legislative districting was not involved in the amendment's adoption. If it had been, it is not credible that the state legislatures would have ratified themselves out of existence. On this point Justice Harlan is completely convincing. But truth is not necessarily relevance, and the clearest case in Harlan's presentation, an objection to the constitution of "reconstructed" Florida on the grounds that the state legislature was "apportioned in such a manner as to give the sparsely-populated portions of the State the control of the Legislature," only confirms that if apportionment meant anything to the Reconstruction Congress it meant Negro political power, not abstract minority control of state legislatures.[51]

In concise terms, Justice Harlan's argument reads: "The problems which concern the Court now were problems when the Amendment was adopted. By the deliberate choice of those responsible for the Amendment, it left those problems untouched."[52] Apportionment was indeed a problem in the 1860's, as well as a century later. But it

49. 377 U.S. at 595.

50. 377 U.S. at 602–08. It may be noted that two years earlier, in his dissent in Baker v. Carr, Justice Frankfurter had relied exclusively on the legislative districting practices of the time and had not appealed to congressional debates in arguing that the fourteenth amendment was not designed to effect state reapportionment. 369 U.S. 186, 310–17 (1962).

51. Reynolds v. Sims, 377 U.S. 533, 605 (1964), quoting Congressman John Farnsworth of Illinois from *Congressional Globe*, 40th Cong., 2d Sess. (1868), pp. 3090–91. Farnsworth continued (*ibid.*): "The sparsely-populated parts of the State are those where there are very few negroes, the parts inhabited by the white rebels, the men who, coming in from Georgia, Alabama, and other States, control the fortunes of their several counties."

52. 377 U.S. at 608.

was not a problem of the same dimensions. And whether or not it was deliberately left untouched at the time, the framers of the fourteenth amendment were not really concerned with it. Their amendment was about Negro rights. Everything else said at the time was in effect obiter dictum. If the Supreme Court had cared to use it, the principle of an adaptable Constitution would have aided in overcoming the historical argument of Justice Harlan. Locational factors could have been added to personal factors in setting constitutional standards for the vote in the twentieth century. Instead, the Court ignored the entire issue, leaving the impression that Justice Harlan's history, though powerless, was both right and relevant.

Historical Trends and the Political Values of the Judiciary

The reasoning by both majority and minority justices in the apportionment cases concerned the course as well as the source of constitutional development. What the majority did not find in original understanding it found in subsequent development. What the dissenters found in the early debates and records was confirmed by their analysis of ongoing history. In simplified form, the justices' attitudes in the cases may be classified as in favor of one person, one vote as a political value; opposed to one person, one vote as a political value; or unwilling to choose either abstractly but demanding that the value be drawn from the American experience. On this basis the Court majority in general held for the newly announced value and the Court minority did not; this was to be expected. But what about the two dominating minds on the Court, Justices Black and Frankfurter? They apparently took the third course. Justice Black believed that "construed in its historical context," and evidently only in that way and only for that reason, the Constitution required a one-person, one-vote rule.[53] Justice Frankfurter believed that the "uniform course of our political history regarding the relationship between population and legislative representation" required no such thing.[54]

The approaches of Justices Black and Frankfurter, expressed in history as intent by one and in ongoing history by the other, were not plucked from a shelf of adjudicatory principles for their aptness

53. Wesberry v. Sanders, 376 U.S. 1, 7 (1964).
54. Baker v. Carr, 369 U.S. 186, 267 (1962).

to the issue of apportionment. They permeate the Justices' entire concept of constitutional law. History to these men is a principle of adjudication not only as a vehicle but also as a value. In the voting cases this attachment to history as the source and sanction of political values is borne out not only from the records as a whole, but also from what amount to counterexamples — evidence that Justice Black abides by his conception of historical values even when deciding against the "liberal" apportionment position, and that Justice Frankfurter, though basing his judicial judgment on an historical relationship as he perceives it, is personally willing to see malapportioned legislatures come to a complete end.

The evidence for Justice Black is his short opinion upholding the constitutionality of a provision of the Georgia Constitution by which the state assembly elects a governor from the two persons having the highest number of votes when no candidate receives a popular majority.[55] In his opinion Justice Black appealed almost exclusively to the antiquity of the Georgia constitutional clause as reason for its validity.[56] Although the dissenters in the case accused the majority of having reversed one of the earliest apportionment cases, this could hardly have been so; four of the five majority justices had also been in the majority in the earlier decision, and Justice Black, for one, joined the Court two years later in extending the apportionment ruling to local units of government when history was not involved.[57] Justice Black and those who joined him in the Georgia gubernatorial case believed firmly in one person, one vote as a political value, but under some circumstances the force of tradition would overcome the force of logic in its implementation.

The evidence from Justice Frankfurter is not quite so clear. He valued both tradition and the concept of community, two factors that would tend to leave malapportioned legislatures as they were — or at least not change apportionment to a strict numerical basis. But first, he never denied the reasonableness of the appellants' goals in Baker v. Carr. In fact, he encouraged the attempt to obtain relief politically even if his rhetoric must have sounded strange to the

55. Fortson v. Morris, 385 U.S. 231 (1966).
56. The opinion begins with the words "Since 1824" and ends: "Article V of Georgia's Constitution provides a method for selecting the Governor which is as old as the Nation itself. Georgia does not violate the Equal Protection Clause by following this article as it was written." 385 U.S. at 232, 236.
57. Avery v. Midland County, 390 U.S. 474 (1968).

Tennessee voters. He asked for "an aroused popular conscience that sears the conscience of the people's representatives." [58] Second, Justice Harlan, who purported to identify himself completely with Justice Frankfurter's views, provides an example of judicial reasoning which quite clearly goes beyond the limits of the senior Justice's beliefs. Justice Harlan offered a defense of unequally populated legislative districts with the implication that "rotten boroughs" are a rational method of promoting political stability: "Rigidity of an apportionment pattern may be as much a legislative policy decision as is a provision for periodic reapportionment. In the interest of stability, a State may write into its fundamental law a permanent distribution of legislators among its various election districts, thus forever ignoring shifts in population." [59] Such a suggestion is not in keeping with Justice Frankfurter's sensitivity to history, society, or the "living law," and one may surmise that it is not a proposition which he would have put forward himself. He was too much a democrat to argue for history, in this case political stability, in the face of the reasonable demands of the people.

Justices Black and Frankfurter provide the best examples of history as a value in modern constitutional law, Justice Black looking to history as intent (or in the Georgia gubernatorial case simply to history as antiquity), and Justice Frankfurter to ongoing history. But in the apportionment cases all the justices claim that their value positions are supported by the American past. Except for Justice Black, who holds out for his understanding of the original purpose of the Constitution, the appeal is to ongoing history, but in two distinctly different manners. The first method of determining and presenting the trends of history is one of general statements and broad strokes. Not particularly concerned with locational factors in voting, this method points to trends towards constitutional equality everywhere. Typical of this claim of the direction of history is Justice Douglas' statement: "The conception of political equality from the Declaration of Independence, to Lincoln's Gettysburg Address, to the Fifteenth, Seventeenth, and Nineteenth Amendments can mean only one thing — one person, one vote." [60] Or Chief Justice Warren's: "History has seen a continuing expansion of the scope of the right of suffrage in this country . . . The democratic ideals of

58. Baker v. Carr, 369 U.S. 186, 270 (1962).
59. 369 U.S. at 348.
60. Gray v. Sanders, 372 U.S. 368, 381 (1963).

equality and majority rule, which have served this Nation so well in the past, are hardly of any less significance for the present and the future." [61] The most substantial expression is that of Justice Fortas, with whom Chief Justice Warren and Justice Douglas concurred, dissenting in the Georgia gubernatorial run-off case:

> Much water has gone under the bridge since the late 1700's and the early 1800's. Our understanding and conception of the rights guaranteed to the people by the "stately admonitions" of the Fourteenth Amendment have deepened, and have resulted in a series of decisions, enriching the quality of our democracy, which certainly do not codify State's rights, governmental theories, or conceptions of human liberties as they existed in 1824, the date when Georgia adopted its present system of choosing a Governor. I have no doubt, for example, that in the early days of the Nation many of the state legislatures were malapportioned . . . But this did not enshrine that condition forever beyond the reach of the Constitution.[62]

This technique of presenting ongoing history in the broadest perspective suggests an Hegelian spirit moving through American history. One person, one vote is the ideal or end towards which the nation is moving. The Supreme Court, aware of this, is leading the country to its destiny, if necessary obscuring or even effacing details of the landscape in order to accomplish the mission. The remarkable opinion of Justice Black in the congressional districting case, although concerned with history as intent rather than ongoing history, may also be considered an example of this technique, for its chief characteristics are those of neither law nor scholarship but of the elucidation of a political principle presumed embedded in the national heritage. It remained for Justice Black's colleagues to extend the principle from the time of the framers down to the present.

The second technique of presenting historical trends in the apportionment cases is the standard essay of ongoing history. It concentrates on what the other technique omits — details. Justice Harlan

61. Reynolds v. Sims, 377 U.S. 533, 555, 566 (1964). In a footnote to the first sentence the Chief Justice explains: "The Fifteenth, Seventeenth, Nineteenth, Twenty-third, and Twenty-fouth Amendments to the Federal Constitution all involve expansions of the right of suffrage. Also relevant, in this regard, is the civil rights legislation enacted by Congress in 1957 and 1960."

62. Fortson v. Morris, 385 U.S. 231, 247 (1966) (notes omitted).

stated what he and Justice Frankfurter found wrong with the first approach: "The failure of the Court to consider any of these matters [of intent, language, contemporary understanding, political practice, subsequent amendments, and constitutional decisions] cannot be excused or explained by any concept of 'developing' constitutionalism. It is meaningless to speak of constitutional 'development' when both the language and history of the controlling provisions of the Constitution are wholly ignored." [63] The historical trends presented by Justices Frankfurter and Harlan therefore brim with the details of constitutional provisions, practices, and debates. Their histories are specific and are confined to the locational factors of voting. Yet for two reasons their conclusions are not always convincing. First, when confronted with a choice between two factors — population on the one hand and geographical-political unit on the other — to describe the "true" principle of apportionment in a state, the dissenters consistently choose the political unit even though the facts would support either alternative.[64] Second and more important, the "compromise between competing political philosophies," to use a phrase of Justice Harlan's, was not a static concept but rather a continual and typically successful attempt of the population principle to erode the gains that the passage of time had presented to the competing philosophy of the political-geographical unit. If there was any trend at all it was towards a victory for the population principle in apportionment whenever the political process permitted a choice. These recurrent waves of success by the population principle cannot be overlooked in any ongoing history of apportionment in America.

History as a Guide to a Standard of Apportionment

In a concurring opinion in the first apportionment decision Justice Douglas said: "Universal equality is not the test; there is room for weighting." [65] With the encouragement of Douglas' own expansive wording about "the conception of political equality" through the course of American history, however, the Court majority abandoned whatever initial sympathy it had held for the view that there was

63. Reynolds v. Sims, 377 U.S. 533, 591 (1964).
64. See Justice Frankfurter dissenting in Baker v. Carr, 369 U.S. 186, 307–24 (1962); and Justice Harlan dissenting in Reynolds v. Sims, 377 U.S. 533, 608–11 (1964).
65. Baker v. Carr, 369 U.S. 186, 244–45 (1962).

room for weighting.[66] By the end of the series of decisions it was clear that the search for guides to a standard of apportionment other than one of mathematical equality was futile. But before this became evident, the opinions, particularly those concurring and dissenting, suggested two distinct types of historical standards that might provide constitutional justification for deviating from a strict population rule. The first of these was the "federal analogy"; the second, the traditions of the individual states.

The "federal analogy" proposes as a constitutional standard for the states the constitutional arrangements of either Congress or the electoral college. Congress deviates from one person, one vote by having equal state representation in the Senate and by the stipulation that each state have at least one delegate to the House of Representatives. The electoral college, in which each state is entitled to as many electors as the sum of its representatives and Senators, is likewise unrepresentative according to the population principle. Even worse, each state casts all its electoral votes for a single presidential candidate, regardless of the popular vote.[67] In the apportionment cases the Supreme Court was faced with the argument that constitutionally established institutions, the Senate and the electoral college, sanctioned representation on a nonpopulation basis elsewhere in the political system. If the practice was legitimate for the Senate, why not for the House? If legitimate for the federal government, why not for the states?

If the states were permitted to deviate as much from the population principle as the national government does, however, then almost any apportionment scheme would be constitutional. Finding no logical place to halt in applying the federal analogy to the states, the

66. The sympathy apparently returned, again under the guidance of Justice Douglas, when the Court unanimously limited the sweep of the one-person, one-vote principle in local elections for offices of a "non-legislative character." Sailors v. Board of Education, 387 U.S. 105 (1967); Dusch v. Davis, 387 U.S. 112 (1967). When the legislative function of the offices became more prominent, however (and was accompanied by a ludicrous population disparity among electoral districts), the Court, by a 5–3 vote, applied the state apportionment holdings to the local level. Avery v. Midland County, 390 U.S. 474 (1968). The ultimate coup to the "room for weighting" notion was administered in Kirkpatrick v. Preisler, 394 U.S. 526 (1969).

67. Worst of all, each state, regardless of population, would cast only a single vote if, on the failure of the electoral college to choose a president by majority vote, the election were to be decided by the House of Representatives in accordance with the twelfth amendment to the Constitution.

Court rejected it altogether. But there are reasons other than logic for rejecting the federal analogy.

When the Court held that congressional districts must contain equal numbers of people, it relied on "the principle solemnly embodied in the Great Compromise." [68] Yet if the truth of the Great Compromise (rather than Justice Black's version) ought really to be a source for contemporary constitutional standards, its most obvious principle is that the two houses of Congress — and therefore by analogy the houses of the state legislatures — may be based on different methods of representation, one of them completely unrelated to population. Yet such a conclusion with regard to the state legislatures is suspect both historically and legally. As the Court put it in the leading case, federalism arose from "unique historical circumstances"; it "averted a deadlock in the Constitutional Convention which had threatened to abort the birth of our Nation." [69] The Court thus isolated the origins of bicameralism on a national basis from the situation in the states, where two-house legislatures had evolved from the colonial experience and the model of the British Parliament. Contemporary state patterns, in short, receive no historical support from the example of Congress. Legally, the federal analogy is even weaker than it is historically. The theory of state representation in the Senate is that individual states are sovereign entities. County, municipal, or other local political jurisdictions are considered in law to be creatures of the states. The states, therefore, cannot claim for their own creations the autonomous right to representation in legislatures that they can claim for themselves as sovereign members of the federal union.

The example of the electoral college as a model for apportionment schemes suffers from the same weaknesses as the system of representation in Congress. It is made an even less apt analogy by the fact that for most of American national history the electoral college has been an anachronism neither fulfilling the function anticipated for it by the framers nor reflecting contemporary theories of democracy. When it was raised as a principal defense in the Georgia county unit case, the Supreme Court rejected the argument without qualification.[70]

In spite of the sound reasons for declaring varieties of the federal

68. Wesberry v. Sanders, 376 U.S. 1, 14 (1964).
69. Reynolds v. Sims, 377 U.S. 533, 574 (1964).
70. Gray v. Sanders, 372 U.S. 368, 376–78 (1963).

analogy inapposite as a standard of apportionment, the Court was not at its most cogent in explaining its position. The force of the analogy was strong enough for the Court, speaking through Chief Justice Warren in one case and Justice Douglas in another, to feel compelled to present historical evidence to prove its case. The evidence was designed to show not merely that the federal plan was the result of political compromise and political theory peculiar to the 1780's, but also that the framers believed in equally apportioned districts in spite of their adoption of the federal plan, and that the electoral college scheme was a poor policy from the start.

First the Court remarks, "The original constitutions of 36 of our States provided that representation in both houses of the state legislatures would be based completely, or predominantly, on population." [71] As Justices Frankfurter, Harlan, and Stewart show from the other side, however, an evaluation of this sort depends on which standard of apportionment, population or geography, is considered primary. Justice Stewart wrote, for instance: "Two-thirds of the States have given effect to factors other than population in apportioning representation in both houses of their legislatures, and over four-fifths of the States give effect to nonpopulation factors in at least one house." [72]

Second, to document that the founders "clearly had no intention of establishing a pattern or model for the apportionment of seats in state legislatures when the system of representation in the Federal Congress was adopted," the Court cites letters of Thomas Jefferson advocating equal representation in both houses of the Virginia legislature. [73] To this it may be answered: (a) Jefferson was not at the Constitutional Convention; (b) his ideas are not typical of those who were at the Convention; (c) the letters cited by the Court were written thirty years after the Convention adjourned; and (d) Jefferson's apportionment plan was not adopted by Virginia.

Third, Chief Justice Warren writes for the Court: "Demonstrative of [the founders' intentions] is the fact that the Northwest Ordinance, adopted in the same year, 1787, as the Federal Constitution, provided for the apportionment of seats in territorial legislatures solely on the basis of population." [74] But the Northwest Ordinance,

71. Reynolds v. Sims, 377 U.S. 533, 573 (1964) (note omitted).
72. Lucas v. Colorado General Assembly, 377 U.S. 713, 761 (1964) (note omitted).
73. Reynolds v. Sims, 377 U.S. 533, 573 (1964),
74. *Ibid.*

adopted not by the framers of the Constitution but by the Confederation Congress they hoped to abolish, also limited voters in the prospective territories to free persons, males, and property holders, and it provided for an upper house (a five-member legislative council), not based on population, to be chosen by Congress from persons nominated by the lower house.

The downgrading of the electoral college through historical argument appears in the opinion for the Court in the Georgia county unit case. Although the case was decided on the basis of a sweeping statement of historical trends, which, the Court said, required a one-person, one-vote interpretation of the Constitution, Justice Douglas nevertheless referred to particular historical sources, including *The Federalist*, in rejecting the electoral college analogy. These references, or Justice Douglas' comment on them, are either banal or needlessly disparaging of the framers' intentions.[75] They demonstrate what may happen when a justice is essentially uninterested in history in constitutional adjudication but feels that history is important enough to necessitate discrediting.

The second historical standard under which modern legislative districting might justifiably deviate from a strict population rule is offered by the traditions of the separate states. As Justice Frankfurter wrote in the initial case, apportionment has involved considerations of "geography, demography, electoral convenience, economic and social cohesions or divergencies among particular local groups, communications, the practical effects of political institutions like the lobby and the city machine, ancient traditions and ties of settled usage, respect for proven incumbents of long experience and senior status, mathematical mechanics, censuses compiling relevant data, and a host of others." [76]

When the Court had concluded its apportionment decisions, Justice Harlan listed ten factors which the Court had held constitutionally impermissible in determining new legislative districts.[77] The first of these was history. In theory, Justice Harlan was not completely correct. Although the Court had said that "history alone" was not a permissible factor "in attempting to justify disparities from population-based representation," [78] it also said: "Indiscriminate districting,

75. See Gray v. Sanders, 372 U.S. 368, 377–78 (1963).
76. Baker v. Carr, 369 U.S. 186, 323 (1962).
77. Reynolds v. Sims, 377 U.S. 533, 622–23 (1964).
78. 377 U.S. at 579.

without any regard for political subdivision or natural or historical boundary lines, may be little more than an open invitation to partisan gerrymandering." [79] Somewhere between these two positions lower courts had held state apportionment plans valid. According to the opinions for the Court, for instance, the federal district court had concluded that New York's districting provisions were "of historical origin," and that one of the tests of invidious discrimination was "whether or not the present complexion of the legislature has a historical basis." [80] The state court in Maryland found that apportionment there "accorded with history, tradition, and reason." [81] And the federal district court in Colorado had accepted the apportionment pattern in that state only after taking into account "a variety of geographical, historical, topographic, and economic considerations." [82] But being in the middle was not enough. The Supreme Court overturned each of the apportionment schemes which the states had sought to justify in part on the basis of history.

Dissenting in the New York case, Justice Stewart defended the use of historical considerations and showed at the same time that the federal analogy, in addition to its theoretical justification, was functionally relevant, even if historically and legally a special case: "As the District Court found, counties have been an integral part of New York's governmental structure since early colonial times, and the many functions performed by the counties today reflect both the historic gravitation toward the county as the central unit of political activity and the realistic fact that the county is usually the most efficient and practical unit for carrying out many governmental programs." [83] What the Supreme Court had done in the apportionment cases, said Justice Stewart, was "to convert a particular political philosophy into a constitutional rule . . . without respect for the many individualized and differentiated characteristics of each State, characteristics stemming from each State's distinct history, distinct geography, distinct distribution of population, and distinct political heritage." [84]

History had failed to maintain the political-question doctrine; it

79. 377 U.S. at 578–79.
80. WMCA, Inc. v. Lomenzo, 377 U.S. 633, 639–40 (1964).
81. Maryland Committee v. Tawes, 377 U.S. 656, 663 (1964).
82. Lucas v. Colorado General Assembly, 377 U.S. 713, 738 (1964).
83. 377 U.S. at 761–62 (note omitted). See also Justice Clark dissenting at 742–43.
84. 377 U.S. at 748.

had been a partial "cause" of the existence of malapportioned legislatures; it had been abused or disregarded in formulating the constitutional principles for apportionment; it had established contradictory political values for the justices; and, finally, it was excluded as a consideration for contemporary apportionment. History had had its days in Court and lost.

CHAPTER VIII

CONSTITUTIONAL INTENT

AND CONSTITUTIONAL CHANGE

Problems

Judicial interpretation of the American Constitution takes place in a political world dominated by the belief in popular sovereignty. From the preamble to the amending article the constitutional text establishes the people as the ultimate source of fundamental law. American history, from Jefferson through Jackson and Lincoln to Franklin Roosevelt, supports this. Judicial review, the power of the courts to declare state or federal law unconstitutional, is the most permanent undemocratic fixture of the constitutional pattern, but it exists at the sufferance of the people. To abide by the concept of popular sovereignty while retaining its powers of judicial review, the Supreme Court is faced with the inseparable problems of constitutional intent and constitutional change. The people are responsible for intent but have entrusted the courts with change. The people establish the Constitution, but the judiciary interprets it. The case studies presented in the preceding chapters offer sufficient evidence that the Supreme Court is faced with real problems in carrying out its trust. But the existence of the problems must generally be inferred from the opinions; the problems are seldom discussed directly. One reason for this is that the Court's most concrete function is to decide cases, not to write essays in legal or political theory. A more important reason, however, is that an adequate theoretical treatment of the difficulties necessarily calls into question the Court's own authority. If this authority could easily be sustained by a theoretical discussion of constitutional intent and constitutional change, the Court might undertake it regularly. But, as this chapter attempts to show, these problems pose both practical and theoretical embarrassments, so much so that, if the Court mentions them at all, it prefers to assert an answer rather than discuss, or even admit, the question, and then only under the legal and political pressures of individual cases. It is the context in which the Court functions, popular sovereignty, that produces the problems in the first place and affects constitutional interpretation in general. But there are three basic and interrelated factors with which the Court must deal in particular. They are (a) that the Constitution is a written and therefore definite document rather than an unwritten tradition or set of practices; (b) that the Constitution is treated largely as a legal rather than a political document and is therefore subject to legal rules of interpretation; and (c) that the Constitution is old.

(a) The Constitution of the United States is a written document. Written documents do not change. Therefore the Constitution of the United States does not change.

This syllogism, almost as poor in sense as it is rich in logic, succinctly demonstrates that there is in America a real problem of constitutional change.[1] The problem lies in the meaning of the word "constitution." In a completely static society the meaning of the word would be unimportant. However defined, the constitution would remain the same. But societies are not static, certainly not American society, and while most people would assent to the major premise of the syllogism, they would not agree with the conclusion. The Constitution does change. The questions must be answered: What is it that changes? How does it change?

Custom dictates that the United States possesses a "Constitution" rather than a "constitution." The difference in orthography reflects the fact that the former is a formal written document describing a pattern of legal rules and institutions that function for political purposes. The latter is a pattern of political relationships which may be, but need not be, defined in legal instruments.[2] Under these

1. A Supreme Court version of the syllogism reads: "The Constitution is a written instrument. As such its meaning does not alter. That which it meant when adopted, it means now." South Carolina v. United States, 199 U.S. 437, 448 (1905).

2. The traditional distinction between written and unwritten constitutions does not do justice to the difference between "Constitution" and "constitution" in America. Henry Steele Commager has suggested the terms "official" and "unofficial" governments. Americans, he says, accept both, "keeping one for ceremonial purposes [incuding Supreme Court opinions] . . . and one for workaday purposes." *The American Mind: An Interpretation of American Thought and Character Since the 1880's* (New Haven: Yale University Press, 1950), p. 315. Herbert J. Spiro's distinction between "formal" and "true" constitutions is concerned with the same phenomena. *Government by Constitution: The Political Systems of Democracy* (New York: Random House, 1959).

definitions the American "constitution" is broader than its "Constitution." It is what Aristotle would have studied for his collection of constitutions and what the British would understand as "constitutional arrangements." To Americans, however, a constitution with a lower-case "c" is largely without meaning. To say that something is constitutional or unconstitutional is to speak about its legal qualities first and its political qualities only by implication. Nevertheless, the United States does possess a constitution, and should it be insisted that a written document must stay the same, it is the constitution rather than the Constitution of the United Sates that changes.[3]

The significance of constitutional changes in the nonjudicial world is at least as great as in the judicial world, and here the broader meaning of "constitution" is indispensable for understanding the process. In 1885 Brooks Adams offered the following proposition: "Modern America is ruled like England, by means of a mass of custom and tradition which silently shapes itself to the changing wants of the people. It would be impossible, even were it desirable, to bind the country by unaltering laws a century old. It is of little moment whether the meaning of our great charter is slowly construed away by the ingenuity of lawyers, or whether it is roughly thrust aside by force; its fate is sealed; it must yield where it

---

3. In the world of judicial constitutional change it has often been asserted that the "meaning" of the Constitution is constant; only the application changes. In the mortgage moratorium case, for instance, Justice Sutherland wrote in dissent: "The provisions of the Federal Constitution, undoubtedly, are pliable in the sense that in appropriate cases they have the capacity of bringing within their grasp every new condition which falls within their meaning. But, their *meaning* is changeless; it is only their *application* which is extensible." Home Building and Loan Ass'n. v. Blaisdell, 290 U.S. 398, 451 (1934) (emphasis in original; note omitted). In another case Justice Sutherland used the same terminology for the majority: "While the meaning of constitutional guaranties never varies, the scope of their application must expand or contract to meet the new and different conditions which are constantly coming within the field of their operation. In a changing world, it is impossible that it should be otherwise." Euclid v. Ambler County, 272 U.S. 365, 387 (1926). Many constitutional lawyers have found this distinction between meaning and application perfectly intelligible. Not only do they believe in an immortal Constitution, but they believe also in immortal constitutional essences or ideas, with a priori definitions. In this scheme the Constitution defines meanings which, when applied to various circumstances, become the judicial contribution to the constitution. Under the influence of pragmatism in philosophy and functionalism in jurisprudence, however, most people now understand that meaning and application are at least interdependent, or that they are identical, or even that meaning depends upon application rather than the other way around.

obstructs." [4] Between the courts on one side and violence on the other lies the slowly moving "mass of custom and tradition" as a force for constitutional change. This mass includes numerous constitutional "usages," essential to the governing of America but not mentioned in the written Constitution.[5]

The most important of these constitutional usages is certainly the party system, which has frustrated the purpose of the electoral college since the time of George Washington and without which American politics is simply unimaginable. A second constitutional usage is judicial review. No matter how this may be sanctioned by lawyers through textual exegesis or by scholars through historical records, the fact remains that judicial review is part of the constitution, not the Constitution.[6] A third important constitutional usage largely unaffected by the written document has been federalism. In the words of Woodrow Wilson: "We have resorted, almost unconscious of the political significance of what we did, to extra-constitutional means of modifying the federal system where it has proved to be too refined by balances of divided authority to suit practical uses . . ." [7]

4. "The Consolidation of the Colonies," *Atlantic Monthly*, 55 (1885), 307–08. Concerning lawyers and force as factors in constitutional change, two points should be noted. First, as often as they mold it by their own resources, courts acknowledge and in effect ratify constitutional change that has taken place beyond the sphere of the judiciary. See Arthur Selwyn Miller, "Notes on the Concept of the 'Living' Constitution," *George Washington Law Review*, 31 (1963), esp. 886–87. Second, violence has not only settled constitutional questions, as with the Civil War, but it has also, in a variety of circumstances, become a political pattern and hence important for an understanding of the constitution. Relations with the Indians, lynchings, industrial strikes, or protests and riots in the 1960's are examples.

5. Herbert W. Horwill, *The Usages of the American Constitution* (London: Oxford University Press, 1925), provides an excellent compilation. Although his juristic notions do not fit American practice, Horwill's British outlook permits his political-constitutional theory to be broader than that of most Americans. For standard American discussions of constitutional practices see Karl N. Llewellyn, "The Constitution as an Institution," *Columbia Law Review*, 34 (1934), 1–40; and Howard Lee McBain, *The Living Constitution: A Consideration of the Realities and Legends of Our Fundamental Law* (New York: Workers Education Bureau Press, 1927).

6. A brief but careful discussion of the subject appears in the introduction by Alan F. Westin to a recent edition of Charles A. Beard, *The Supreme Court and the Constitution* (Englewood Cliffs, N.J.: Prentice-Hall, 1962). The volume also includes an extensive bibliography.

7. *Congressional Government* (Boston: Houghton, 1885), p. 243. See also Louis Henkin, "Voice of a Modern Federalism," in Wallace Mendelson (ed.), *Felix Frankfurter: The Judge* (New York: Reynal, 1964), pp. 66–108; and Arthur Selwyn Miller, "Technology, Social Change, and the Constitution," *George Washington Law Review*, 33 (1964), 17–46.

Finally there is the growth of executive power. The Constitution looked forward to "executive departments," but the size and scope of the federal administration and the relations between executive agencies and Congress are part of a constitutional world about which the Constitution says nothing and in the development of which the judiciary has played no role.[8]

(b) Since Americans consider their constitution a written document, they are usually more concerned with constitutional interpretation — constitutional law — than with constitutional practices such as those mentioned above. The question then arises: In what way does constitutional interpretation relate to the constitutional document? The answer is: In a legal way. The Supreme Court is a court of law, bound by oath and legal function to expound a written document. No matter how political the issue, the Court presents its argument in a legal form, attending to many of the same considerations that would be applied to the interpretation of any other legal document, such as a contract or a statute. Certain rules of construction apply generally. The words, unless obviously employed in a special sense, should be given their natural meaning. The document should be presumed internally consistent. And the meaning of the document should be determined and applied with a view towards the social and legal worlds of which that meaning will become a part.

The most important assumption in legal construction, however, is that the authors of a document said what they meant to say in the document itself. Yet the correct interpretation of a document may nevertheless depend upon the use of sources external to it. Although these sources are consulted only to determine a document's meaning, by an easy chain of reasoning the search for textual meaning may become a search for the author's intentions. In this way the "intent of the framers" enters into constitutional interpretation.

The distinction between meaning and intention, between documents and people, appears clear. Contemporary legal theory comes out flatly in favor of the former: the search must be for the meaning of documents, not the intentions of people. According to Julius Stone, "The error of substituting *author's intention* for *meaning of*

8. Perhaps the most important field in which executive practice under the Constitution has changed since the time of the founders is foreign policy. See in general J. William Fulbright, "American Foreign Policy in the 20th Century under an 18th Century Constitution," *Cornell Law Quarterly,* 47 (1961), 1–13. Although the character of Senator Fulbright's answer has changed since this article was written, the question of constitutional change and constitutional usage in the field of foreign policy remains as he posed it.

language is that it ignores the fact that a written work, once created, acquires a meaning which, though still dependent on men's usage, is still independent of its creator's motives; and interpretation is precisely a search for this meaning." [9] In the words of Morris Cohen: "If the legislative will is to be obeyed, people must be governed by what the statute actually says, that is, by the ordinary meaning that the language employed usually conveys. In the long run it would undermine the power of legislatures if the words they used were generally set aside by speculations as to what they intended but did not say." [10] But contemporary theory notwithstanding, jurists from Blackstone to the present have made speculations as to what was intended but not actually written down.[11] There is a host of concepts — aim, purpose, object, design — which apply to both documents and people simultaneously and which help to mediate between the meaning of words and the intention of legislators.[12] But these terms also obscure the difference between meaning and intention. The consequence has been, in the phrasing of John Marshall, that "where the mind labors

9. *Legal System and Lawyers' Reasoning* (Stanford: Stanford University Press, 1964), p. 32 (emphasis in original).

10. *The Meaning of Human History* (La Salle, Ill.: Open Court, 1947), pp. 55–56. See also Cohen, *Law and the Social Order* (New York: Harcourt, Brace, 1933), pp. 128–39.

11. Blackstone wrote that "the most universal and effectual way of discovering the true meaning of a law, when the words are dubious, is by considering the *reason* and *spirit* of it; or the cause which moved the legislator to enact it." *Commentaries*, I, *61. A century and three quarters later Learned Hand wrote: "Of course it is true that the words used, even in their literal sense, are the primary, and ordinarily the most reliable, source of interpreting the meaning of any writing: be it a statute, a contract, or anything else. But it is one of the surest indexes of a mature and developed jurisprudence not to make a fortress out of the dictionary; but to remember that statutes always have some purpose or object to accomplish, whose sympathetic and imaginative discovery is the surest guide to their meaning." Cabell v. Markham, 148 F. 2d 737, 739 (2d Cir. 1945). See also Oliver Wendell Holmes, "The Theory of Legal Interpretation," in *Collected Legal Papers* (New York: Harcourt, Brace and Howe, 1920), pp. 203–09; Felix Frankfurter, "Some Reflections on the Reading of Statutes," *Columbia Law Review,* 47 (1947), 527–46; and "A Symposium on Statutory Construction," *Vanderbilt Law Review,* 3 (1950), 365–584.

12. The word "intent" also applies to both people and documents. "Intention," however, is properly applied only to people, and the more specialized word "intendment" only to documents. For an analysis of the Supreme Court's use of history, organized around the distinctions among "intent," "purpose," and "meaning" — the entire continuum of terms — see John G. Wofford, "The Blinding Light: The Uses of History in Constitutional Interpretation," *University of Chicago Law Review,* 31 (1964), 502–33.

to discover the design of the legislature, it seizes every thing from which aid can be derived." [13] In constitutional law this has meant that the Supreme Court, if only because it is interpreting a legal document, searches for the intent of the framers.

(c) The crucial factor that gives rise to the problem of intent and change in constitutional adjudication is that the Constitution is old. It is the antiquity of the Constitution that distinguishes it from most other documents that courts are called on to interpret. It is its antiquity along with its special legal and political significance in American life that distinguishes it from the constitutions of other countries. The age of the Constitution raises the questions of changes in meaning, of historical sources, and of the relevance of historical intent to contemporary problems.

The first effect of the passage of time since the Constitution was adopted is that the meaning of the text has changed, both as a whole and in the case of particular words and phrases. Especially if it is assumed that the Constitution was a single coherent text at the time of its adoption, then the meaning of the entire document is different today from what it was in the eighteenth century. The framers' views of the world — socially, politically, economically, philosophically, and legally — were different from our own. Although it is the inarticulate premise of all historical interpretation that earlier views of the world can be understood by the present, not all historians and almost no jurists come to grips with the changes in world views over time. If anything is certain with respect to constitutional meaning, it is that if the entire Constitution means something definite today, this is not what it meant in 1789.[14]

13. United States v. Fisher, 2 Cr. 358, 386 (1805).
14. "One is prone to assume," wrote the authors of a study of the commerce clause of the Constitution, "that, when words abide, meanings remain; yet some fifteen decades of cultural change — and their restless impact upon language — lie between us and the words of the Constitution." Walton H. Hamilton and Douglass Adair, *The Power to Govern: The Constitution — Then and Now* (New York: Norton, 1937), p. 42. The problem of archaic words and changing language is not, of course, confined to law. The most notable area in which it arises is religion. Literature, especially poetry, is another important area. And primitive societies must cope with the problem quite as much as more advanced ones. As one anthropologist reports: "It often happens that traditions become incomprehensible to the informants who relate them, either because the language has become archaic (which is often the case with fixed texts), or because the events spoken of bear reference to customs which no longer exist, and which are thus unfamiliar to the informants." Jan Vansina, *Oral Tradition: A Study in Historical Methodology* (Chicago: Aldine, 1965), p. 44.
The most significant contemporary attempt to study the entire Constitu-

The Constitution as a whole is seldom subjected to a coherent interpretation. It is explained in cases and in commentary piecemeal according to the clause at issue. Since language itself does not change at a uniform pace, this is the only kind of interpretation which does justice to differences in the meanings of words. Explaining the true meaning of a document, as historians well know, sometimes requires and is almost always aided by the use of modern language. The most delicate aspect of this explanation will center on those words and phrases that still make perfect sense, but not the same sense that was imparted to them when they were first set down. In Justice Holmes's explanation: "A word is not a crystal, transparent and unchanged; it is the skin of a living thought and may vary greatly in color and content according to the circumstances and the time in which it is used." [15] In the constitutional world, according to Justice Frankfurter, we ask "not what words did Madison and Hamilton use, but what was it in their minds which they conveyed." [16]

The second effect of the passage of time on the determination of constitutional intent is the great difficulty of discovering precisely what was in the minds of the framers. The entire endeavor was derided by Justice Jackson from the bench: "Just what our forefathers did envision, or would have envisioned had they foreseen

---

tion in terms of its original meaning is the two-volume work of the late William Winslow Crosskey, *Politics and the Constitution in the History of the United States* (2 vols.; Chicago: University of Chicago Press, 1953). Crosskey views the Constitution as a completely internally consistent document whose provisions must be given a legal (rather than a political) interpretation and may be understood only by first compiling a special "dictionary of 1787" for crucial words. Crosskey's study and the passions it aroused well illustrate the problems of historical intent and constitutional change. Almost no reviewer of the work, regardless of his position on Crosskey's historical arguments (or policy goals), dared to follow the author's leap across the historical chasm and agree that more than a century and a half of constitutional development should be repealed on the basis of new discoveries as to the original meaning of the constitutional document.

15. Town v. Eisner, 245 U.S. 418, 425 (1918).

16. Concurring in Dennis v. United States, 341 U.S. 494, 523 (1951). Jacobus ten Broek collects several instances of constitutional interpretation which have depended upon the special meaning of words at the time of the adoption of the Constitution. "Admissibility and Use by the United States Supreme Court of Extrinsic Aids in Constitutional Construction," *California Law Review*, 26 (1938), 301. For a treatment of the problem generally and more broadly, see Charles H. McIlwain, "Some Illustrations of the Influence of Unchanged Names for Changing Institutions," in Paul Sayre (ed.), *Interpretations of Modern Legal Philosophies* (New York: Oxford University Press, 1947), pp. 484–97.

modern conditions, must be divined from materials almost as enigmatic as the dreams Joseph was called upon to interpret for Pharaoh. A century and a half of partisan debate and scholarly speculation yields no net result but only supplies more or less apt quotations from respected sources on each side of any question. They largely cancel each other." [17] This skepticism is the product not only of unwillingness to yield control over the Constitution to earlier generations, but also of the daily task of reading conflicting histories presented by lawyers to demonstrate the sanction of the founders on both sides of the same case. But historians as scholars can generally state the matter more objectively than can advocates as historians. From the historian's point of view, determining the original purpose of the Constitution is no different from many other research activities. The chief questions are what material to admit as evidence and how much weight to give it.

The legal restrictions against inquiring into motive, as distinguished from purpose, are not applicable to the historian so long as he is concerned not with the legal effect of a document but with the circumstances surrounding its appearance. Yet since the difference between motive and purpose is not always clear, the exclusion of evidence in court under the former heading does not always bar its return under the latter one. In addition, some of the reasons for the rule excluding motive from law are equally applicable to historical research. Psychological, not to say psychoanalytic, interpretations of characters in history are dubious in many instances either because of a scarcity of relevant data or because of lack of adequate training and insight on the part of the historian.[18] The task of the historian who would apply psychology to the framers of the Constitution is made doubly difficult by the fact that it is not just the mind of a

17. Concurring in Youngstown v. Sawyer, 343 U.S. 579, 634–35 (1952). Jackson continues, in a footnote with specific references to the works of well-known interpreters, "A Hamilton may be matched against a Madison . . . Professor Taft is counterbalanced by Theodore Roosevelt . . . It even seems that President Taft cancels out Professor Taft."

18. Erik H. Erikson's *Young Man Luther* (New York: Norton, 1958) is generally considered the most successful attempt to apply psychoanalytic insights to an historical figure. The technique is being increasingly advocated for historians. See, e.g., William L. Langer, "The Next Assignment," *American Historical Review,* 63 (1958), 283–304; H. Stuart Hughes, *History as Art and as Science: Twin Vistas on the Past* (New York: Harper and Row, 1964), pp. 42–67; Erikson, *Insight and Responsibility* (New York: Norton, 1964), pp. 159–215; and the review article by Bruce Mazlish, "Inside the Whales," *Times Literary Supplement,* July 28, 1966, pp. 667–69.

single individual which must be analyzed but the minds of a group of men — at least the entire Constitutional Convention and possibly all persons involved in the campaign for ratification. Although small-group theory may provide insights about the sociology of the Convention, neither it nor social psychology offers any real aid to the question of historical intent. It is necessary to agree with the modern Court's most noted historian that "the devil himself knoweth not the mind of men" and to stick to the ostensible import of the records left by the actors of the time.[19]

In the case of the adoption of the Constitution, the records of the actors consist of the Articles of Confederation, acts taken under that charter, and the evidence of the political difficulties which led up to the Constitutional Convention;[20] the official journal, the draft proposals, and the several sets of notes, particularly those of Madison, taken at the Convention;[21] the federalist and antifederalist literature published during the ratification campaign;[22] the records of the state

19. Justice Frankfurter dissenting in Leland v. Oregon, 343 U.S. 790, 803 (1952). The warning for jurists came over three decades ago: "The judgment of the Court rests upon the ruling that another purpose, not professed, may be read beneath the surface, and by the purpose so imputed the statute is destroyed. Thus the process of psychoanalysis has spread to unaccustomed fields." Justice Cardozo dissenting in United States v. Constantine, 296 U.S. 287, 298–99 (1935).

20. See Chapter III for the use of Confederation materials in determining the purpose of the contract clause. The political-expression cases show that events before and during the Revolution may also be relevant to the determination of constitutional intent.

21. The most satisfactory edition of these is Max Farrand (ed.), *The Records of the Federal Convention of 1787* (3 vols.; New Haven: Yale University Press, 1911), recently reprinted. The material in this edition is arranged by date no matter what the source. The government publication, C. C. Tansill (ed.), *Documents Illustrative of the Formation of the Union of the American States* (Washington: Government Printing Office, 1927) contains essentially the same material, arranged by source. Unfortunately, it is miserably indexed. An exhaustive compilation of documents pertaining to the adoption of the Constitution is currently being prepared at the National Archives. The Preface and Introduction to the Farrand edition contain information on the scope, accuracy, and original publication dates of the various records of the Convention.

22. It is natural that Americans — and the Supreme Court — should be familiar almost exclusively with the writing of the victors of this campaign, essentially Hamilton, Madison, and Jay, in *The Federalist,* of which there are many editions. On the use of *The Federalist* in constitutional law see Charles W. Pierson, "*The Federalist* in the Supreme Court," *Yale Law Journal,* 33 (1924), 728–35; and Jacobus ten Broek, "Use by the United States Supreme Court of Extrinsic Aids in Constitutional Construction," *California Law Review,* 27 (1939), 157–71. Ten Broek discusses three doctrines that the Supreme

ratifying conventions;[23] early governmental practice, especially the debates and legislation of the First Congress;[24] and the personal writings of men considered to be framers.[25]

The difficulties posed by this material lie not so much in the nature of the sources as in the nature of the problem. It is not a unique historical task to deal with fragmentary sources, or to reconstruct group intent in the preparation of a document, or to recognize that a document contains compromises and a certain amount of general, even designedly imprecise, language. What is distinctive about the historical problem in this instance is that it is not merely historical. It is also political. Because it is concerned with the Constitution, historical research on the intent of the framers at once becomes a contemporary public issue with contemporary public consequences.

Court has held in justification of the use of *The Federalist*: that the papers are authoritative due to their authorship; that they are intrinsically excellent; and that they were widely disseminated and known by the members of the state ratifying conventions. A convenient collection of statements by the opposition is Cecelia M. Kenyon (ed.), *The Antifederalists* (Indianapolis: Bobbs-Merrill, 1966).

23. The standard edition of these is Jonathan Elliot (ed.), *The Debates in the Several State Conventions, on the Adoption of the Federal Constitution* (5 vols.; Washington, 1836–1845). Legally, it is the state ratifying conventions which should be controlling in constitutional interpretation if history is to be the guide. Madison, whose notes of the Philadelphia Convention had not yet been published, wrote a correspondent in 1831: "Another error has been in ascribing to the *intention* of the *Convention* which formed the Constitution, an undue ascendancy in expounding it. Apart from the difficulty of verifying that intention, it is clear, that if the meaning of the Constitution is to be sought outside of itself, it is not in the proceedings of the Body that proposed it, but in those of the State Conventions, which gave it all the validity and authority it possesses." Letter to N. P. Trist, December 1831, *The Writings of James Madison*, ed. Gaillard Hunt (9 vols.; New York: Putnam's Sons, 1900–1910), IX, 477. Ten Broek, writing in 1938, found no case "in which the Court relied to any appreciable degree upon debates or proceedings in the ratifying Conventions." *California Law Review*, 26 (1938), 454, n. 78. Perhaps the opinions in the apportionment case of Wesberry v. Sanders, 376 U.S. 1 (1964) would qualify, however. See esp. 376 U.S. at 15–17 (for the Court) and at 33–39 (Justice Harlan dissenting).

24. See Chapter IV on the presidential removal power. The use of the First Congress in constitutional interpretation is discussed in ten Broek, *California Law Review*, 27 (1939), 171–79.

25. Madison and Hamilton are the most obvious; Madison was notoriously inconsistent in his views, while Hamilton did not attend the entire Constitutional Convention and was uninfluential when he did. James Wilson should certainly rank with them in view of his work at the Convention and afterwards. Washington and Franklin are cited on account of their names, as is Jefferson, who was in France at the time.

The storm raised half a century ago — and still — by Charles Beard's *An Economic Interpretation of the Constitution* developed not because the interpretation was economic, but because it was "of the Constitution."

The antiquity of the Constitution raises not only the historical problem of determining original intent and the semantic problem of comprehending changes in word meaning over time. It raises also the judicial problem of determining the relevance of constitutional intent to the contemporary situation. From one viewpoint, relevance is a matter of judgment and frame of reference concerning the subject matter. But the Supreme Court is faced with more than the case-by-case question of the topical relevance of historical material. The permanent problem of relevance posed by the Constitution's antiquity is the constitutional-legal one. Confronted with a clear original understanding of the Constitution, a judge may elect to follow it because it is his sworn duty. He believes that under the doctrine of popular sovereignty only the people, through the amending process, possess the right to alter the basic charter governing the country. But, confronted with the same meaning, another judge may choose to ignore the original understanding of the Constitution. His conception of the Constitution emphasizes the need for contemporary viability of judicial interpretation if the Constitution is to continue to play its political role in American life. In either case, the judge ultimately elects to abide or not to abide by the intent of the framers as a result of the interaction of two factors: contemporary topical relevance and his belief about the constitutional function of the Court.

To isolate the time factor in discussing the relevance of constitutional intent in general, one might ask whether the intent or the purpose of a very recent constitutional amendment should be strictly adhered to in its judicial interpretation. Legal theory is presumably indifferent to time. It makes no difference when a clause was incorporated into the Constitution (except in the instances of later amendments superseding earlier text). Judges are expected to give effect to the clause whether they agree with its meaning or not and whether it was ratified yesterday or almost two centuries ago. The question reduces to how to ascertain the meaning. In the case of a contemporary amendment, those who framed and ratified it are alive and certainly expect to have their intentions closely followed, and judges are likely to agree. But do the judges agree because they believe that in all cases constitutional intent is the soundest guide to constitutional interpretation, or because they believe that the meaning of the Constitution, no matter when the language was adopted, must be a contemporary meaning? If it is for the first reason, then the antiquity of the Constitution is significant, popular sovereignty is adhered to in a formal way, and constitutional "development" is, from a legal point of view, a misleading or useless conception. If the second, then the antiquity of the Constitution counts for nothing, popular sovereignty becomes the equivalent of an enlightened contemporary public will, and constitutional development replaces constitutional origins as a principle of adjudication.

Proposed Solutions

To the problems of constitutional interpretation posed by popular sovereignty, the written and legal nature of the Constitution, and the passage of time, three types of solutions have been proposed.[26] The first emphasizes constitutional intent and therefore formal amendment as the most appropriate instrument of constitutional change. The second is a two-clause theory of constitutional interpretation — that some parts of the Constitution are fixed as of the time of their adoption while others are subject to judicial adaptation. The third is a general theory of constitutional development.

In the eighteenth century a written constitution was viewed by many as the literal realization of the social contract. In contrast to John Marshall's belief that "a constitution is framed for ages to come," [27] Thomas Jefferson proposed that each generation literally renew its acceptance of the social contract by plebiscite.[28] To the extent the renewal of the entire Constitution may be accomplished by periodic formal amendment, the people can still retain close control over the fundamental law. Formal amendment would not

26. These do not include the "mass of custom and tradition" discussed above, or the various theories of formal executive or congressional responsibility for expounding the Constitution. For a thorough examination of the congressional theories, see Donald G. Morgan, *Congress and the Constitution, A Study of Responsibility* (Cambridge, Mass.: Harvard University Press, 1966).

27. Cohens v. Virginia, 6 Wheat. 264, 387 (1821).

28. See his letter to James Madison, Sept. 6, 1789, *Writings,* ed. Paul L. Ford (10 vols.; New York: Putnam's Sons, 1892–1899), V, 115–24; and to Samuel Kerchevall, July 12, 1816, *Writings,* X, 43–44. Although Jefferson took his plan seriously as theory, he ignored it in practice, for he was President at the time the second generation should have adopted or re-adopted a constitution.

only solve the problem of popular sovereignty, it would also lighten the burden on the judiciary in interpreting the Constitution. If amendments were relatively frequent, their intent would be no more difficult to determine and no more embarrassing to apply than the intent of a recent statute. The problem of accommodating past and present would be greatly diminished. But the amending process is designedly cumbersome in America, and some eighteenth-century theorists notwithstanding, the country has generally preferred to adapt the Constitution rather than adopt amendments. As Marshall suggested in Marbury v. Madison, the people themselves "can seldom act," and the problem of constitutional change returns to the judiciary.[29]

If the Constitution is interpreted with rigid literalism, or if constitutional change were to take place normally by amendment, then the intent theory of constitutional construction could remain intact. Once judicial responsibility for constitutional change is permitted, however, new theories are required to explain and justify the Court's actions. There exists a cluster of theories attempting to bind the Supreme Court partially, but not wholly, to the words or concerns of the Constitution as adopted. These are the two-clause theories of constitutional interpretation. A two-clause theory states that there are two distinct groups of constitutional clauses, one immutable and not subject to judicial construction, the other subject to change over time through judicial interpretation. The two-clause theories may be classified either according to how the different types of clauses are ascertained or according to the subject matter of the clause, no matter how ascertained.

Two basic methods have been proposed for determining the difference between clauses which are and clauses which are not amenable to judicial construction. They are the textual and historical methods. According to the textual approach, one can tell from the

29. 1 Cr. 137, 176 (1803). For a sound and brief discussion see Paul A. Freund, "To Amend — or Not to Amend — the Constitution," *New York Times Magazine*, Dec. 13, 1964, p. 33. For comments on the relationship of formal amendment and judicial interpretation to social stability, see Fritz F. Heimann, "Professor Crosskey and the Founding Fathers," *Iowa Law Review*, 39 (1953), 146. William S. Livingston, *Federalism and Constitutional Change* (Oxford: Clarendon Press, 1956), is a study of the significance of the formal amending process for federal constitutions. A most insightful essay on permanence and change in the American Constitution is Edmond Cahn, "An American Contribution," in Cahn, *Supreme Court and Supreme Law* (Bloomington: Indiana University Press, 1954), pp. 1–25.

constitutional text itself which clauses, phrases, or words are specific and not subject to construction, and which are general and therefore may be construed by the courts. At the extremes this is a proposition difficult to dispute. All would agree that a six-year term for Senator is specific and that the power of Congress to regulate commerce among the states is general. But these two examples are unrepresentative of most constitutional provisions. For instance, is the prohibition against the impairment of contracts by the states a general or specific clause? Chief Justice Hughes, elaborating a textual two-clause theory in the mortgage moratorium case, thought it general; four dissenters thought not.[30] Further, there appear to be some clauses which are neither specific nor general until seized on by the Court. What kind of clause is it that requires Congressmen to be "chosen . . . by the people"? Until the apportionment cases this clause seemed only to distinguish the House of Representatives from the Senate (which was to be "chosen by the legislature" of each state). But under the guidance of Justice Black the clause was given a meaning general enough to lift it from its role as a linguistic aid and at the same time specific enough to be responsible for the rule of one person, one vote.[31]

Justice Frankfurter proposed a two-clause theory of interpretation which appears partly textual (for general clauses) and partly historical (for specific clauses):

> Broadly speaking two types of constitutional claims come before this Court. Most constitutional issues derive from the broad standards of fairness written into the Constitution (e.g., "due process," "equal protection of the laws," "just compensation"), and the division of power as between States and Nation. Such questions, by their very nature, allow a relatively wide play for individual legal judgment. The other class gives no such scope. For this second class of constitutional issues derives from very specific provisions in the Constitution. These had their source in definite grievances and led the Fathers to proscribe against recurrence of their experience. These specific grievances and the safeguards against their recurrence were not defined by the Constitution. They were defined by history. Their meaning was so

30. Home Building and Loan Ass'n. v. Blaisdell, 290 U.S. 398, 426, 473 (1934). See above, p. 41.
31. Wesberry v. Sanders, 376 U.S. 1 (1964).

settled by history that definition was superfluous. Judicial enforcement of the Constitution must respect these historic limits. The prohibition of bills of attainder falls . . . among these very specific constitutional provisions.[32]

The first provisions listed appear to be nonhistorical because "by their very nature" they allow judicial latitude in interpretation. The second set of claims appears to be historical because the claims refer to "specific grievances" in the eighteenth century. But both sets are historical in an important respect. As Justice Frankfurter said on another occasion: "Some words are confined to their history; some are starting points for history." [33] The clauses involving specific grievances are confined to history as the intent of the framers. The issues involving broader constitutional clauses may utilize ongoing history. One set is static, the other evolutionary, but both require history for their elucidation. Yet the issues deriving from the specific provisions of the Constitution can be limited in their interpretation not merely because of their history but also because of their wording in the Constitution. The treason clause, requiring the testimony of two witnesses to the same overt act, is a good example of a clause specific as to both text and history.

The two-clause theory of Justice Frankfurter has merit because it is both descriptive and prescriptive. It describes roughly what the Court has done with respect to different kinds of constitutional claims (even though Justice Frankfurter is the only one to articulate a two-clause rationale); and it proposes that the two-clause method should continue to be utilized by the Court. In the case in which the theory was first suggested, however, Justice Black had proposed for the Court a new line of constitutional development for a clause which Justice Frankfurter felt was confined by its history.[34] Justice Frankfurter, although agreeing with the outcome of the case, opposed any doctrinal innovation to reach the decision. He would have

32. Concurring in United States v. Lovett, 328 U.S. 303, 321 (1946). For other, less detailed expressions of this theory by Justice Frankfurter see his opinions for the Court in Rochin v. California, 342 U.S. 165, 169–70 (1952), and in Ullman v. United States, 350 U.S. 422, 426–29 (1956).

33. "Some Reflections on the Reading of Statutes," *Columbia Law Review,* 47 (1947), 537.

34. The clause Justice Black proposed utilizing prohibited a congressional bill of attainder (art. 1, sec. 9). Justice Frankfurter preferred to base judgment on the due process clause of the fifth amendment. The case is United States v. Lovett, 328 U.S. 303 (1946).

preferred instead to extend more readily serviceable constitutional principles. Doctrinal innovation, Justice Frankfurter implied in speaking of the clause at issue in this case, was a thing of the past. This attitude, indeed, suggests one reason why the Court may have been reluctant to accept Justice Frankfurter's two-clause theory of constitutional construction. By confining the development of constitutional concepts to already marked channels, the stream not only becomes wider (the concepts embrace more) but also muddier (it is less easy to see the original source of the concept in the Constitution). To Justice Frankfurter this is simply natural legal evolution. But to a Court which depends on a document for its authority, it is not clear that the structural simplicity achieved by having a few clauses dominate constitutional adjudication is preferable to the directness with which decisions could be explained from the constitutional text if more clauses were permitted to play a role.

The second two-clause theory which distinguishes constitutional clauses on an historical basis is the theory of open-ended intent proposed by Alexander Bickel.[35] This theory is more in the traditional pattern of constitutional construction than Justice Frankfurter's because it proposes not that history in general be a guide to distinguishing among constitutional clauses, but that the intent of the framers in particular determine whether a provision is permitted to develop and expand. The Court, said Bickel, should attempt "to discover what if any thought was given to the long-range effect, under future circumstances, of provisions necessarily intended for permanence."[36] Open-ended intent is the theory most impregnable from attack by the proponents of popular sovereignty since it assumes that the people intended the Court to adapt particular constitutional clauses to changing circumstances. Yet if some clauses are open-ended, others must be close-ended, and here is where the difficulty of the theory lies. One type of clause can be distinguished from the other only on the basis of historical evidence, and Bickel offered no examples of either type beyond the equal protection clause, which was said to be open-ended. Unfortunately, it is just this kind of historical evidence that is hardest to come by. Framers of constitutional provisions almost always have their minds on contemporary

35. The theory, proposed in conjunction with the fourteenth amendment and the school segregation cases, is discussed above as applied to the sit-in cases (pp. 116–17). The original article is "The Original Understanding and the Segregation Decision," *Harvard Law Review,* 69 (1955), 1–65.

36. *Ibid.,* 59.

circumstances and particular purposes. To ask that constitutional adjudication depend upon the definite conclusions of history as to the framers' ideas on "long-range effect" is almost certainly to ask for what cannot be given.

Although there are variations in the classification schemes proposed by the several two-clause theorists, there is general agreement among them that constitutional clauses defining the powers of government and the rights of individuals belong to one group — admitting of broad construction or possessed of open-ended intent; and that clauses defining the organization of government and particular procedures at law belong to the other group — admitting of only narrow construction or confined by history to a specific meaning. Justice Frankfurter, in the passage quoted above, spoke of "broad standards of fairness" and governmental powers on the one hand, and of "specific provisions" on the other. Edward Corwin's proposal is similar and more thorough:

> It will be generally found that words which refer to governing institutions, like "jury," "legislature," "election," have been given their strictly historical meaning, while words defining the subject-matter of power or of rights like "commerce," "liberty," "property," have been deliberately moulded to the views of contemporary society. Nor is the reason for this difference hard to discover. Not only are the words of the former category apt to have the more definite, and so more easily ascertainable historical denotation, but the Court may very warrantably feel that if the people wish to have their governmental institutions altered, they should go about the business in accordance with the forms laid down by the basic institution. Questions of power or of right, on the other hand, are apt to confront the Court with problems that are importunate for solution.[37]

Corwin suggested that "historical interpretation" (intent history) was the canon of constitutional construction applied to the first set of clauses, and "adaptive interpretation" (ongoing history) the canon for the second set.

However they are labeled, the two-clause theories ultimately re-

---

37. "Judicial Review in Action," *University of Pennsylvania Law Review,* 74 (1926), 659–60 (notes omitted). For a similar scheme see Willard Hurst, "The Role of History," in Cahn, *Supreme Court and Supreme Law,* p. 57.

duce to the old categories of loose and strict construction arising from the disputes between John Marshall and Thomas Jefferson. But the two-clause theories suggest a more complex reality than did the earlier disputes. They suggest that the Court employs both kinds of construction simultaneously, though for different parts of the Constitution. And they offer substantial reasons why this should be the case rather than simply taking one side or the other on the basis of political expediency or of the most abstract constitutional theory. Between the strictures imposed by a "plain words" and original-intent approach to the Constitution, permitting change only through amendment, and the complete freedom from text and history some-times advanced on the ground that the Court is a thoroughly politi-cal institution, the two-clause theories provide a reasonable explana-tion and guide to constitutional interpretation.

A two-clause theory, no matter how adequate from a scholarly standpoint, is not a theory of constitutional change that has been espoused by many members of the Court. Rather, two more general theories of constitutional development appear to reflect better the views of the Court as a whole.[38] The first is that constitutional change inheres in the nature of the Constitution: that it was part of the framers' broad intention that the Constitution be adapted to the changing needs of society. This is the loose or broad construc-tionist view that stretches from John Marshall ("a constitution in-tended to endure for ages to come"[39]) to Earl Warren ("For the Constitution to have vitality, this Court must be able to apply its principles to situations that may not have been foreseen at the time those principles were adopted"[40]).

The second view of general constitutional change reaches similar results without emphasizing the broadness of original intent. Post-Darwinian in its formulation, it recognizes and makes a principle of the evolutionary nature of law. As Woodrow Wilson expressed it: "The Constitution was founded on the law of gravitation. The government was to exist and move by virtue of the efficacy of

38. A good short essay on the general nature of constitutional change is Walton Hamilton, "1937 to 1787, Dr.," in Conyers Read (ed.), *The Constitu-tion Reconsidered* (New York: Columbia University Press, 1938), pp. vii–xvi. An excellent study of constitutional change in one area sensitive to the entire process of constitutional development is Hamilton's "The Path of Due Process of Law," *ibid.*, pp. 167–90.

39. McCulloch v. Maryland, 4 Wheat. 316, 415 (1819).

40. Concurring in Estes v. Texas, 381 U.S. 532, 564 (1965).

'checks and balances.' The trouble with the theory is that government is not a machine, but a living thing. It falls, not under the theory of the universe, but under the theory of organic life. It is accountable to Darwin, not to Newton." [41] To John Marshall the Constitution was "designed to approach immortality as nearly as human institutions can approach it." [42] But Justice Holmes speaks of "organic, living institutions." [43] The evolutionary approach to the Constitution keeps an eye on history from the founding to the present, history as intent merging into ongoing history and that merging into contemporary law and politics. Although evolution suggests the use of ongoing history only, the more refined form of this approach insists on using intent also. The best-known expression of the view is Justice Holmes's statement: "The case before us must be considered in the light of our whole experience, and not merely in that of what was said a hundred years ago." [44] Not merely, but also. In Holmes's language again, the significance of constitutional words is to be gathered "by considering their origin and the line of their growth." [45] Not one or the other, but both.

A combination, such as this, of the two kinds of history is the

41. *The New Freedom* (New York: Doubleday, Page, 1913), p. 47. Perry Miller believes that the evolutionary principle was almost, but not quite, grasped by American lawyers during the first half of the nineteenth century. *The Life of the Mind in America from the Revolution to the Civil War* (New York: Harcourt, Brace and World, 1965), pp. 128–30. See also Edward S. Corwin, "The Impact of Evolution on the American Political and Constitutional Tradition," in Stow Persons (ed.), *Evolutionary Thought in America* (New York: Braziller, 1956), pp. 182–99.

42. Cohens v. Virginia, 6 Wheat. 264, 387 (1821).

43. Gompers v. United States, 233 U.S. 604, 610 (1914). Compare the following judgment of Holmes's predecessor on the bench, Horace Gray (who sat during the years that Woodrow Wilson was forming the same opinion): "Gray viewed the Federal Constitution as a living organism that meant one thing in 1789, another in 1860, and still another in his own time." Robert M. Spector, "Legal Historian on the United States Supreme Court: Justice Horace Gray, Jr., and the Historical Method," *American Journal of Legal History*, 12 (1968), 209. It may be noted that, at the same time Holmes in law and Wilson in political science were searching for the explanations for social phenomena beyond static forms and mechanical analogies, Frederick Jackson Turner was stating the theme for history: "Behind institutions, behind constitutional forms and modifications, lie the vital forces that call these organs into life and shape them to meet changing conditions." "The Significance of the Frontier in American History" (1893), in Ray Allen Billington (ed.), *Frontier and Section: Selected Essays of Frederick Jackson Turner* (Englewood Cliffs, N.J.: Prentice-Hall, 1961), p. 37.

44. Missouri v. Holland, 252 U.S. 416, 433 (1920).

45. Gompers v. United States, 233 U.S. 604, 610 (1914).

Court's most successful attempt to overcome the problems of constitutional intent and constitutional change. It recognizes that the Constitution does not usually change according to its own plan of amendment, yet constitutional change is continual. When the Constitution is discussed in terms of a theory (that of evolution) to which change itself is integral, then the "Constitution" has become once more the "constitution" that John Marshall said he was expounding. And yet justices have by no means surrendered their "sworn duty to construe the Constitution . . . to effectuate the intent and purposes of the Framers." [46] The principle of popular sovereignty on which the Constitution is based and the legal cast of the American mind will probably always prevent the complete and candid acceptance in the judicial world of the idea that constitutional development is as legitimate in theory as it is manifest in practice. And the American attitude towards history and towards the Constitution, to which this study turns next, will very likely permit the dilemma to continue unresolved.

46. Justice Goldberg concurring in Bell v. Maryland, 378 U.S. 226, 288–89 (1964).

CHAPTER IX

HISTORY, THE CONSTITUTION,

AND THE COURT IN AMERICAN LIFE

This chapter is an exploration in political sociology. Standing apart from the concerns of constitutional jurists, it examines the way in which the distinctive American attitudes towards history, the Constitution, and the Supreme Court affect the justices' use of history in constitutional law.

History in American Life

The American attitude towards history is a determinant of the political culture of which the justices of the Supreme Court are influential members and to which the Court addresses its opinions. Constitutional law is not pronounced principally for the benefit of the legal profession but for the American people as a whole. The arguments and the language of constitutional opinions are designed to take this into account. The Court maintains its constitutional authority in part by reinforcing the political principles and political bonds of the country. These principles and bonds are derived from history and may often be expressed best in historical terms. Thus, when the Supreme Court declares the meaning of the Constitution by celebrating the American past, it does so not for legal reasons alone. It is following the custom of the country.

It is well to begin at the beginning. There are in American history two groups of founding fathers, one for the time of settlement in the seventeenth century and the other for the era of national independence in the late eighteenth century. In many ways the two groups have been treated as one. As Louis Hartz has said, there has been "a colossal blending and confusion of figures in the heroic era of American history. The men of the *Mayflower* sink into the ranks of the men of the Revolution . . ." [1] One reason for this telescoping of more than a century and a half of history into a single political-historical concept is that both foundings lead to the same decisive point in the story of America, the establishment of an independent nation. Corollary to this is the fact that the views of the two groups of founders concerning their own place, and America's place, in history were very much the same. Both groups saw themselves, or the land whose fortunes had become their own, as endowed with a mission.[2]

The belief that America and Americans are endowed with a mission, set apart from the rest of the world and therefore from world history, is an enduring one. For the first founders, in the seventeenth century, the belief in a mission was largely theological.[3] For the second set of founders the belief in a mission was much more secular and political, though still dependent on a faith in the guiding hand of God. As heirs of a combined tradition, we still regard the more solemn moments of politics as a quasi-religious experience and consider religion in general a cornerstone of the polity.[4]

According to the mission viewpoint, Americans are a chosen people. They have been set apart by a natural and providential design from old-world intrigues, wars, intolerance, royalty, feudalism. America was in effect created *de novo* by the hand of God. Made manifest by being established on a continent unspoiled by the civili-

1. *The Founding of New Societies* (New York: Harcourt, Brace and World, 1964), p. 81. See also Daniel J. Boorstin, *The Genius of American Politics* (Chicago: University of Chicago Press, 1953), p. 12.

2. The following are generally relevant to this discussion: Boorstin, *The Genius of American Politics*; Henry Steele Commager, *The Search for a Usable Past, and Other Essays in Historiography* (New York: Knopf, 1967), title essay; Wesley Frank Craven, *The Legend of the Founding Fathers* (New York: New York University Press, 1956); Max Lerner, *America as a Civilization* (New York: Simon and Schuster, 1957), chap. 1; Reinhold Niebuhr, *The Irony of American History* (New York: Scribner's, 1952); David W. Noble, *Historians against History* (Minneapolis: University of Minnesota Press, 1965); Clinton Rossiter, "The American Mission," *American Scholar*, 20 (1951), 19–28; Ernest Lee Tuveson, *Redeemer Nation: The Idea of America's Millenial Role* (Chicago: University of Chicago Press, 1968).

3. By "first founders" is meant here those who influenced the American conception of history, and this means primarily those whose settlement was religiously motivated. Jamestown and the Virginia adventurers have a secure place in American history, but compared to the Puritans and Pilgrims they have had little influence on our attitude towards history.

4. See Robert N. Bellah, "Civil Religion in America," *Daedalus,* Winter 1967, pp. 1–21.

zation and ways of Europe, America was, like ancient Israel, responsible to a divine destiny.[5] Also like ancient Israel, America was exempt from the ordinary course of history. Having repudiated Europe and severed ties with the past, America was able to float free in historical time and, like the Hebrews, to believe in an essentially ahistorical reality.[6] It is this belief, a consequence of the mission viewpoint, that helps account for the unhistorical approach of Americans towards the Founding Fathers and towards the nation's past generally.[7]

For purposes of understanding the use of history in constitutional law, special attention must be given to the role that history played in making the Constitution. Justice Frankfurter has stated the theme: "The Founders of this Nation were not imbued with the modern cynicism that the only thing that history teaches is that it teaches nothing. They acted on the conviction that the experience of man sheds a good deal of light on his nature." [8] The eighteenth century, though not concerned with historical process, was deeply interested in history. History, if correctly studied, would yield immutable laws of society in the same way that Newtonian mechanics described nature.[9] This was the application of reason to history — and the other way around. No matter how they might disagree on politics,

5. See especially Niebuhr, *Irony of American History,* pp. 24, 46, 70.

6. See Commager, *Search for a Usable Past,* pp. x, 12; Morris R. Cohen, *The Meaning of Human History* (La Salle, Ill.: Open Court, 1947), pp. 15–16; J. A. Harrison, "Time and the American Historian," *South Atlantic Quarterly,* 64 (1965), 362–66; Louis Hartz, *The Liberal Tradition in America, An Interpretation of American Political Thought since the Revolution* (New York: Harcourt, Brace and World, 1955), chap. 1; Jacob Neusner, *History and Torah, Essays on Jewish Learning* (New York: Schocken, 1965).

7. It doubtless accounts for much else besides. In Reinhold Niebuhr's view: "A nation with an inordinate degree of political power is doubly tempted to exceed the bounds of historical possibility, if it is informed by an idealism which does not understand the limits of man's wisdom and volition in history." *Irony of American History,* p. 143. This is also a theme of J. William Fulbright, *The Arrogance of Power* (New York: Random House, 1967). David W. Noble, in his study of the acceptance and promulgation of the theory of an "American mission" by historians from George Bancroft to the present, concludes that "if Americans have no past, they have no future; they are doomed by the burden of innocence to repeat endlessly that only in America is there no historical drama; they are fated to deny the reality of their existence." *Historians against History,* p. 177. See also Roland Van Zandt, *The Metaphysical Foundations of American History* (The Hague: Mouton, 1959).

8. Concurring in Youngstown v. Sawyer, 343 U.S. 579, 593 (1952).

9. See in general R. N. Stromberg, "History in the Eighteenth Century," *Journal of the History of Ideas,* 12 (1951), 295–304.

eighteenth-century American leaders were one with Bolingbroke in believing that "history is philosophy teaching by examples." [10] Nothing in eighteenth-century America was more diligently studied, more appealed to for authority, or more advocated for the education of youth and the spread of civic virtue than history.[11]

In the crisis that began with the Stamp Act and ended with the Declaration of Independence the American colonists argued their case against Parliament and the King largely in the language of Whig history and the supposedly ancient Anglo-Saxon rights of Englishmen.[12] Following the custom of the times they often signed their published statements with classical tag names, such as Brutus, Cato, or, as with *The Federalist*, Publius. The culminating American application of history to public affairs took place at the Constitutional Convention. James Madison arrived in Philadelphia with a detailed study he had made: "Of Ancient and Modern Confederacies." [13] From the beginning of the Convention to the end the framers backed their political theory with, and sometimes derived it from, the lessons of history. Historical arguments, which to the eighteenth-century mind were not mere embellishment, extended from leagues of

10. *Letters on the Study and Use of History* (London, 1752), I, 15. For the classic expression of this see David Hume, *An Inquiry Concerning Human Understanding,* sec. 8, part 1.

11. Henry Steele Commager writes that "no other American generation has been so deeply immersed in or preoccupied with history. Indeed, we might say with considerable justice that the Founding Fathers thought history too serious a business to be left to the historians. It was the concern of all, but especially of statesmen . . ." "Leadership in Eighteenth-Century America and Today," in *Freedom and Order: A Commentary on the American Political Scene* (New York: Braziller, 1966), p. 160. For a detailed study of colonial reading habits and use of history, see H. Trevor Colbourn, *The Lamp of Experience*: Whig History and the Intellectual Origins of the American Revolution (Chapel Hill: University of North Carolina Press, 1965).

The relation of the study of history to the legal profession is manifest on almost every page of Blackstone's *Commentaries,* which was a staple in American colonial libraries. See Daniel J. Boorstin, *The Mysterious Science of the Law* (Boston: Beacon Press, 1958), esp. pp. 31–61. The *Letters* of Lord Mansfield on the proper preparation for the law, widely circulated in the 1790's, were devoted almost exclusively to a recitation, with specific book, chapter, and page references, of those portions of ancient, modern, and British history essential for the legal profession. For a modern American expression see Charles E. Wyzanski, Jr., "History and Law," *University of Chicago Law Review,* 26 (1959), 237–44.

12. See Colbourn, *Lamp of Experience.*

13. See Irving Brant, "The Madison Heritage," *New York University Law Review,* 35 (1960), 882–902.

Greek city-states to modern Europe.[14] The framers had no doubt
that their most sympathetic British cousin was correct in saying, "In
history, a great volume is unrolled for our instruction, drawing the
materials of future wisdom from the past errors and infirmities of
mankind." [15] When *The Federalist* papers were presented to the
citizens of New York in the fall of 1787, the Convention's historical
learning and historical tone were displayed for all. At the end of the
third consecutive paper devoted entirely to the history of confedera-
tions, Publius wrote: "I make no apology for having dwelt so long on
the contemplation of these federal precedents. Experience is the
oracle of truth; and where its responses are unequivocal, they ought
to be conclusive and sacred." [16] This view of Publius, although exag-
gerated with respect to the significance of history in the Constitutional Convention, has come down to the present. But there is a
crucial difference. The American attitude towards history today is
held captive by the success of the eighteenth-century Founding
Fathers. We have come to regard *their* experience as both conclusive
and sacred. When the Supreme Court uses history as intent, it is this
phenomenon of our political culture to which it is anchored.

In the nineteenth century, the application of the American view
of history was influenced by fast-changing economic relationships
and Darwinian ideas. The mission doctrine of the American purpose,
in combination with territorial expansion (manifest destiny) and material prosperity, led to a widespread faith in historical progress.
But these same conditions led to an intensification of the nonhistorical

14. Two of the chief writers relied on by the framers, Montesquieu and
Thomas Mably (on Polybius), were notoriously inaccurate in describing the
functioning of the British constitution and Greek federalism. (And Polybius
himself was not very accurate in describing the Roman government.) A full
examination of the framers' use of history is Raoul S. Naroll, "Clio and the
Constitution: The Influence of the Study of History upon the Federal Convention of 1787" (unpub. diss. University of California, Los Angeles, 1953).
Naroll studies both the effect of historical arguments on the framing of the
Constitution and the validity of the history used. His work is organized
according to constitutional issues, such as federation, representation, congres-
sional procedure, and the distribution of powers. See also Gilbert Chinard,
"Polybius and the American Constitution," *Journal of the History of Ideas*, 1
(1940), 38–58; Colin B. Goodykoontz, "The Founding Fathers and Clio,"
Pacific Historical Review, 23 (1954), 111–23; and Richard M. Gummere, *The
American Colonial Mind and the Classical Tradition* (Cambridge, Mass.:
Harvard University Press, 1963), esp. pp. 173–90.

15. "Reflections on the Revolution in France," *The Writings and Speeches
of Edmund Burke* (12 vols.; Boston: Little, Brown, 1909), III, 418.

16. *The Federalist*, No. 20 (Wright ed., p. 185).

cast of the American mind, which has continued to the present. Though fascinated by the past, Americans prefer to concentrate on producing something new. The United States, obviously not a traditional society in the anthropologist's sense, is not nearly so burdened with tradition as other developed societies. The Constitution may appear static, with the nation's political values enshrined in the story of its origin, but the society is dynamic and always in motion. The United States, says a prominent sociologist, "is probably the first large society in history to have change and innovation 'built into' its culture." [17] Yet far from giving Americans a greater appreciation of historical change, this has only reinforced the notion that history is that moment in time when the Founding Fathers bequeathed their values and deeds to the present. The present needs to be concerned only with itself. When Henry Ford exclaimed that history was bunk, he did not mean only that it was lies, but also that it was useless in an era of material progress.[18] In taking this somewhat paradoxical stance towards the past, Americans have ignored the warnings of the Founding Fathers against hero-worship[19] and have been unable to extend their own involvement in change as a way of life to a more adequate view of history as a succession of related events. The Founding Fathers, almost from the beginning, have been gods, a popular acceptance of Carlyle's great-man theory of history.[20] Americans are as ahistorical in outlook as ever.

The timelessness of the past makes it particularly easy for Americans to use history in contemporary public life, both in politics and in culture. The United States is far from being alone in using history for contemporary purposes, but, especially in its political use of history, it is distinguished from other countries in two important

17. Daniel Bell, *The End of Ideology* (Glencoe, Ill.: The Free Press, 1960), pp. 35–36; see also p. 89.

18. For commentary on this proposition see Cohen, *Meaning of Human History*, p. 16; and C. Wright Mills, *The Sociological Imagination* (New York: Grove Press, 1961), p. 157.

19. See e.g., Thomas Jefferson to Samuel Kerchevall, July 12, 1816, *Writings*, ed. Paul L. Ford (10 vols.; New York: Putnam's Sons, 1892–1899), X, 42; and John Adams in the preface to his *Defence of the Constitutions of Government of the United States of America*, quoted in Craven, *Legend of the Founding Fathers*, p. 74.

20. See in general Craven, *Legend of the Founding Fathers*: and David D. Van Tassel, *Recording America's Past* (Chicago: University of Chicago Press, 1960), esp. pp. 66–76. On the charisma of George Washington see Marcus Cunliffe, *George Washington: Man and Monument* (Boston: Little, Brown, 1958).

ways. First, the American past is a unified and positive tradition. Disagreement over its implications for present policy never brings into question which history one should be faithful to. The Founding Fathers are *the* founding fathers. Elsewhere the situation is different. In France, for instance, royalist and revolutionary traditions contribute conflicting strands to political argument in a nation that has long debated politics in terms of history. There is no consensus concerning historical values to which all Frenchmen can appeal.[21] In England, Anglo-Saxon and Norman lines of heritage have converged as far as political debate is concerned, but Whig and Tory histories continue.[22] In German public life various myths from the past and about the past have achieved historical status largely because of the absence or weakness of political unity. The "two souls" within Goethe's breast are reflected in a history too diffuse and contradictory to support a single political tradition.[23] Only in the United States has history seemed so single-minded and continuous that the authority of the Founding Fathers is undisputed and indisputable.

The second distinguishing characteristic of the American use of history is that the expression of its unity corresponds closely to actuality. It is not a history imposed by political authorities. While American history is often made use of for official purposes, it does not have to be made up for these occasions. The contrast here is with the unified history enforced by twentieth-century totalitarian states. History in these countries has been alternately invented, revised, and obliterated on the premise that what men believe about the past determines their attitude towards public policy. In the words of the Party slogan of *1984:* "Who controls the past controls the future; who controls the present controls the past."[24] With a

21. For uses of the past in French political history see Jacques Barzun, "Romantic Historiography as a Political Force in France," *Journal of the History of Ideas,* 2 (1941), 318–29; Stanley Mellon, *The Political Uses of History: A Study of Historians in the French Restoration* (Stanford: Stanford University Press, 1958); Harold T. Parker, *The Cult of Antiquity and the French Revolutionaries* (Chicago: University of Chicago Press, 1937).

22. For a specialized study see Olive Anderson, "The Political Uses of History in Mid Nineteenth-Century England," *Past & Present,* no. 36 (April 1967), pp. 87–105.

23. For a specialized study see August Nitschke, "German Politics and Medieval History," *Journal of Contemporary History,* 3 (1968), 75–92.

24. George Orwell, *1984* (New York: Harcourt, Brace, 1949), p. 35. At the height of the era of Hitler and Stalin the sensitivity of American historians to this situation extended to literary criticism and to completely innocent value systems. See Perry Miller reviewing Van Wyck Brooks, *New England: Indian Summer* (1940), in the *Journal of the History of Ideas,* 2 (1941), 122.

single tradition that adequately reflects historical reality, Americans have been fortunate in the material provided by the past.[25]

Because history is the principal source of American political values and national cohesion, historical material is often in evidence in public life. As with the Supreme Court, the history used in American politics takes the form of both history as intent and ongoing history. But the differences between the political and judicial uses of history are important. The most significant of these is that in politics history has no legal compulsion. Thus in politics the story of the founders performs a symbolic function only. More recent ongoing history may actually influence the particular actions of public figures. Further, the use of history in public affairs is a pragmatic one, and the test of its success is its reliability as a means of prediction.[26] The validity of history as a principle of adjudication, on the other hand, depends on its accuracy, its relevance to the decision reached, and how it relates to other principles used in the judicial opinion. Since the direct effect of a judicial decision is largely independent of the reasoning of the opinion, its historical observations are of little predictive interest.

In the political as in the judicial world, it is not possible to determine the extent to which history is a source of policy and the extent to which it is only a source of argument in justification of policy. History is undoubtedly used in both ways. In shaping public policy, where the rules are much less formal than in adjudication, the role of history as a source for decisions can be accounted for only by the general observation that the springs of human action are tied to an evaluation of experience, and this in turn depends in part on the society's outlook on the past. Public officials who rely on historical justification for their policies are likely to be sincere about it, though

25. Since Charles A. Beard and the Progressive Era, dissenting versions of the American past have been common, though never conquering. A recent example is Barton J. Bernstein (ed.), *Towards a New Past: Dissenting Essays in American History* (New York: Pantheon, 1968). Of critical historical and public importance today are the legacy of black slavery and the aims of American foreign policy since the late nineteenth century. Current dispute over "consensus" history — whether the American past is actually unified and without serious and permanent conflicts — is a real concern, but it is so for professional historians, not for the popular mind.

26. This is the point of Arthur M. Schlesinger, Jr., "On the Inscrutability of History," *Encounter,* November 1966, pp. 10–17. For a discussion of the background and theory of the use of history in the formulation of public policy, see Sidney Hook, "Objectivity and Reconstruction in History," in Hook (ed.), *Philosophy and History* (New York: New York University Press, 1963), pp. 252–53.

as much at an unconscious as at a conscious level. Arthur Schlesinger, Jr., has said that "one cannot . . . reduce the function of history in public policy to that of mere rationalization, for historical models acquire a life of their own. Once a statesman begins to identify the present with the past, he may in time be carried further than he intends by the bewitchment of analogy." [27]

In American political life, history has played an especially important role in presidential activities and in the conduct of foreign affairs. The presidency requires considerable symbolic and ceremonial use of history.[28] Beyond this, several Presidents, notably Jefferson, Theodore Roosevelt, Wilson, and Kennedy, have had a strong personal, even professional, interest in the subject.[29] In foreign affairs the use of history has resembled its use in constitutional law. Expounders of foreign policy have relied strongly on the spirit and admonitions set down in early documents by the founders, especially Washington's Farewell Address and the Monroe Doctrine. Of especial importance in foreign policy has been the relationship between history and diplomacy. Not only have secretaries of state and the diplomatic corps typically been well trained in and acutely conscious of history, but professional historians have often become diplomats or aided in other aspects of foreign policy.[30] Finally, the most durable problems

27. "On the Inscrutability of History," p. 10. An excellent example of the control that conscious historical analogy may have over public affairs is that of "Munich" in recent American foreign policy. This is examined in Schlesinger's article and in J. William Fulbright, "The Fatal Arrogance of Power," *New York Times Magazine,* May 15, 1966, p. 28.

28. The best evidence of what the office requires can be obtained by reading presidential inaugural addresses. These are conveniently collected in *Inaugural Addresses of the Presidents of the United States from George Washington 1789 to Lyndon Baines Johnson 1965* (Washington: Government Printing Office, 1965).

29. For modern times, see George E. Mowry, "The Uses of History by Recent Presidents," *Journal of American History,* 53 (1966), 5–18. For Harry Truman see his *Mr. Citizen* (New York: Bernard Geis, 1960), pp. 143–70, 209–18. On John F. Kennedy see Arthur M. Schlesinger, Jr., *A Thousand Days: John F. Kennedy in the White House* (Boston: Houghton Mifflin, 1965), pp. 59–60, 109–13; and the eulogy in *American Historical Review,* 69 (1964), 602.

30. Preeminent among historian-diplomats of the nineteenth century are George Bancroft and John Lothrop Motley; in the twentieth century Claude Bowers, William E. Dodd, and George F. Kennan stand out. For the role of history in American foreign policy generally see Francis L. Loewenheim (ed.), *The Historian and the Diplomat: The Role of History and Historians in American Foreign Policy* (New York: Harper and Row, 1967); also William T. Hutchinson, "The American Historian in Wartime," *Mississippi Valley Historical Review,* 29 (1942), 163–86.

of American foreign policy may be seen as a direct outgrowth of America's own charmed past. These problems often reduce to the question, "If we could do it, why can't they?" [31] At the same time, the sense of an American mission has given a moral and even self-righteous tone to many debates over foreign affairs.[32]

In American cultural life, as well as in the public arena, history plays a significant role. Henry Steele Commager has suggested that "nothing in the history of American nationalism is more impressive than the speed and the lavishness with which Americans provided themselves with a usable past: history, legends, symbols, paintings, sculpture, monuments, shrines, holy days, ballads, patriotic songs, heroes, and — with some difficulty — villains." [33] The most conspicuous cultural reminders of the past are landmarks and buildings. Although the American attitude towards these has been one of neglect and often destruction, the apparent need for them has led just those persons who did so much to bring about change to restore or reconstruct historic sites almost from scratch. The Williamsburg of John D. Rockefeller, Jr., and the Fort Dearborn of the Ford ("history is bunk") family are examples.

Much of American literature is pervaded with historical locale and action — from the nineteenth century, when defining America and creating its history were much the same thing, to the modern era, with its evocations of the past as in Carl Sandburg's life of Lincoln, Robert Frost's "The Gift Outright," and the popular historical novels.[34] Finally, the evidence of history in American culture may

31. See Carl N. Degler, "The American Past: An Unsuspected Obstacle in Foreign Affairs," *American Scholar*, 32 (1963), 192–209; and Robert L. Heilbroner, *The Future as History* (New York: Grove Press, 1961), esp. chaps. 1 and 4.

32. The hearings conducted by Senator Fulbright in 1966 and 1967 on American policy in Asia bring out the difficulties of this attitude. The statements of Fulbright, George Kennan, and Henry Steele Commager are especially relevant.

33. *The Search for a Usable Past*, p. 13. For the suggestion that popular history is more essential to the United States, as a nation of immigrants, than to other people, see *ibid.*, p. 22; and Esmond Wright, "A National Catechism," *New York Times Book Review*, Nov. 6, 1966, p. 1.

34. Henry Steele Commager has written of the leading nineteenth-century authors: "These were the Founding Fathers of American literary nationalism, and their achievement was scarcely less remarkable than that of the Founding Fathers of political nationalism." *The Search for a Usable Past*, pp. 25–26. Among contemporary poets who have made American history into art are William Carlos Williams, Steven Vincent Benét, and Robert Lowell. For a study of a case that does not quite fit the pattern of these men, see Leland D.

be seen in the widely appreciated work of historians. The writing of such men as Bruce Catton and Arthur Schlesinger, Jr., the popularity of *American Heritage* magazine, and the foundation-supported publication of lengthy "complete papers" series attest to the national interest. It is historians, indeed, whether mythmakers such as Parson Weems, great narrators such as Bancroft, Prescott, and Parkman, or modern professionals, who have laid the foundation for what we know about the past, and who therefore provide the basis for the use of history in contemporary public life.[35]

Woodrow Wilson, who wrote history as a scholar and used it as a politician, claimed much for his profession. History, he wrote, "is a high calling and should not be belittled. Statesmen are guided and formed by what we write, patriots stimulated, tyrants checked. Reform and progress, charity and freedom of belief, the dreams of artists and the fancies of poets, have at once their record and their source with us." [36] Americans who are neither scholars nor politicians claim much the same thing for the past. History is exalted in America, permitting the past to become moral interpreter of the present.[37] The reason for this is partly that the nation's fundamental political

Peterson, "Ezra Pound: The Use and Abuse of History," *American Quarterly*, 17 (1965), 34–47. A critical study of the relation between artistic merit and fidelity to historical truth is David Levin, *In Defense of Historical Literature* (New York: Hill and Wang, 1967). A recent cause célèbre in this regard is William Styron, *The Confessions of Nat Turner* (New York: Random House, 1966).

35. For suggestive remarks on the differences between amateur and professional historians in handing down the tradition of a society, see the anthropological study by Jan Vansina, *Oral Tradition: A Study in Historical Methodology* (Chicago: Aldine, 1965), p. 41. A good concise essay on the history of American history is Edward N. Saveth, "Historical Understanding in Democratic America," in Saveth (ed.), *Understanding the American Past* (Boston: Little, Brown, 1954), pp. 3–64. Important special studies relevant to the transmission of American history to the public are Herman Ausubel, *Historians and Their Craft* (New York: Columbia University Press, 1945); Clifford L. Lord (ed.), *Keepers of the Past* (Chapel Hill: University of North Carolina Press, 1965); and Van Tassel, *Recording America's Past*. For a general survey of the role of nonprofessionals in transmitting an image of the American past to the public, see Thomas A. Bailey's presidential address to the Organization of American Historians, "The Mythmakers of American History," *Journal of American History*, 55 (1968), 5–21.

36. "The Variety and Unity of History," an address delivered at the Universal Exposition, St. Louis, 1904, in Loewenheim, *Historian and Diplomat*, pp. 186–87.

37. On this subject in general see Herbert Butterfield, *The Whig Interpretation of History* (New York: Scribner's, 1951).

principles stem from a definite era in history, that of the founders; and partly that — in the absence of a common religion, a common original homeland, or an articulate social philosophy — a shared history provides one of the strongest bonds of the American political culture. This is the social-political significance of history in American life. In evaluating the Supreme Court's use of history, it is this role as much as the legal role that must be taken into account.

Constitution and Court in the American Mind

In the beginning was the Constitution; and the Constitution was with the Founding Fathers; and the Constitution was the Founding Fathers.

This, without much exaggeration and with most of its connotations, describes the relation between the American attitudes towards history and towards the Constitution. The Constitution, like the era from which it came, is an object of almost religious adoration. There have been times, particularly during crises such as the Progressive Era and the Great Depression, when serious and loyal citizens, criticizing the Constitution as archaic and unworkable under modern conditions, have proposed drastic revision.[38] But these exceptions have been small and futile. Change, perhaps, but a new Constitution, no.

America has been a nation of Constitution-worshippers almost from the beginning.[39] "The laws and the Constitution of our government," declared a state judge in a charge to the jury in 1791, "ought

38. An effort to rewrite the Constitution (caused by contemporary crisis) has been undertaken by Rexford G. Tugwell and the Center for the Study of Democratic Institutions. See Tugwell, "Constitutional Reform: Let Law Catch Up with Life," *The Center Magazine,* vol. I, no. 2 (January 1968), pp. 50–54, and "Rewriting the Constitution," *The Center Magazine,* vol. I, no. 3 (March 1968), pp. 18–25; also, Scott Buchanan, "So Reason Can Rule: The Constitution Revisited," Occasional Paper of the Center for the Study of Democratic Institutions (Santa Barbara, Calif., 1967). The national director of the Congress of Racial Equality (CORE), speaking to the Platform Committee of the Republican Party Convention in 1968, held that the Constitution was never intended to apply to Negroes, that it offered no aid to ghetto problems, and that a new social contract was therefore needed.

39. For a good account of Constitution-worship in the late eighteenth century see Frank I. Schechter, "The Early History of the Tradition of the Constitution," *American Political Science Review,* 9 (1915), 707–34. For a biting and immodest account pervaded with theological terminology, see H. Von Holst, *The Constitutional and Political History of the United States* (Chicago, 1889), vol. 1, chap. 2, "The Worship of the Constitution and Its Real Character."

to be regarded with reverence. Man must have an idol. And our political idol ought to be our Constitution and laws. They, like the ark of the covenant among the Jews, ought to be sacred from all profane touch." [40] The same thought has continued to the present.[41] "Founding Fathers" itself is a phrase that in both expression and orthography connotes a sacredness. Led by the charismatic figure of George Washington, this group has exercised a constitutional control comparable to that of ancestral spirits in a primitive society.[42] An historian writing about that era has said: "The first function of the founders of nations, after founding itself, is to devise a set of true falsehoods about origins — a mythology — that will make it desirable for nationals to continue to live under common authority, and, indeed, make it impossible for them to entertain contrary thoughts." [43] One of the most important of these "true falsehoods" is the accepted story of the chaos and uselessness of the Confederation period. With the Founding Fathers, particularly Washington, providing a spiritual and physical link between the two heroic points, Revolution and Constitution, it has been relatively easy virtually to expunge the Articles of Confederation from historical memory as out of keeping with a sanctified era.[44] The Constitution has been accorded the status of the original, as well as the true, faith and fundamental law.

40. Quoted in Schechter, "Early History," p. 733.

41. Surely the most idolatrous expression in book length is *The Constitution of the United States: Yesterday, Today — and Tomorrow?* (New York: Doran, 1922), by James M. Beck, Solicitor General under Calvin Coolidge. The epigraph for the book, from Proverbs (xxii, 28), sets the tone: "Remove not the ancient Landmark, which thy fathers have set." A series of learned Sunday school sermons, the book's three hundred pages form a unique combination of anecdotes and piety with a pinch of unconsciously insightful metaphor and analysis. Today such expressions are briefer, though unchanged in tone: e.g., Irving Brant's "The written Constitution stands like a tablet on Mt. Sinai, reading 'This is the Law'" (*The Bill of Rights: Its Origin and Meaning* [Indianapolis: Bobbs-Merrill, 1965], p. 8); or a recent expression of Mormon doctrine, "We stand for the Constitution of the United States as having been divinely inspired" (*Deseret News* [Salt Lake City], July 1, 1968, p. 14).

42. For anthropological insights that are useful in understanding the social roles of the Constitution and the Supreme Court see the survey by Max Gluckman, *Politics, Law and Ritual in Tribal Society* (Chicago: Aldine, 1965).

43. Forrest McDonald, *E Pluribus Unum: The Formation of the American Republic, 1776–1790* (Boston: Houghton Mifflin, 1965), p. ix.

44. The deposing of the Articles began with the earliest postconstitutional history of the country, Jedidiah Morse, *The History of America in Two Books* (1790), in which the author simply "omitted the Confederation interlude, allowing his readers to believe that the Constitution came directly out of the revolution." Van Tassel, *Recording America's Past*, pp. 44–45. This view was reinforced a century later by John Fiske, *The Critical Period in American*

Several attributes have served to place the Constitution at the center of American political culture and have contributed to its conserving and stabilizing character. From the beginning the Constitution has emanated an aura both religious and legal. Among the Puritans the idea of a covenant represented religion and law simultaneously.[45] By the end of the eighteenth century a high regard for written constitutions was natural in a country concerned with religion, raised under colonial charters, and accustomed to expressing its political aims in legal language.[46] According to Daniel Boorstin, "The American Revolution could be framed in legal language because that language spoke for the literate community. The great issues of American politics, through the Civil War in the 19th century and the New Deal in the 20th would be cast in legal language — the sacred test of 'constitutionality' — precisely because Americans saw the revered legal framework as the skeleton on which the community had grown. In this use of a legal test for politics there was a kind of conserving narcissism not often found among non-primitive nations." [47]

Religion and law are supplemented by two other conservative forces associated with the Constitution, history and written permanence. Standing at the focal point of American history, the Constitution participates in all the respect accorded the era of the founders. It is the living evidence of the national heritage. The fact that the Constitution is a written document means that under it all change must be measured or rationalized against a text that itself does not change. This, in a society founded in an age of reason and brought up in an age of rational technology, is a difficult burden for an aging document to bear. But the advantages of a written constitution were

History (Boston: Houghton, 1888). In the early twentieth century James Beck was affected by the mythology: "A few wise and noble spirits, true Faithfuls and Great Hearts, led a despondent people out of the Slough of Despair until their feet were again on firm ground and their faces turned towards the Delectable Mountains of peace, justice, and liberty." *Constitution of the United States,* p. 21.

45. See Perry Miller, *The New England Mind: The Seventeenth Century* (Cambridge, Mass.: Harvard University Press, 1954), pp. 398–462.

46. In general see William C. Morey, "The Genesis of a Written Constitution," *Annals of the American Academy of Political and Social Science,* 1 (1890–91), 529–57; and Benjamin F. Wright, "The Early History of Written Constitutions in America," in *Essays in History and Political Theory in Honor of Charles Howard McIlwain* (Cambridge, Mass.: Harvard University Press, 1936), pp. 344–71.

47. *The Americans, The Colonial Experience* (New York: Random House, 1958), p. 205.

very early recognized. As Jefferson wrote: ". . . it is still certain that tho' written constitutions may be violated in moments of passion or delusion, yet they furnish a text to which those who are watchful may again rally and recall the people: they fix too for the people principles for their political creed." [48] The most "watchful" to whom the Constitution has furnished a text has been the Supreme Court. A written constitution provides the chief justification for the Court to "recall the people" and fix even more permanently the principles for their political creed.[49] Although it is ultimately the political success of the United States which has led to the veneration of the Constitution, and not the reverse, the Constitution itself has contributed to that success by serving as a central support for other institutions in the society.

The Constitution, then, is primarily a symbol, a symbol of national political cohesion. H. Stuart Hughes has written about the role of symbols in this sense: "Those of us who define our vision of history in terms of a retrospective cultural anthropology have stressed the central importance of symbols in establishing the common values of a given culture. These symbols may be of all types and degrees of specificity — religious, aesthetic, moral — yet they have in common their power to hold together heterogeneous manifestations of the human spirit whose inner connection people seldom express in logical form. The symbol conveys the implicit principles by which the society lives, the shared understanding of assumptions which require no formal proof." [50] If the Constitution does not fulfill its symbolic function, then all that is contained in its text about the distribution and limitation of powers and the rights and duties of citizens is unlikely to be respected. As the Supreme Court's handling of first-amendment history illustrates, constitutional text has no meaning without constitutional spirit. The most rationally oriented expounders

48. Letter to Joseph Priestly, June 19, 1802, in *Writings* (Ford ed.), VIII, 159–60.

49. Justice Black has declared that the absence of a written constitution was a source of British tyranny in the eighteenth century. See "The Bill of Rights," *New York University Law Review,* 35 (1960), 869. For similar thoughts *in extenso* see Edmond Cahn, "The Parchment Barriers," *American Scholar,* 32 (1962), 21–39. Unfortunately for these views, however, Great Britain, still without a written constitution, and almost all other countries, with one, demonstrate that there is no correlation between a written constitution and political prosperity. See, e.g., the essays in Arnold J. Zurcher (ed.), *Constitutions and Constitutional Trends since World War II* (New York: New York University Press, 1951).

50. *History as Art and as Science: Twin Vistas on the Past* (New York: Harper and Row, 1964), pp. 80–81.

of the American legal tradition have recognized this primary symbolic function of the Constitution.[51] Max Lerner has summed it up:
"Beyond all these [facts that have fed the Constitutional cult] there
is the human need for roots, which finds expression by clinging to
some strong symbol of allegiance." [52]

The Supreme Court is the living manifestation of the constitutional
symbol. According to Paul Freund, "We accept the Court as a
symbol in the measure that, while performing its appointed tasks,
it manages at the same time to articulate and rationalize the aspi-
rations reflected in the Constitution." [53] This uncolored language
explains accurately what the Court has done to account for its place
in American society. But the relation of the Court to the Constitution, like the symbolic role of the Constitution itself, has more often
been expressed in quasi-religious terms which are accurate at a
different level: "Since the Constitution is America's covenant, its
guardians are the keepers of the covenant and therefore touched
with its divinity. As the tenders of the sacred flame the justices of
the Supreme Court cannot help playing the role of a sacerdotal
group. By reason of its technical function every priesthood exercises
a political power: since they alone are privy to the mysteries on
which the destiny of the tribe depends, the priests must be consulted
on what is permissible and what is taboo in tribal policy." [54] Such
metaphor seems valid in the light of recent work in social anthro-

51. See Morris R. Cohen, *Law and the Social Order* (New York: Harcourt,
Brace, 1933), p. 202; Oliver Wendell Holmes, "John Marshall," in *Collected
Legal Papers* (New York: Harcourt, Brace and Howe, 1920), pp. 270–71; Justice
Brandeis concurring in Whitney v. California, 274 U.S. 357 (1927); and Justice
Frankfurter in the flag-salute cases, Minersville v. Gobitis, 310 U.S. 586 (1940)
(for the Court), and Board of Education v. Barnette, 319 U.S. 624, 646 (1943)
(dissent).

52. *America as a Civilization,* p. 442. See also the following essays written in
the mid-1930's to call attention to the fact that the symbolic power of the
Constitution was in danger of decaying and losing its capacity to promote
needed social change: Edward S. Corwin, "The Constitution as Instrument and
as Symbol," *American Political Science Review,* 30 (1936), 1071–85; W. Y.
Elliott, "The Constitution as the American Social Myth," in Conyers Read
(ed.), *The Constitution Reconsidered* (New York: Columbia University Press,
1938), pp. 209–24; and Max Lerner, "Constitution and Court as Symbols," *Yale
Law Journal,* 46 (1937), 1290–1319. On symbols in American political culture
generally see Carl N. Degler, *Out of Our Past: The Forces that Shaped Modern
America* (New York: Harper and Row, 1962), pp. 91–104, 367–86, 441–52.

53. *The Supreme Court of the United States* (Cleveland: World, 1961), p.
89.

54. Lerner, *America as a Civilization,* pp. 442–43. See similarly Henry Steele
Commager, "Democracy and Judicial Review," in his *Freedom and Order,* p.
12.

pology.[55] One might also compare the role of the Court to that of the elders of the Areopagus in Athenian society, or the nocturnal guardians in Plato's *Laws*.[56] For the many intelligent and sympathetic foreigners who find the worship of a legal document and respect for its interpreters beyond rational comprehension, Henry Steele Commager proposes institutional analogies: "Americans alone of western peoples made constitutionalism a religion and the judiciary a religious order and surrounded both with an aura of piety . . . The Supreme Court, in time, became the most nearly sacrosanct of American institutions — became to Americans what the Royal Family was to the British, the Army to the Germans, the Church to the Spaniards." [57]

Although the Constitution and the Court may be described in similar language drawn from various fields other than government, there is a crucial difference between the two. While the religion is almost beyond criticism, the priesthood is not. The Supreme Court and the justices, though not the Constitution, regularly undergo searching scrutiny by the legal profession and often scathing denunciation from politicians — from Thomas Jefferson, through Andrew Jackson and Franklin Roosevelt, to the Congresses of the 1950's and 1960's. In the words of a British observer who took a long-range view of these controversies and the American attitudes toward the Constitution and the Court, "At the first sound of a new argument over the United States Constitution and its interpretation the hearts of Americans leap with a fearful joy. The blood stirs powerfully in their veins and a new lustre brightens in their eyes. Like King Harry's men before Harfleur, they stand like greyhounds in the slips, straining upon the start." [58]

55. See Gluckman, *Politics, Law and Ritual in Tribal Society.*
56. Analogies dependent more on Freud than Frazer have been attempted, but less successfully. Jerome Frank, *Law and the Modern Mind* (New York: Coward-McCann, 1930), is the most extensive and influential. Frank saw in judges the universal need for a father-figure. One of the more modest statements of a recent article surveying this broad and marvelously indefinite field is that "once the assumption is made that the Supreme Court is an unconscious parent-symbol, then the emotional storm aroused by the court-packing plan [of 1937] no longer appears so inexplicable." C. G. Schoenfeld, "On the Relationship between Law and Unconscious Symbolism," *Louisiana Law Review* 26 (1965), 64. Max Lerner has said that the Constitution provides "womb-retreat" for Americans, especially for the lower middle class ("Constitution and Court as Symbols," p. 1316). An important general study is Franz Rudolf Bienenfeld, "Prologemena to a Psychoanalysis of Law and Justice," *California Law Review,* 53 (1965), 957–1028, 1254–1336.
57. *The American Mind* (New Haven: Yale University Press, 1950), p. 361.
58. Quoted from *The Economist,* May 10, 1952, p. 370, by Justice Frankfurter concurring in Youngstown v. Sawyer, 343 U.S. 579, 594 (1952).

Because the Supreme Court is both participant and referee in this most serious of national political pastimes, it must fortify itself with symbols of its own. Among these are certain physical trappings, such as the "marble palace" of the Court building, the elevated bench, and the sudden appearance, from behind a curtain, of men in black robes. Neither Congress nor the executive enjoys such impressive ritual.[59] The Court also profits from its own antiquity and from the mystery of the law in general. Most important, however, the Court invokes the principal political symbol of the country more consistently and intensively than does any other institution. It often seems to regard the Constitution as its own.[60]

The care and deference with which the Court treats the Constitution accounts for the continuous transfer of authority from the impersonal to the personal symbol of government. Through the Constitution the Court must satisfy the basic political desires of the nation. It must preserve constitutional continuity by mediating successfully between an unchanging Constitution and a changing world. Although the Court enunciates principles which are presumed to exist somewhere in the meaning of the written Constitution, it is never required to deal with the entire document — nor with the total political cohesion which it represents — at one time. Case by case the Supreme Court takes from the constitutional world individual phrases, clauses, doctrines, and traditions. It interprets, reinterprets, alters, and sometimes manhandles them. But then it replaces them;

59. William Howard Taft, who was closely attuned to the value of judicial folkways, remarked: "It is well that judges should be clothed in robes, not only that those who witness the administration of justice should be properly advised that the function performed is one different from, and higher, than that which a man discharges as a citizen in the ordinary walks of life; but also in order to impress the judge himself with constant consciousness that he is a high-priest in the temple of justice . . ." Quoted from a speech of 1908, in Alpheus Thomas Mason, *William Howard Taft: Chief Justice* (New York: Simon and Schuster, 1964), p. 58.

The relation of ritual to the functions and functioning of law was a topic much seized on by some legal realists, such as Jerome Frank. But the wider relation between ritual and society, discussed by anthropologists and a few gifted historians, such as Johann Huizinga (e.g., in *Homo Ludens*), presents a much more persuasive case and context for understanding the place of legal ceremony in social relations.

60. In addition to the literature on constitutional symbolism cited above, see Alpheus Thomas Mason, "Myth and Reality in Supreme Court Decisions," *Virginia Law Review*, 48 (1962), 1385–1406; Arthur Selwyn Miller, "Some Pervasive Myths about the United States Supreme Court," *St. Louis University Law Journal*, 10 (1965), 153–89; and Harry P. Stumpf, "The Political Efficacy of Judicial Symbolism," *Western Political Quarterly*, 19 (1966), 293–303.

and the constitutional world continues to revolve very much as before.[61] The Constitution is like a patchwork quilt in the care of the Supreme Court. The sources of the quilt are old; they are varied; and individual parts may be changed. But they are all made to fit together; the entity as a whole retains the same outward shape; and, above all, the function of keeping the body politic warm and secure continues to be fulfilled.

61. This process is similar to the "moving classification system" which Edward H. Levi proposes for describing evolution in the legal system as a whole. See *An Introduction to Legal Reasoning* (Chicago: University of Chicago Press, 1949), and "The Nature of Judicial Reasoning," in Sidney Hook (ed.), *Law and Philosophy* (New York: New York University Press, 1964), pp. 263–81.

CHAPTER X

CONSTITUTIONAL LAW AND

THE AMERICAN PAST

The Supreme Court performs two overlapping roles in American political life. The first is to maintain and enunciate a political-legal order through formal adjudication. The second is to preserve the social-political bonds of the nation. The legal function is in its nature exclusive to the judiciary. The social function is widely shared with other governmental and nongovernmental institutions. But both functions require the qualifying and mediating term "political" because the Court's overriding task, in both cases, is to provide constitutional — that is, political — continuity. Although there is no sound way of separating the Court's legal and social roles according to kinds of cases in constitutional law (and most cases exhibit both roles simultaneously), the distinction between the legal and the social functions of the Court is of considerable aid in understanding the Supreme Court's uses of history.

In performing its legal function the Court uses history as one of several vehicles of adjudication. Along with the constitutional text, constitutional doctrine, precedent, and social facts, history is a category of legal reasoning which contributes first to deciding a case and then to explaining the decision in an opinion. In this role history is either internal to the law, taking the form of precedent and legal history, or external to the law in the form of general history. It is in the area of general history that the Court's legal function meets its most intractable problems, those of constitutional intent and constitutional change. In the first case study presented above, the mortgage moratorium case, these problems were central to the issue before the Court. They took the forms of the two basic types of general history, the intent of the framers and ongoing history since that time. In each of the succeeding case studies the Court has similarly sought the support of these two types of history. History as intent is the more strictly legal form of history because its use is an attempt to determine the meaning of the Constitution today on the basis of the meaning given to it by the people who adopted it. This explanation of the use of history as intent points out the chief defect of the approach, that the Constitution is no longer the instrument of the framers' government, but of our own. It is for this reason that ongoing history, through which the Constitution can adapt to changing circumstances and serve contemporary Americans, has developed as a second principle of adjudication using historical materials.

Within its limited range, there are several varieties of history as intent. The most obvious of these is the reliance on the Philadelphia Convention of 1787 and the Congresses which have proposed constitutional amendments since that time. The apportionment cases and the sit-in case used this form of history as intent. The state ratifying conventions were used in the congressional apportionment case. *The Federalist*, the principal contemporaneous commentary, was referred to in all cases in which the original constitutional text was under discussion. In the mortgage moratorium case the "history of the times" explained the original meaning of the contract clause. In the case on the presidential removal power, the First Congress was treated as if it were a second session of the Constitutional Convention. The Court considered the entire seventeenth- and eighteenth-century background of freedom of speech and press in determining the meaning of the first amendment. Under every guise the words of the leading founders contributed to the intent history used by the Supreme Court.

The forms of ongoing history are more various than those of intent history. There are four distinguishable types. The first is closely related to history as intent, stating with John Marshall that the Constitution was "intended to endure for ages to come." [1] Carried to the extreme, this notion of intent makes specific intent history needless in constitutional interpretation. But no matter how understood, it permits the Court to argue that the framers intended that the Constitution was designed to meet changing circumstances. Ongoing history is thus sanctioned by intent history. This was the argument of the Court majority in the mortgage moratorium case, and of a unanimous Court in the case which applied freedom of expression to picketing in labor disputes. This use of ongoing

1. McCulloch v. Maryland, 4 Wheat. 316, 415 (1819).

history, since the framers "intended" that it be used, is the most satisfying justification of the use of history from both the legal and social views of the Supreme Court's function. Under this theory the Constitution can stand still at the same time that it moves forward — a fair description of what actually happens.

The two-clause theories of constitutional intent are a refinement of the theory of adaptation-by-intent. They permit the Court to restrict some provisions of the Constitution to an historically determined meaning and to expand other provisions to acquire contemporary meaning. Which clauses are "open" and which "closed" to development depends upon either the intent of the framers or the historical or linguistic specificity of the constitutional text. None of the two-clause theories based on history (in contrast to those based on the constitutional text) was explicitly relied on in the case studies. But the dissenters in the mortgage moratorium case certainly believed that the contract clause was limited by its history, and Justice Goldberg concurring in the sit-in cases adopted the argument of Alexander Bickel and proposed that the equal protection clause was not limited by its history.

The second use of ongoing history by the Court is the most common: an historical essay that traces a constitutional issue over a span of years. This use is the clearest example of viewing history as process rather than event, and of viewing law in terms of evolution and development rather than immanent meaning. Although the history they trace has a relatively static meaning, Justice Brandeis dissenting in the presidential removal power case and Justice Frankfurter dissenting in the apportionment case wrote scholarly essays typical of this use of ongoing history.

The third and fourth varieties of ongoing history depart, in different ways, from traditional conceptions of history. One depicts the American past in the boldest strokes, citing a few important men, events, or documents as representative of the true spirit of the Constitution. This was the approach of Chief Justice Warren and Justice Douglas in the apportionment cases and, in a completely different setting, of Justice Black in the free expression cases. The final variety of ongoing history looks backward from the present instead of forward from the past. It is not interested in where we came from but in "what this country has become." [2] Contemporary

2. Justice Holmes for the Court in Missouri v. Holland, 252 U.S. 416, 434 (1920).

evidence fortifies ongoing history as a principle of adjudication. In the cases discussed, this was the view of the past taken by Justice Goldberg in the sit-ins after he had presented his argument from constitutional intent. It was the chief argument of the Court, as Justice Goldberg pointed out, in the original school desegregation decisions.

A classification of the Court's uses of history such as the one just presented shows how history is used, but, except to explain its relation to the legal problems of constitutional intent and change, it does not explain *why* history is used. For this, one must turn from the legal-political function to the social-political function of the Court. From the viewpoints of the lawyer and the historical or legal scholar, the use of history in support of the social-political function of the Court is a bothersome phenomenon. The lawyer who uses history does not "need" it as an historian does; he only "needs" to win his case. The lawyer's use of history, states a federal judge flatly, "is entirely pragmatic or instrumental. His history may be fiction, from the standpoint of a scholarly historian, but if it produces victory, it has served its purpose." [3] The scholar, on the other hand, is only marginally concerned with the outcome of cases. His standard is historical truth, and his interest, therefore, is in the reasoning of the Court. The impression left by the scholars' articles is that the Court should either write only accurate history or give up the practice entirely.

In contrast to these outlooks, the world of the judge in a constitutional case is that of neither advocacy nor scholarship. It is, in the highest sense of the word, politics. The judge is not trained as an historian nor does he believe that the adversary process, the best that we have for resolving disputes at law, necessarily yields historical truth. In any event, that is not principally what he is looking for. His job is to decide cases and explain his decision. Further, although Supreme Court opinions certainly advocate, their chief purpose is to convince the public, not legal or scholarly superiors. The justices, in short, are bound to neither courtroom nor classroom. Their world is the public world of the Constitution, where the people (who are

3. Edward Dumbauld, "The Lawyer's Use of Historical Materials" (a paper delivered to the Southern Historical Association on Nov. 8, 1963), p. 2. One of the country's most able and experienced practicing constitutional lawyers, however, advises his colleagues that history "must be both accurate and reliable." Frederick Bernays Wiener, *Briefing and Arguing Federal Appeals* (Washington: BNA, Inc., 1961), p. 186.

not lawyers) are less concerned with individual cases and their reasoning than with constitutional trends and their impact on national life; and where the people (who are not historians) are less concerned with the literal intent of the framers or the accuracy of subsequent history than with the constitutional significance of the past for the present.[4] For most Americans the Court acts as constitutional symbol, as conscience, educator, legitimizer, and guardian of the nation's political values. In these roles history becomes a value or a means of transmitting values. It is not a mere instrument of decision, as the lawyers would have it, nor is it a research project, as the historians sometimes view it.

The transmission of the American heritage, history as well as political values, is not entrusted to any one institution, and the Court is less directly important in this than, for instance, the schools. But the Court is the only public and official institution consciously and continuously concerned with relating past, present, and future in American life. It is expected to develop the values of society by looking both to origins and to ends and by applying the lesson of one and the vision of the other to contemporary situations. Because of the American attitude towards the era of the Founding Fathers, both origins and ends may be supplied by history as intent. As the story of origins, the era of the Founding Fathers provides important legal values for constitutional interpretation. This is demonstrated on the one hand by the practice of referring to the framers' intentions for specific provisions of the Constitution, and on the other hand by accepting the ratification of the Constitution as the literal evidence of popular sovereignty and as the indirect sanction by the people of the legitimacy of judicial review. As the story of ends, the era of the Founding Fathers provides important social and symbolic values for constitutional law. The Court regularly refers to this aspect of intent history in explaining or refashioning the principles for which the nation stands.

4. For those who are especially backward-looking or legal-minded, Court opinions can make particularly painful reading. Among conservative writings for the layman, see L. Brent Bozell, *The Warren Revolution: Reflections on the Consensus Society* (New Rochelle, N.Y.: Arlington House, 1966), e.g., pp. 41–54; Lyman A. Garber, *Of Men and Not of Law: How the Courts Are Usurping the Political Function* (New York: Devin-Adair, 1966), e.g., pp. 102, 103, 147; and the publications of the Virginia Commission on Constitutional Government, especially "The Supreme Court of the United States, A Review of the 1964 Term," pp. 1, 3, 7, 15, 25, 56–59.

The two roles of intent history, legal and social, are linked by ongoing history. History as intent represents the extreme terms in the two expressions describing the functions of the Court: legal-political and political-social. Ongoing history represents the middle term. Ongoing history is more constructively political than either aspect of intent history. It is the means of relating past to future and legal values to social values. Ongoing history ultimately insures constitutional continuity.

Justice Brandeis is the outstanding example of a jurist keenly aware of the legal and social functions of the Court, and therefore of the political role that mediates them. At the same time, Justice Brandeis viewed the Court as a teacher to the nation of both scholarly and moral truths. His use of history served all of these purposes. In his dissenting opinion in the *Myers* case, where the practices of the executive removal power are traced from the eighteenth century to the present, Justice Brandeis was concerned with the legal function of the Court and used history to educate in an academic fashion.[5] In his concurring opinion in the *Whitney* case, where he voiced a contemporary philosophy of free expression through the mouths of the Founding Fathers, he was concerned with the social function of the Court and used history to educate in political morality.[6]

The use of history by Justice Brandeis is a reminder, but no guarantee, that history can be used successfully. The chief guides to this success must be the correspondence of the Court's history to reality, insofar as this can be determined, and, at the same time, its demonstrated relevance to the issues involved in the case. Yet Justice Brandeis, who valued certainty in the law, might have agreed with the statement of the leading twentieth-century British legal historian, "For certainty in the law a little bad history is not too high a price to pay."[7] And he might have agreed that for the

5. For a law clerk's recollections of how such an historical essay was fashioned see Dean Acheson, *Morning and Noon* (Boston: Houghton Mifflin, 1965), p. 86. Mark DeWolfe Howe has suggested that Justice Brandeis "played a large part in making elaborate historical investigation an instrument of decision" on the Court. "Split Decisions," *New York Review of Books,* July 1, 1965, p. 16.

6. In viewing the Supreme Court as educator, Justice Brandeis was following the intent of the framers and the earliest practices of the national judiciary. See Ralph Lerner, "The Supreme Court as Republican Schoolmaster," *Supreme Court Review* (1967), 127–80.

7. William Holdsworth, *Essays in Law and History* (Oxford: Clarendon Press, 1946), p. 24.

progress of the law some bad history may even be necessary.[8] But how bad a history? And how much of it? The world of the judge is relatively unrestrained with respect to the use of history, compared to the worlds of the lawyer and the historian. Lawyers may lose poorly presented cases. But judges win them all. Historians rise and fall in their open society on the basis of the quality of their work. Judges can exercise their power to the very limits of irresponsibility. Sanctions against judges for poor opinions, and therefore for the poor use of history, are basically a matter of individual standards and sensitivity to colleagues and critics.[9] Nevertheless, the Supreme Court as a whole cannot indulge in historical fabrication without thereby appearing to approve the deterioration of truth as a criterion for communication in public affairs. On this point Sidney Hook has written: "To the extent that dignity and honesty in the conduct of human affairs rest on the belief in [historical] objectivity, reflection on it goes to the very heart of the question concerning the nature and possibility of liberal civilization . . . There is a difference between using our knowledge of the history of the past in order to influence the future, to help bring about events we regard desirable and to forestall those which are undesirable, and making or manufacturing a history of the past solely with an eye to achieve our aims." [10] It does make a difference if Supreme Court history is false.

When the Court's history is wrong, however, this is seldom due to a simple misstatement of verifiable fact. Rather, the Court's history is misleading in its interpretation. In Macaulay's expression,

8. See, e.g., Philip B. Kurland, "Magna Carta and Constitutionalism in the United States: 'The Noble Lie,'" in Samuel E. Thorne, et al., *The Great Charter* (New York: Random House, 1965), pp. 48–74.

9. A composite of the societies studied by an anthropologist suggests that where there is an oral tradition there is likely to be a group of men whose special duty it is to preserve the official history of the tribe. The considerable political power enjoyed by this group derives almost solely from the fact that its members can accurately recite the tribe's cherished traditions, and they may be punished and rewarded according to their performance. Jan Vansina, *Oral Tradition: A Study in Historical Methodology* (Chicago: Aldine, 1965), esp. pp. 15, 33, 79–80.

10. "Objectivity and Reconstruction in History," in Hook (ed.), *Philosophy and History* (New York: New York University Press, 1963), pp. 257, 255. The same thoughts, applied to the Supreme Court's use of history, appear throughout Mark DeWolfe Howe, *The Garden and the Wilderness: Religion and Government in American Constitutional History* (Chicago: University of Chicago Press, 1965); and Alfred H. Kelly, "Clio and the Court: An Illicit Love Affair," *Supreme Court Review* (1965), 119–58.

"A history in which every particular incident may be true may on the whole be false." [11] This describes Chief Justice Taft's opinion in the postmaster removal case, Justice Goldberg's opinion in the sit-in case, and Justice Black's opinion in the reapportionment case. What makes these opinions more vulnerable than any Macaulay had in mind, however, is that they appear on the record alongside a contrary interpretation of the same facts.[12] Although this is perhaps the unseemly price of the valuable practice of dissenting opinions, it points out clearly that the plainer the historical record and the more significant the historical argument to the reasoning of the justices, the higher the price of historical abuse.

It cannot successfully be demanded that only perfect history should be permitted in the *United States Reports*. But the imperfections which are bound to exist due to incomplete scholarship or permissible latitude of interpretation can be reduced if two basic facts are recognized. First, history may be distinguished from other principles of adjudication by its effects upon the public. Abuse of the constitutional text is a matter of interest chiefly to scholars and semanticists. The distortion of precedent is the concern particularly of lawyers. Disagreement over contemporary social evidence is expected, but it is limited to experts as far as the law is concerned. History, however, belongs to the public memory. Its use and misuse affects the political values of the nation. This is especially so when it is the Supreme Court that is declaring the meaning of the past, for it speaks with special public authority. This is to say again that where it matters most to society, it matters most that the story be a true one. "I appeal to the [historical] record," argued Senator Pepper unsuccessfully in the postmaster removal case, "because when this great tribunal declares the law we all bow to it; but history remains history, in spite of judicial utterances upon the subject." [13] The second point to be considered in improving the Supreme Court's use of the past is that the historical story can be a true one without being destructive of the Court's opinion. The argument of Chief

11. "History," in *Critical, Historical and Miscellaneous Essays and Poems* (3 vols.; Philadelphia: David McKay, n.d.), I, 304.

12. For an excellent study of this practice in one field of constitutional law see John Roche, "The Expatriation Cases: 'Breathes there the Man, with Soul so Dead . . . ?'" *Supreme Court Review* (1963), 325–56. Roche discovered the development of a history and an "anti-history," both equally distorting the historical record in order to support contradictory ideologies of expatriation, and both appearing in all recent litigation on the issue.

13. Myers v. United States, 272 U.S. 52, 70 (1926).

Justice Hughes in the mortgage moratorium case, although it has not often been emulated, is the only honorable way out of the legal trap which the intent theory of constitutional interpretation imposes on the Court. It may be said plainly, as Hughes said it, that loyalty to the purpose of the Constitution does not require strict adherence to its words as put down in the eighteenth century. In situations where the historical record is more ambiguous than it was in the matter of the contract clause, it is easier to state, as Justice Brennan did in a concurring opinion, that "an awareness of history and an appreciation of the aims of the Founding Fathers do not always resolve concrete problems." [14] But this is done as seldom where it is painless as where it is not.

If the Supreme Court recognizes that the Constitution need not be interpreted solely in the light of its history, and if the history that is employed is substantially in accord with the views of disinterested scholars, then the Court has overcome two of the most significant drawbacks to the use of history in constitutional law. An important problem remains, however: a standard of relevance. Yet while it would be highly desirable to suggest general criteria for determining the relevance of history to the subject matter of a case, for several reasons the exercise is not a very fruitful one. At the outset one must acknowledge that relevance is in the mind of the opinion-writer, is very much determined by the outcome he wishes to reach, and is related to the particular political and legal audience of the case. The fundamental subjectivism of the first fact and the particularism of the second and third cloud the entire endeavor of attempting to formulate general criteria of relevance.

Several other considerations concerning historical relevance in constitutional adjudication must also be borne in mind. First, once one justice makes an historical assertion in a draft opinion, it may be challenged in detail by another justice, forcing an equally detailed, though originally unintended, reply. What might have gone unnoticed in its initial form becomes a central point of contention. What looks irrelevant from outside the Court has a human logic inside the Court that will not be halted by the advice of critics.[15]

14. Abington School District v. Schempp, 374 U.S. 203, 234 (1963). Justice Brennan's opinion is an unusual and sensitive attempt to explain why history should — and then to demonstrate how history can — be treated with respect yet without obeisance.

15. This explanation for the use of history is a possibility in the sit-in cases. See above, Chapter VI, note 42.

Next, one might suppose that, as with other principles of adjudication, judges utilize history in their opinions when it reasonably serves the purpose of arriving at the outcome desired. If this were the basic standard, we would expect to see history relied on whenever a strong support could be constructed from it, and ignored when the contrary was the case. The facts, however, show that some justices utilize historical material when it adds almost nothing to, or even detracts from, the opinion in the minds of outside observers, while others ignore history even when it might prove a great aid to the decision. Some judges simply are history-minded and others are not.[16] It is difficult to imagine that criticism as to historical relevance will much affect the basic temperament of mature men in this respect.

Finally, apart from the justices as persons, it is very difficult to label in advance particular types of history as relevant or irrelevant to judicial decisions. Ongoing history, because it eventually merges into contemporary experience, has about it a living authenticity that should almost always keep it from being irrelevant. It is a matter of historical continuity. Yet even in the hands of Justice Frankfurter, its master, ongoing history showed its limits when it could not meet the issue of the permanently malapportioned legislature. On the other side, it might be said that history as intent, so long as it is not binding, is always relevant since it imparts an original meaning to the Constitution. But the more apropos this history is to the current controversy in terms of subject matter, the more difficult it will be to claim it is not binding. Justice Sutherland's history of the contract clause was both correct and, as much as history could be, directly to the point. Chief Justice Hughes acknowledged this and went on to decide the case by other principles. Yet it cannot be asserted in advance that such intent history is an irrelevant consideration simply because it should not by itself carry the day. The equal relevance of Hughes's ongoing and Sutherland's intent history, in fact, is what gives the *Blaisdell* case its classic dimensions and forces

16. It has been claimed that Horace Gray, who sat on the Court from 1881 to 1902, was "the most history-centered, his reasoning taking place more through the historical or chronological process than did that of any other member of the high court" — including Story, Holmes, and Frankfurter. Robert Spector, "Legal Historian on the United States Supreme Court: Justice Horace Gray, Jr., and the Historical Method," *American Journal of Legal History*, 12 (1968), 181. Further studies of individual justices' ways with history, based on both their opinions and their biographies, would certainly contribute to an understanding of the use of history by the Court as an institution.

its readers to recognize that problems of history are inherent in constitutional law. The "gap in history" discussed in connection with the fourteenth amendment suggests a final difficulty to proposing standards for historical relevance in constitutional law. If constitutional law is evolving law, it might appear most irrelevant of all to attempt to leapfrog a settled pattern of decisions on the ground of newly discovered historical error at the outset. But such throwbacks may offer just the insight that history can provide for constitutional adjudication. Whichever way one turns, there is no sure guide for establishing in advance of the particular issue which history, if any at all, can be helpful in determining and justifying a constitutional decision.

In the discussion of truth and relevance as basic to the proper use of history by the Supreme Court, the issue of the Court's freedom from the control of the past has been raised at several points. This freedom must underlie any use of history in constitutional law. As Paul Freund has written: "Of history it may be said briefly that its usefulness varies inversely with the weight of the demands made upon it." [17] Yet not to be bound or weighed down by the past does not mean to ignore it. In the formulation of a philosopher who never concerned himself with the American Constitution: "We must know the right time to forget as well as the right time to remember and instinctively see when it is necessary to feel historically and when unhistorically . . . The unhistorical and the historical are equally necessary to the health of an individual, a community, and a system of culture." [18] The health of constitutional law depends on the same recognition.

Justice Holmes, who knew the most legal history but seldom employed it on the Court, began with the premise that "the present has a right to govern itself so far as it can." [19] But he agreed that it was inevitable that the past should govern the living to a considerable extent. The reason was not a matter of legal theory but simply the fact that we are the products of our experience. "The past," Holmes

17. *On Law and Justice* (Cambridge, Mass.: Harvard University Press, 1968), p. 68.

18. Friedrich Nietzsche, *The Use and Abuse of History* (New York: Liberal Arts Press, 1957), p. 8. Nietzsche's classification of the uses of history and his discussion of the values and dangers of each make this one of his most sound and appealing essays.

19. *Collected Legal Papers* (New York: Harcourt, Brace and Howe, 1920), p. 139.

said, "gives us our vocabulary and fixes the limits of our imagination." [20] The value of a thorough knowledge of history, he believed, was that it "sets us free and enables us to make up our own minds dispassionately" whether to enforce an old law that no longer serves a legitimate social purpose; "its chief good is to burst inflated expectations." [21] There is another side to the use of history, however, one emphasized by Holmes's followers after the apparent success of the earlier campaign to free the present from the past. This is the use of history to free the present from itself. History, as Jerome Frank wrote, "liberates from the fetters of the present, for it suggests that there were other ways of doing things than those we now employ." [22] We may benefit from the thoughts and experience of others who faced similar problems, regardless of when they lived.

In neither case — liberation from the past or from the present — is history a binding force. Justices of the Supreme Court are ultimately bound only by contemporary wisdom, perhaps largely their own, and it is against this that the decisions and the reasoning of the Court must be measured. Holmes looked forward, he said, "to a time when the part played by history in the explanation of dogma shall be very small, and instead of ingenious research we shall spend our energy on a study of the ends sought to be attained and the reasons for desiring them." [23] History, in short, would yield to philosophy.[24]

But history could not yield all the way. As much as a justice's philosophic outlook is a chief determinant of his vote, philosophy

20. *Ibid.*
21. *Ibid.*, p. 225.
22. *Fate and Freedom* (New York: Simon and Schuster, 1945), p. 32. Compare Morris R. Cohen, *The Meaning of Human History* (La Salle, Ill.: Open Court, 1947), p. 291.
23. *Collected Legal Papers*, p. 195.
24. This is the point of Paul Freund's gentle criticism of the use of history by the Court's most avid Holmesian. "Mr. Justice Frankfurter," in Wallace Mendelson (ed.), *Felix Frankfurter: A Tribute* (New York: Reynal, 1964), pp. 160–61. See also the works of Charles P. Curtis, who knew Holmes and his position well, battled unceasingly against the use of history in constitutional law and the intent theory of constitutional interpretation, and called on the Court to articulate a contemporary philosophy for the country in its constitutional adjudication. *Lions Under the Throne* (Boston: Houghton Mifflin, 1947); *It's Your Law* (Cambridge, Mass.: Harvard University Press, 1954); *Law as Large as Life: A Natural Law for Today and the Supreme Court as Its Prophet* (New York: Simon and Schuster, 1959).

itself is neither free from the past nor a substitute for historical materials in the explanation of a decision. Of all people who respected Holmes as a thinker, Morris Cohen gave the most attention and the soundest advice on the relations among law, history, and philosophy. Law, he insisted, was a means, not an end, and the end is a "just life between living human beings here and now." [25] While history alone "cannot establish standards of value or of what is desirable in law," a knowledge of history is necessary for the adequate solution of moral problems.[26] When this knowledge enters the process of adjudication in constitutional law, it is the task of the Supreme Court to show that it illumines but does not blind the path to a solution to the problems of today.

25. *Law and the Social Order* (New York: Harcourt, Brace, 1933), p. 34.
26. *Ibid.*, p. 191; also, *The Meaning of Human History*, p. 291; see in general Cohen, *Reason and Nature* (Glencoe, Ill.: The Free Press, 1953), pp. 369–85.

APPENDIX, SELECTED BIBLIOGRAPHY, INDEXES

APPENDIX

THE FIRST CONGRESS AND THE PRESIDENTIAL

REMOVAL POWER: VOTING PATTERNS IN THE

HOUSE OF REPRESENTATIVES, JUNE 1789

(*This appendix accompanies the argument in the text, pp. 61–64.*)

In deciding Myers v. United States, the case which granted the President extensive power to remove executive officers, the Supreme Court relied in large part on the "decision of 1789" of the First Congress.[1] In establishing the department of foreign affairs in that year, Congress provided that the chief clerk of the department would be responsible for the official records "whenever the . . . principal officer shall be removed from office by the President of the United States." From the proceedings of Congress in 1789, Chief Justice Taft, in his opinion for the Court, intended to prove that the meaning of the decision of the First Congress was that the legislators recognized the inherent constitutional right of the President to remove the secretary of foreign affairs without first obtaining the consent of the Senate.

An exact analysis of the debates in the House of Representatives regarding the "decision of 1789" is not possible. A variety of opinions were expressed not only by the membership as a whole but by individual Congressmen.[2] Since less than half the members spoke in debate, any inferences from the complex patterns presented by the three roll-call votes taken during the House's consideration of the bill are matters of conjecture. But informed conjecture still illuminates the basic dispute over the true meaning of the action of Congress. This appendix presents in tabular form several descriptions of the voting of the House of Representatives in the debate over the establishment of the department of foreign affairs in June 1789.

1. 272 U.S. 52 (1926).
2. Edward S. Corwin, "Tenure of Office and the Removal Power under the Constitution," *Columbia Law Review*, 27 (1927), 361–62, gives several examples of this.

In his *Myers* decision Chief Justice Taft classified only those Congressmen who both participated in debate and voted on the final passage of the bill. The following tabulation, based on the Taft opinion, shows that by this classification the decision of 1789 was a victory for the group led by James Madison, those who thought the Constitution vested the removal power in the President alone.[3]

25 Congressmen were classified by Chief Justice Taft.

14 of them voted for the amended bill (Madison's group).

11 voted against it. Of these, 8 thought the removal power lay in the President with the consent of the Senate; 2 thought removal was possible only by impeachment; and for 1 no reason is given.

Justice McReynolds, dissenting in the case, also classified only those Congressmen who participated in debate. He arranged them, however, not by how they voted on the final passage of the bill, but according to how they viewed the removal power in the debate over the bill. The following tabulation shows that Madison's group, by this classification, was in the minority.[4]

24 Congressmen were classified by Justice McReynolds.

16 of them were Constitutionalists. Of these, 9 thought the Constitution vested the removal power in the President alone (Madison's group), and 7 thought the Constitution vested the power elsewhere.

8 of them were Congressionalists. Of these, 3 thought that Congress should say nothing, and 5 thought that Congress should vest the removal power elsewhere.

The classification in Justice Brandeis' dissenting opinion is based on the same data Justice McReynolds employed, but it is a more refined representation of how the Congressmen viewed the removal power of the President. It likewise supports the conclusion that Madison's group was a minority, consisting, in fact, of only one quarter of those participating in debate.[5]

24 Congressmen were classified by Justice Brandeis.

13 were Constitutionalists. Of these, 6 thought the removal power

3. 272 U.S. at 126.
4. The tabulation is drawn from 272 U.S. at 194.
5. The tabulation is drawn from 272 U.S. at 284–85.

lay in the President alone (Madison's group); 5 thought the power lay in the President with the consent of the Senate; and 2 thought removal was possible only by impeachment.
7 were Congressionalists.
4 were unclassifiable. Of these, 1 favored the power in the President but did not distinguish between a legislative and a constitutional grant.

Edward Corwin, who published an exhaustive assault on the *Myers* decision six months after it was handed down, offered two classifications, both designed to show that Chief Justice Taft and the Court majority had erred in claiming that Madison's group represented the true sentiment of the House of Representatives. Corwin admits that some members of Congress are difficult to classify and, in fact, disagrees with Justice Brandeis in at least three cases (Sherman, Huntington, and Ames). Corwin's first classification is comparable to those of Justices McReynolds and Brandeis.[6] The different totals of speakers are probably explainable by the use of various criteria of relevance applied to the speaker, or by including the earlier perfunctory debate when the bill was first proposed in May 1789, or simply by miscounting in the examination of the voluminous record.

27 Congressmen were classified by Corwin.
20 were Constitutionalists. Of these, 10 thought the removal power lay in the President alone (Madison's group); 7 thought the power lay in the President with the consent of the Senate; and 3 thought removal was possible only by impeachment.
7 were Congressionalists.

This tabulation, like those drawn from the dissents of Justices McReynolds and Brandeis, shows clearly that the House was split roughly in thirds among Presidential Constitutionalists (Madison's group), Senatorial Constitutionalists, and Congressionalists. In addition, there were two or three impeachment Constitutionalists.

But Corwin's study goes further. He proposes that from the roll-call votes taken in the House a logical classification can be constructed, independent of whether or how Congressmen expressed themselves in debate. While Corwin's information is not originally presented in tabular form, and his footnote from which the figures

6. Corwin, "Tenure of Office," 361.

are drawn is not completely clear on several of the individual votes, Table 1 appears to represent his intention.[7] The descriptions at the right in the table are the only logically consistent political positions that can be held on the basis of the voting combinations presented at the left. Vote 1 is for the addition to the bill of "Whenever [he] shall be removed." Vote 2 is for the deletion from the bill of "removable by the President." The two motions, sponsored by the Presidential Constitutionalists (Madison's group), resulted in incorporating that group's views into the final act by splitting the opposition. In Vote 1 the Congressionalists and in Vote 2 the Senatorial Constitutionalists voted "yes" with Madison's Presidential Constitutionalists. In this way the "yes" vote won in both cases, although those who voted "yes" both times did not amount to a majority in either one of the two votes.

Table 1

Vote 1	Vote 2	Number in both votes	Classification
Yes	Yes	16	Presidential Constitutionalists
No	Yes	15	Senatorial Constitutionalists
No	No	2	Impeachment Constitutionalists
Yes	No	15	Congressionalists

The technique of voting classification can be carried one step further, however, since there were three roll-call votes in the House, the final one a vote for the passage of the bill as amended. Mathematically there are eight possible combinations of "yes" and "no" ballots over the three votes. In Table 2, where these are listed, the classification of Congressmen is determined, as in the previous table, by the voting records in Vote 1 and Vote 2. Madison's group voted "yes" in all three votes. (A recount from the roll-call listing shows that the number of Congressmen of the first two lines of Table 1, representing Corwin's classification, should be reversed.[8] This, in addition to depriving Madison's group of one vote from Corwin's figures, explains why the Senatorial Constitutionalists have more votes in Table 2 than in Table 1. Other groups have fewer votes

7. *Ibid.*
8. *Annals of the Congress of the United States* (Washington: Gales and Seaton, 1834), I, 580, 585.

in Table 2 because not every Congressman who participated in Vote 3 had participated in Votes 1 and 2.[9])

Table 2

Vote 1	Vote 2	Vote 3	*Number in all three votes*	Classification
Yes	Yes	Yes	13	Presidential Constitutionalists
Yes	Yes	No	1	
No	Yes	No	16	Senatorial Constitutionalists
No	Yes	Yes	0	
No	No	Yes	1	Impeachment Constitutionalists
No	No	No	1	
Yes	No	Yes	10	Congressionalists
Yes	No	No	2	

In view of the fact that fewer than half the members of the House spoke during the debate, that those who did speak typically offered several grounds for their beliefs, that some men very likely changed their minds during the course of the debate, and that a few might have been confused by either the arguments or the parliamentary tactics and so could offer no rational explanation for their voting patterns, these figures are probably as close as one can approach the "truth" of the decision of 1789. This truth, needless to say, does not correspond with the claim of the opinion of the Court in the *Myers* case. If Madison is accepted as the leader of the Presidential Constitutionalists, then his loyal followers, at least in terms of the voting record, numbered only 13 of the 44 members of the House who cast three ballots. This fraction, which does not even represent a plurality, is less than one third. If one uses as the denominator the 53 members who participated in any of the three votes, or the 54 who participated in the non-roll-call vote at the beginning of the debate over the bill (and hence were interested enough to be present at some of the discussion), or the complete membership of the House of Representatives at the time, 59, then the fraction supporting the views of Madison — and the Court majority in *Myers* — is reduced to less than one fourth.

9. Information for Vote 3 comes from *Annals*, I, 591.

The Chief Justice wrote for the Court in Myers v. United States: "[Madison's] arguments in support of the President's constitutional power of removal independently of Congressional provision, and without the consent of the Senate, were masterly, and he carried the House." [10] Yes, Madison's arguments were masterly — but his politics were even more so. It was Madison's votes, not his views, that carried the House and account for the "decision of 1789."

10. 272 U.S. at 115.

SELECTED BIBLIOGRAPHY

Aiken, Charles. "*Stare Decisis*, Precedent, and the Constitution," *Western Political Quarterly*, 9 (1956), 87–92.

Anastaplo, George. Book review of Leonard Levy, *Freedom of Speech and Press in Early American History*, in *New York University Law Review*, 39 (1964), 735–41.

Anderson, William. "The Intention of the Framers: A Note on Constitutional Interpretation," *American Political Science Review*, 49 (1955), 340–52.

Arendt, Hannah. *Between Past and Future: Six Exercises in Political Thought*. New York: Viking, 1961.

Bailey, Thomas A. "The Mythmakers of American History," *Journal of American History*, 55 (1968), 5–21.

Beard, Charles A. "Historiography and the Constitution," in Conyers Read (ed.), *The Constitution Reconsidered*, pp. 159–66. New York: Columbia University Press, 1938.

Becker, Carl. "Afterthoughts on Constitutions," in Conyers Read (ed.), *The Constitution Reconsidered*, pp. 387–97. New York: Columbia University Press, 1938.

Becker, Theodore L. *Political Behavioralism and Modern Jurisprudence: A Working Theory and Study in Judicial Decision-Making*. Chicago: Rand McNally, 1964.

Bickel, Alexander M. "Is the Warren Court Too 'Political?'" *New York Times Magazine*, Sept. 25, 1966, p. 30.

———— "The Original Understanding and the Segregation Decision," *Harvard Law Review*, 69 (1955), 1–65.

———— "The Passive Virtues," *Harvard Law Review*, 75 (1961), 40–79.

———— *Politics and the Warren Court*. New York: Harper and Row, 1965.

Bischoff, Ralph F. "The Role of Official Precedents," in Edmond Cahn (ed.), *Supreme Court and Supreme Law*, pp. 76–83. Bloomington: Indiana University Press, 1954.

Black, Hugo L. "The Bill of Rights," *New York University Law Review*, 35 (1960), 865–81.

Blawie, James L. and Marilyn J. "The Judicial Decision: A Second Look at Certain Assumptions of Behavioral Research," *Western Political Quarterly*, 18 (1965), 579–93.

Boorstin, Daniel J. *The Genius of American Politics*. Chicago: University of Chicago Press, 1953.

———— *The Mysterious Science of the Law*. Boston: Beacon Press, 1958.

Boudin, Louis B. "The Problem of *Stare Decisis* in our Constitutional Theory," *New York University Law Quarterly Review*, 8 (1931), 589–639.

Bozell, L. Brent. *The Warren Revolution: Reflections on the Consensus Society.* New Rochelle, N.Y.: Arlington House, 1966.

Brant, Irving. *The Bill of Rights: Its Origin and Meaning.* Indianapolis: Bobbs-Merrill, 1965.

———— "The Madison Heritage," *New York University Law Review,* 35 (1960), 882–902.

———— "Seditious Libel: Myth and Reality," *New York University Law Review,* 39 (1964), 1–19.

Broek, Jacobus ten. "Admissibility and Use by the United States Supreme Court of Extrinsic Aids in Constitutional Construction," *California Law Review,* 26 (1938), 287–308.

———— "Use by the United States Supreme Court of Extrinsic Aids in Constitutional Construction," *California Law Review,* 26 (1938), 437–54, 664–81; 27 (1939), 157–81, 399–421.

Broiles, R. David. "Principles of Legal Reasoning," *Mercer Law Review,* 17 (1966), 389–96.

Butterfield, Herbert. *The Whig Interpretation of History.* New York: Scribner's, 1951.

Cahill, Fred V., Jr. *Judicial Legislation: A Study in American Legal Theory.* New York: Ronald, 1952.

Cahn, Edmond. "An American Contribution," in Cahn (ed.), *Supreme Court and Supreme Law,* pp. 1–25. Bloomington: Indiana University Press, 1954.

———— "The Parchment Barriers," *American Scholar,* 32 (1962), 21–39.

Cardozo, Benjamin N. *The Growth of the Law.* New Haven: Yale University Press, 1924.

———— *The Nature of the Judicial Process.* New Haven: Yale University Press, 1921.

———— *The Paradoxes of Legal Science.* New York: Columbia University Press, 1928.

Chafee, Zechariah, Jr. "Do Judges Make or Discover Law?" *Proceedings of the American Philosophical Society,* 91 (1947), 405–20.

———— *Free Speech in the United States.* Cambridge, Mass.: Harvard University Press, 1941.

Chamberlain, D. H. "The Doctrine of Stare Decisis as Applied to Decisions of Constitutional Questions," *Harvard Law Review,* 3 (1889), 125–31.

Chinard, Gilbert. "Polybius and the American Constitution," *Journal of the History of Ideas,* 1 (1940), 38–58.

Cohen, Morris R. *Law and the Social Order.* New York: Harcourt, Brace, 1933.

———— *The Meaning of Human History.* La Salle, Ill.: Open Court, 1947.

———— *Reason and Law.* Glencoe, Ill.: The Free Press, 1950.

———— *Reason and Nature.* Glencoe, Ill.: The Free Press, 1953.

Colbourn, H. Trevor. *The Lamp of Experience: Whig History and the Intellectual Origins of the American Revolution.* Chapel Hill: University of North Carolina Press, 1965.

—— "Thomas Jefferson's Use of the Past," *William and Mary Quarterly*, 15 (1958), 56–70.

Commager, Henry Steele. *Freedom and Order: A Commentary on the American Political Scene*. New York: Braziller, 1966.

—— *The Search for a Usable Past, and Other Essays in Historiography*. New York: Knopf, 1967.

Corwin, Edward S. "The Constitution as Instrument and as Symbol," *American Political Science Review*, 30 (1936), 1071–85.

—— "Judicial Review in Action," *University of Pennsylvania Law Review*, 74 (1926), 639–71.

—— "Moratorium over Minnesota," *University of Pennsylvania Law Review*, 82 (1934), 311–16.

—— "Tenure of Office and the Removal Power under the Constitution," *Columbia Law Review*, 27 (1927), 353–99.

Craven, Wesley Frank. *The Legend of the Founding Fathers*. New York: New York University Press, 1956.

Crosskey, William Winslow. *Politics and the Constitution in the History of the United States*. 2 vols. Chicago: University of Chicago Press, 1953.

Curtis, Charles P. *It's Your Law*. Cambridge, Mass.: Harvard University Press, 1954.

—— *Law as Large as Life: A Natural Law for Today and the Supreme Court as Its Prophet*. New York: Simon and Schuster, 1959.

—— *Lions Under the Throne*. Boston: Houghton Mifflin, 1947.

—— "The Role of the Constitutional Text," in Edmond Cahn (ed.), *Supreme Court and Supreme Law*, pp. 64–70. Bloomington: Indiana University Press, 1954.

Daly, John J. *The Use of History in the Decisions of the Supreme Court, 1900–1930*. Washington, D.C.: The Catholic University of America Press, 1954.

—— "The Use of History in the Supreme Court, 1873–1887," unpub. M.A. thesis, The Catholic University of America, 1950.

Degler, Carl N. *Out of Our Past: The Forces that Shaped Modern America*. New York: Harper and Row, 1962.

Douglas, William O. "Stare Decisis," *Columbia Law Review*, 49 (1949), 735–58.

Downer, L. J. "Legal History — Is it Human?" *Melbourne Law Review*, 4 (1963), 1–16.

Duberman, Martin. "The Limitations of History," *Antioch Review*, 25 (1965), 283–96.

Dumbauld, Edward. "The Lawyer's Use of Historical Materials," a paper read at a meeting of the Southern Historical Association, Nov. 8, 1963.

Elliott, W. Y. "The Constitution as the American Social Myth," in Conyers Read (ed.), *The Constitution Reconsidered*, pp. 209–24. New York: Columbia University Press, 1938.

Farrand, Max. *The Framing of the Constitution of the United States.* New Haven: Yale University Press, 1913.

Fisher, Sidney G. "The Legendary and Myth-Making Process in Histories of the American Revolution," *Proceedings of the American Philosophical Society,* 51 (1912), 53–75.

Foran, William A. "John Marshall as a Historian," *American Historical Review,* 43 (1937), 51–64.

Frank, Jerome. *Fate and Freedom.* New York: Simon and Schuster, 1945.

―――― *Law and the Modern Mind.* New York: Coward-McCann, 1930.

Frankfurter, Felix. *Mr. Justice Holmes and the Supreme Court.* 2d ed. Cambridge, Mass.: Harvard University Press, 1961.

―――― "Some Reflections on the Reading of Statutes," *Columbia Law Review,* 47 (1947), 527–46.

Freund, Paul A. "An Analysis of Judicial Reasoning," in Sidney Hook (ed.), *Law and Philosophy: A Symposium,* pp. 282–89. New York: New York University Press, 1964.

―――― "Mr. Justice Frankfurter," in Wallace Mendelson (ed.), *Felix Frankfurter: A Tribute,* pp. 147–63. New York: Reynal, 1964.

―――― *On Law and Justice.* Cambridge, Mass.: Harvard University Press, 1968.

―――― "Review of Facts in Constitutional Cases," in Edmond Cahn (ed.), *Supreme Court and Supreme Law,* pp. 47–51. Bloomington: University of Indiana Press, 1954.

―――― *The Supreme Court of the United States: Its Business, Purposes, and Performance.* Cleveland: World, 1961.

―――― "To Amend — or Not to Amend — the Constitution," *New York Times Magazine,* Dec. 13, 1964, p. 33.

Friedrich, Carl Joachim. "Law and History," *Vanderbilt Law Review,* 14 (1961), 1027–48.

Fulbright, J. William. "American Foreign Policy in the 20th Century under an 18th Century Constitution," *Cornell Law Quarterly,* 47 (1961), 1–13.

Garraty, John A. (ed.). *Quarrels That Have Shaped the Constitution.* New York: Harper and Row, 1964.

Gluckman, Max. *Politics, Law and Ritual in Tribal Society.* Chicago: Aldine, 1965.

Goebel, Julius, Jr. "Constitutional History and Constitutional Law," *Columbia Law Review,* 38 (1938), 555–77.

Goldberg, Edward M. "Mr. Justice Harlan, the Uses of History, and the Congressional Globe," *Journal of Public Law,* 15 (1966), 181–86.

Goodykoontz, Colin B. "The Founding Fathers and Clio," *Pacific Historical Review,* 23 (1954), 111–23.

Graham, Howard Jay. "Crosskey's Constitution: An Archeological Blueprint," *Vanderbilt Law Review,* 7 (1954), 340–65.

Gray, John Chipman. *The Nature and Sources of the Law,* 2d ed. New York: Macmillan, 1927.

Hamilton, Walton H. "1937 to 1787, Dr.," in Conyers Read (ed.), *The*

Constitution Reconsidered, pp. vii–xvi. New York: Columbia University Press, 1938.

Harnett, Sister Ellen Mary. "The Use of History in the Supreme Court under Charles Evans Hughes," unpub. M.A. thesis, The Catholic University of America, 1956.

Harrison, J. A. "Time and the American Historian," *South Atlantic Quarterly,* 64 (1965), 362–66.

Hartz, Louis. *The Liberal Tradition in America: An Interpretation of American Political Thought since the Revolution.* New York: Harcourt, Brace and World, 1955.

Heilbroner, Robert L. *The Future as History: The historic currents of our time and the direction in which they are taking America.* New York: Grove Press, 1961.

Holcombe, Arthur N. "The Political Interpretation of History," *American Political Science Review,* 31 (1937), 1–11.

Holmes, Oliver Wendell. *Collected Legal Papers.* New York: Harcourt, Brace and Howe, 1920.

Hook, Sidney. "Objectivity and Reconstruction in History," in Hook (ed.), *Philosophy and History: A Symposium,* pp. 250–74. New York: New York University Press, 1963.

Horwill, Herbert W. *The Usages of the American Constitution.* London: Oxford University Press, 1925.

Howe, Mark DeWolfe. *The Garden and the Wilderness: Religion and Government in American Constitutional History.* Chicago: University of Chicago Press, 1965.

——— "Split Decisions," *New York Review of Books,* July 1, 1965, p. 14.

Hughes, Charles Evans. *The Supreme Court of the United States: Its Foundations, Methods and Achievements — An Interpretation.* New York: Columbia University Press, 1928.

Hughes, H. Stuart. *History as Art and as Science: Twin Vistas on the Past.* New York: Harper and Row, 1964.

Hurst, Willard. *Justice Holmes on Legal History.* New York: Macmillan, 1964.

——— "The Role of History," in Edmond Cahn (ed.), *Supreme Court and Supreme Law,* pp. 55–58. Bloomington: Indiana University Press, 1954.

Jones, J. Walter. *Historical Introduction to the Theory of Law.* Oxford: Clarendon Press, 1965.

Kelly, Alfred H. "Clio and the Court: An Illicit Love Affair," *Supreme Court Review* (1965), 119–58.

Klinkhamer, Sister Marie Carolyn. "John Marshall's Use of History," *Catholic University Law Review,* 6 (1956), 78–96.

——— "The Use of History in the Supreme Court, 1789–1835," *University of Detroit Law Journal,* 36 (1959), 553–78.

Kurland, Philip B. "The Court Should Decide Less and Explain More," *New York Times Magazine,* June 9, 1968, p. 34.

Lerner, Max. *America as a Civilization*. New York: Simon and Schuster, 1957.

—— "Constitution and Court as Symbols," *Yale Law Journal*, 46 (1937), 1290–1319.

Lerner, Ralph. "The Supreme Court as Republican Schoolmaster," *Supreme Court Review* (1967), 127–80.

Levi, Edward H. "The Nature of Judicial Reasoning," in Sidney Hook (ed.), *Law and Philosophy: A Symposium*, pp. 263–81. New York: New York University Press, 1964.

Levy, Leonard W. *Freedom of Speech and Press in Early American History: Legacy of Suppression*. New York: Harper Torchbooks, 1963.

Llewellyn, Karl N. "The Constitution as an Institution," *Columbia Law Review*, 34 (1934), 1–40.

Loewenheim, Francis L. (ed.). *The Historian and the Diplomat: The Role of History and Historians in American Foreign Policy*. New York: Harper and Row, 1967.

Loewenstein, Karl. "Reflections on the Value of Constitutions in our Revolutionary Age," in Arnold J. Zurcher (ed.), *Constitutions and Constitutional Trends since World War II*, pp. 191–224. New York: New York University Press, 1951.

Lord, Clifford L. (ed.). *Keepers of the Past*. Chapel Hill: University of North Carolina Press, 1965.

Lyon, Charles Stuart. "Old Statutes and New Constitution," *Columbia Law Review*, 44 (1944), 599–638.

McBain, Howard Lee. *The Living Constitution: A Consideration of the Realities and Legends of Our Fundamental Law*. New York: Workers Education Bureau Press, 1927.

McCloskey, Robert G. *The American Supreme Court*. Chicago: University of Chicago Press, 1960.

Mason, Alpheus Thomas. "Myth and Reality in Supreme Court Decisions," *Virginia Law Review*, 48 (1962), 1385–1406.

Miller, Arthur Selwyn. "Notes on the Concept of the 'Living' Constitution," *George Washington Law Review*, 31 (1963), 881–918.

—— "Some Pervasive Myths about the United States Supreme Court," *St. Louis University Law Journal*, 10 (1965), 153–89.

—— "Technology, Social Change, and the Constitution," *George Washington Law Review*, 33 (1964), 17–46.

Miller, Perry. *The Life of the Mind in America from the Revolution to the Civil War*. New York: Harcourt, Brace and World, 1965.

Mills, C. Wright. *The Sociological Imagination*. New York: Grove Press, 1961.

Morey, William C. "The Genesis of a Written Constitution," *Annals of the American Academy of Political and Social Science*, 1 (1890–91), 529–57.

Morgan, Donald G. *Congress and the Constitution: A Study of Responsibility*. Cambridge, Mass.: Harvard University Press, 1966.

Mowry, George E. "The Uses of History by Recent Presidents," *Journal of American History*, 53 (1966), 5–18.

Murphy, Paul L. "Time to Reclaim: The Current Challenge of American Constitutional History," *American Historical Review*, 69 (1963), 64–79.

Naroll, Raoul S. "Clio and the Constitution: The Influence of the Study of History upon the Federal Convention of 1787," unpub. diss. University of California, Los Angeles, 1953.

Niebuhr, Reinhold. *The Irony of American History*. New York: Scribner's, 1952.

Nietzsche, Friedrich. *The Use and Abuse of History*, trans. Adrian Collins. New York: Liberal Arts Press, 1957.

Noble, David W. *Historians against History: The Frontier Thesis and the National Covenant in American Historical Writing since 1830*. Minneapolis: University of Minnesota Press, 1965.

O'Brien, Joseph A. "The Use of History in the Supreme Court, 1864–1873," unpub. M.A. thesis, The Catholic University of America, 1950.

Pierson, Charles W. "*The Federalist* in the Supreme Court," *Yale Law Journal*, 33 (1924), 728–35.

Popper, Karl R. "Towards a Rational Theory of Tradition," *Rationalist Annual* (London), 1949, pp. 36–55.

Pound, Roscoe. *Interpretations of Legal History*. New York: Macmillan, 1923.

Powell, Thomas Reed. "From Philadelphia to Philadelphia," *American Political Science Review*, 32 (1938), 1–27.

—— "The Logic and Rhetoric of Constitutional Law" (originally published 1918), in Robert G. McCloskey (ed.), *Essays in Constitutional Law*, pp. 85–101. New York: Knopf, 1957.

Roche, John P. "The Expatriation Cases: 'Breathes there the Man, with Soul so Dead . . .?'" *Supreme Court Review* (1963), 325–56.

Schechter, Frank I. "The Early History of the Tradition of the Constitution," *American Political Science Review*, 9 (1915), 707–34.

Schlesinger, Arthur M., Jr. "The Historian and History," *Foreign Affairs*, 41 (1963), 491–97.

—— "The Historian as Artist," *The Atlantic*, 212 (July 1963), 35–41.

—— "On the Inscrutability of History," *Encounter*, November 1966, pp. 10–17.

Smith, Page. *The Historian and History*. New York: Knopf, 1964.

Spector, Robert M. "Legal Historian on the United States Supreme Court: Justice Horace Gray, Jr., and the Historical Method," *American Journal of Legal History*, 12 (1968), 181–210.

Stevens, Richard G. "Reason and History in Judicial Judgment: Mr. Justice Frankfurter's Treatment of Due Process," unpub. diss. University of Chicago, 1963.

Stone, Julius. *Legal System and Lawyers' Reasoning*. Stanford: Stanford University Press, 1964.

Stromberg, R. N. "History in the Eighteenth Century," *Journal of the History of Ideas*, 12 (1951), 295–304.

Swindler, William F. "Legal History — Unhappy Hybrid," *Law Library Journal*, 55 (1962), 98–110.

Vansina, Jan. *Oral Tradition: A Study in Historical Methodology*, trans. H. M. Wright. Chicago: Aldine, 1965.

Van Tassel, David D. *Recording America's Past: An Interpretation of the Development of Historical Societies in America, 1607–1884*. Chicago: University of Chicago Press, 1960.

Van Zandt, Roland. *The Metaphysical Foundations of American History*. The Hague: Mouton, 1959.

Wechsler, Herbert. "Toward Neutral Principles of Constitutional Law," *Harvard Law Review*, 73 (1959), 1–35.

Welch, James E. "Roger B. Taney: Historical Allusion in his Supreme Court Decisions," unpub. M.A. thesis, The Catholic University of America, 1950.

Wiener, Frederick Bernays. *Uses and Abuses of Legal History: A Practitioner's View*. London: Bernard Quaritch, 1962.

Wiggins, James R. "Lawyers as Judges of History," *Proceedings of the Massachusetts Historical Society*, 75 (1964), 84–104.

Wilson, Woodrow. "The Variety and Unity of History," in Francis L. Loewenheim (ed.), *The Historian and the Diplomat: The Role of History and Historians in American Foreign Policy*, pp. 171–87. New York: Harper and Row, 1967. (Address delivered 1904.)

Wofford, John G. "The Blinding Light: The Uses of History in Constitutional Interpretation," *University of Chicago Law Review*, 31 (1964), 502–33.

Wright, Benjamin F. "The Early History of Written Constitutions in America," in *Essays in History and Political Theory in Honor of Charles Howard McIlwain*, pp. 344–71. Cambridge, Mass.: Harvard University Press, 1936.

Wyzanski, Charles E., Jr. "History and Law," *University of Chicago Law Review*, 26 (1959), 237–44.

Yoder, Edwin M., Jr. "The American Uses of the Past," *Virginia Quarterly Review*, 41 (1965), 108–18.

INDEX OF CASES

GENERAL INDEX